49.00/36.75

D1088090

Looking at
Picture Books

Looking at
Picture Books

By John Warren Stewig

Highsmith PRESS

Fort Atkinson, Wisconsin

Published by Highsmith Press
W5527 Highway 106
P.O. Box 800
Fort Atkinson, Wisconsin 53538-0800

1-800-558-2110

The paper used in this publication meets the minimum requirements of
American National Standard for Information Science —
Permanence of Paper for Printed Library Material.
ANSI/NISO Z39.48-1992.

Library of Congress Cataloging in Publication

Stewig, John W.

Looking at picture books / by John Warren Stewig.
     p.   cm.

   Includes bibliographical references and index.

   ISBN 0-917846-29-X

   1. Picture books for children--United States--Authorship.
2. Illustration of books--United States. 3. Children's stories,
English--History and criticism. I. Title.

PN147.5.S74 1995

741.6 ' 42 ' 0973--dc20   94-35026

Materials in *Looking at Picture Books* were used with permission from the following:

Chapter 1

From *Crafty Chameleon* by Mwenye Hadithi and Adrienne Kennaway. Copyright © 1987 by Bruce Hobson and Adrienne Kennaway. By permission of Little, Brown and Company.

From *Frog and Toad Are Friends* by Arnold Lobel. Copyright © 1970 by Arnold Lobel. Selection reprinted by permission of HarperCollins Publishers.

Hetty and Harriet. Reprinted with the permission of Atheneum Books for Young Readers, an imprint of Simon & Schuster Children's Publishing Division from *Hetty and Harriet* by Graham Oakley. Copyright © 1981 Graham Oakley.

John Gilpin and Other Stories by Randolph Caldecott. London: Frederick Warne Ltd.

From *Maria Teresa* by Petra Mathers. Illustrations copyright © 1985 by Petra Mathers. Selection reprinted by permission of HarperCollins Publishers.

From *The Owl-Scatterer* by Howard Norman. Text copyright © 1986 by Howard Norman; Illustrations copyright © 1986 by Michael McCurdy. By permission of Little, Brown and Company.

Pyramid of the Sun, Pyramid of the Moon. Reprinted with the permission of Atheneum Books for Young Readers, an imprint of Simon & Schuster Children's Publishing Division from *Pyramid of the Sun, Pyramid of the Moon* by Leonard Everett Fisher. Copyright © 1988 Leonard Everett Fisher.

Chapter 2

From *Everett Anderson's Friend* by Lucille Clifton. Illustrations by Ann Grifalconi. Illustrations copyright ©1976 by Ann Grifalconi. Reprinted by permission by Henry Holt and Company.

From *Farm Day* by Claire Henley. Reprinted by permission of J.M. Dent & Sons Ltd.

From *The Garden of Abdul Gasazi* by Chris Van Allsburg. Copyright © 1979 by Chris Van Allsburg. Reprinted by permission of Houghton Mifflin Company. All rights reserved.

From *Go Away, Stay Away* by Gail Haley. Published by Scribner, 1977. Republished by New River Pub., 1988. Reprinted by permission of Gail Haley.

From *Mr. Grumpy's Outing* by John Burningham. Copyright ©1970 by John Burningham. Reprinted by permission of Henry Holt and Company, Inc.

From *The Nightingale* by Eva le Gallienne, illustrations by Nancy Ekholm Burkert. Illustrations copyright © 1985 by Nancy Ekholm Burkert. Selection reprinted by permission of HarperCollins Publishers.

Illustration by Donald Crews from his *Parade*. Copyright © 1983 by Donald Crews. By permission of Greenwillow Books, a division of William Morrow & Company, Inc.

Rapunzel. Illustration copyright © 1982 by Trina Schart Hyman from *Rapunzel* by Barbara Rogasky. All rights reserved. Reprinted by permission of Holiday House, Inc.

Seven Blind Mice. Illustration by Ed Young reprinted by permission of Philomel Books from *Seven Blind Mice*, copyright © 1992 by Ed Young.

Illustration by Pat Hutchins from her *What Game Shall We Play?* Copyright © 1990 by Pat Hutchins. By permission of Greenwillow Books, a division of William Morrow & Company, Inc.

Chapter 3

From *Abuela* by Arthur Dorros. Copyright © 1991 by Arthur Dorros, text. Used by permission of Dutton Children's Books, a division of Penguin Books USA Inc.

From *Annie and the Wild Animals* by Jan Brett. Copyright © 1985 by Jan Brett. Reprinted by permission of Houghton Mifflin Company. All rights reserved.

From *The Big Pets* by Lane Smith. Copyright © 1991 by Lane Smith. Used by permission of Viking Penguin, a division of Penguin Books USA Inc.

From *Burt Dow Deep-Water Man* by Robert McCloskey. Copyright © 1963, renewed ©1991 by Robert McCloskey. Used by permission of Viking Penguin, a division of Penguin Books USA Inc.

Illustration from *Crow Chief* by Paul Goble. Copyright © 1992 by Paul Goble. Used by permission of Orchard Books, New York.

From *Elephant Cat* by Nicola Bayley. Reprinted by permission of Walker Books Limited.

The Gold Coin. Reprinted with the permission of Atheneum Books for Young Readers, an imprint of Simon & Schuster Children's Publishing Division from *The Gold Coin* by Alma Flor Ada, illustrated by Neil Waldman. Illustrations copyright © 1991 Neil Waldman.

From *If At First You Do Not See* by Ruth Brown. Copyright © 1982 by Ruth Brown. Reprinted by permission of Henry Holt and Company, Inc.

Jason Goes to Show-And-Tell. Illustration by Linda Weller from *Jason Goes to Show-and-Tell* by Colleen Sutherland. Copyright © 1992 by Linda Weller. Reprinted by permission of Boyds Mills Press, Inc.

Illustration from *My Mama Needs Me* by Mildred Pitts Walter, illustrated by Pat Cummings. Copyright © 1983 by Pat Cummings. By permission of Lothrop, Lee & Shepard Books, a division of William Morrow & Company, Inc.

Illustration by Ann Jonas from her *Round Trip*. Copyright © 1983 by Ann Jonas. By permission of Greenwillow Books, a division of William Morrow & Company, Inc.

From *Tree of Cranes* by Allen Say. Copyright ©1991 by Allen Say. Reprinted by permission of Houghton Mifflin Company. All rights reserved.

From *The Twelve Days of Christmas* by Louise Brierley. Reprinted by permission of Walker Books Limited.

We Keep a Pig in the Parlor by Suzanne Bloom. Copyright © 1988 by Suzanne Bloom. Reprinted by permission of Clarkson N. Potter, a division of Random House, Inc.

From *The World from My Window* by Sheila White Samton. Re-issued by Caroline House, Boyd's Mills Press, Inc., 1991. Reprinted by permission of Sheila White Samton.

From *Zoo* by Anthony Browne. Copyright © 1992 by Anthony Browne. Reprinted by permission of Alfred A. Knopf, Inc.

Chapter 4

From *Africa Dream* by Eloise Greenfield, illustrations by Carole Byard. Illustrations copyright © 1977 by Carole Byard. Selection reprinted by permission of HarperCollins Publishers.

From *The Ballad of Belle Dorcas* by William Hooks, illustrated by Brian Pinkney. Illustrations copyright © 1990 by Brian Pinkney. Reprinted by permission of Alfred A. Knopf, Inc.

The Cat's Purr. Reprinted with the permission of Atheneum Books for Young Readers, an imprint of Simon & Schuster Children's Publishing Division from

From *The Tale of Peter Rabbit* by Beatrix Potter. Copyright © Frederick Warne & Co., 1902, 1987. Reprinted with permission of Frederick Warne.

The Tale of Peter Rabbit. Illustration by David McPhail from *The Tale of Peter Rabbit* by Beatrix potter. Illustration copyright © 1986 by David McPhail. Reprinted by permission of Scholastic Inc.

Chapter 6

From *Changes* by Anthony Browne. Copyright © 1990 by Anthony Browne. Reprinted by permission of Alfred A. Knopf, Inc.

From *Follow the Drinking Gourd* by Jeanette Winter. Copyright © 1988 by Jeanette Winter. Reprinted by permission of Alfred A. Knopf.

From *From the Hills of Georgia* by Mattie Lou O'Kelley. Copyright © 1983 by Mattie Lou O'Kelley. By permission of Little, Brown and Company.

From *In Search of the Last Dodo* by Ann and Reg Cartwright. Reprinted by permission of The Bodley Head.

From *Mr. Rabbit and the Lovely Present* by Charlotte Zolotow, illustrations by Maurice Sendak. Illustrations copyright © 1962 by Maurice Sendak. Selection reprinted by permission of HarperCollins Publishers.

Illustration by John L. Steptoe from his *Mufaro's Beautiful Daughters: An African Tale*. Copyright © 1987 by John L. Steptoe. By permission of Lothrop, Lee & Shepard Books, a division of William Morrow & Company, Inc. with the approval of the Estate of John Steptoe.

Pictures of Home by Colin Thompson. Copyright © 1992 by Colin Thompson. Used by permission of the publisher, Green Tiger Press/ a division of Simon & Schuster, New York.

Red Light, Green Light by Margaret Wise Brown, illustrations by Leonard Weisgard. Illustrations copyright © 1992 by Leonard Weisgard. Reprinted by permission of Scholastic Inc.

Shadow. Reprinted with the permission of Atheneum Books for Young Readers, an imprint of Simon & Schuster Children's Publishing Division from *Shadow* translated and illustrated by Marcia Brown. Illustrations copyright © 1982 by Marcia Brown.

Stevie. Copyright © 1969 by John L. Steptoe. Use permitted by HarperCollins Publishers with the approval of the Estate of John Steptoe.

Contents

Illustrations

Color plates

The following illustrations appear in the color plate section following page 174. Text and further description relating to these illustrations can be found on the following pages:

Black and white illustrations

Chapter 1

Chapter 5

Chapter 6

Preface

Many of us remember with fondness a picture book from our childhood. You may recall the cozy charm of *The Little Family* by Lois Lenski which entertained generations of youngsters. Perhaps your favorite was the adventures of the mallard family in the now-classic *May Way for Ducklings* by Robert McCloskey. Or, you may be among those captivated by the delicious scariness of the monsters in *Where the Wild Things Are* by Maurice Sendak. It doesn't make any difference which of the many vibrant picture books remain vivid in your memory. What is important is that you understand, even if you haven't consciously thought about it, the ways in which such books can capture and hold children's attention. In the process, picture books enrich children's understanding of language, pictures, and how the two work together.

My purpose in writing this book is to help you move beyond this intuitive appreciation from childhood into the more conscious awareness of picture books possible for adults. Together, we will think about picture books, why and how they are made, and the effects they can have on children's learning and development.

One outcome of this process is that you may become a more discerning consumer of picture books. To accomplish this, we'll consider information about picture books, because information can enhance appreciation. An example is when a knowledgable listener attends the performance of a Gustav Mahler symphony. If the listener knows that in the second movement, the key will shift from major to minor, before the theme returns in inverted form, her or she is prepared to appreciate more deeply the interplay of ideas in the music. Similarly, if you understand what the author was doing with the often deceptively simple language in the picture book, as well as what the artist was doing with the materials chosen to create the visual symbols in the illustrations, you'll be better prepared to respond to the book as an artistic unit.

A second outcome of this process is that you'll glean ideas about how you can share your enthusiasm for picture books with children at all age levels. You may be a librarian serving children in a school media center. Or you may be a teacher working with a group of children to enhance their understanding of and appreciation for finely crafted language and striking visual art. In either case, you'll find, embedded into each chapter in this book, ideas for how to engage children in directed looking at pictures, so they can become more skilled observers. In contrast, you may be a children's librarian working in a public library. If so, your task might be to bring parents and teachers in contact with this book, as a source for enhancing their interactions with children. No matter why your interest in picture books has drawn to this book, my intent is to lead you to a deeper appreciation of the very best of picture books.

The book opens with a general consideration of picture books, attending particularly to how the two components work together. Most people who write about this genre comment on the interrelated nature of the words and pictures. Separately, each component must be strong. The language must be evocative, distinguished in both vocabulary and syntax, while using additional resources, like imagery, available to a skilled writer. The other equally critical component is the art, created today with a widening array of materials, and using an equally impressive variety of visual styles, to challenge children to perceive in new ways. Together, these two components interact to create a final effect greater than either could separately.

Chapter two looks at the visual components of the illustrations. First, we consider the elements of the pictures themselves: line, shape, color, proportion, detail and space. In this chapter, as throughout the book, the ideas are explained in the context of examples of exemplary picture books, both classics enjoyed by generations of children, and books published this year selected because of their quality.

Chapter three examines how artists incorporate these disparate visual elements into complete works of art, using compositional principles. In this chapter, we look closely at the principles of: unity, proximity, similarity, continuity, variety, dominance, rhythm and movement, and balance. In this chapter we'll look at individual books exemplifying effective use of each of these principles, as well as identifying how all of them are exemplified in a single book.

Chapter four explores another element which controls the final look of any picture book: the media used by the artist. There is a wider selection of materials artists can choose from today, and they are selecting and combining these in exciting new ways. In addition, the technical improvements in photography make it possible to reproduce these combinations of materials with impressive clarity.

The art an illustrator creates, incorporating the visual elements and compositional principles through the media chosen, is always seen in a context. That context is the book as a whole, a unity which has other design qualities. Any book is a visual object or artifact, with size, shape, and orientation, either vertical or horizontal. Physical components include such things as binding, endpapers and type of paper. Other components include page arrangement and type faces selected. We too seldom focus consciously on these elements, but they are powerful determinants of the total visual impact. Chapter five examines all of the different physical features which enhance the enjoyment of picture books.

Finally, chapter six embeds picture book art in a larger context, the general development of art movements. Visual art has a history, in which interest in varying kinds of representations has led to succeeding movements. These general trends have often originated in particular times or places, but their influence has spread to other times and places. What goes on in the art world affects what goes on in picture book art; this is explored in chapter six. Specific links which librarians and teachers can make for children are suggested. The book concludes with an annotated bibliography of books, not about picture books, per se, but rather about the visual arts in general. The purpose of including this is to make more apparent the links between art, and the art of picture books.

Throughout this book, I've described individual books for you which I feel are especially effective. But I hope you'll also notice the many suggestions to look at particular books in relation to other books. Frequently, there are suggestions to compare and contrast, looking for relationships in elements, principles, mediums or formats. This is because we sense more completely the characteristics of anything, as we think consciously about similarities and difference with other things. To return to the illustration given earlier, we perceive, and can respond more deeply to Mahler's music, as we know how it is like and unlike that of, for instance, Frederick Delius. So, throughout this book, I've suggested that rather than thinking of books as isolated objects, we need to see them in relation to other books we know. That's not only important as we adults seek to learn more about picture books, but also as we work with children.

I would like to note that in the discussion of particular pages, you'll notice indications such as "...on the 12th opening." Since most picture book pages are not numbered, this convention of speaking about a particular opening, provides a method for indicating where a reference is located. To determine the opening in the book, count from the first page on which text appears. Throughout this book, indications of size are given, width first, then height.

Any book, to be effective, must move beyond the writer's individual vision, to set the ideas in the larger context of other people's thoughts. Throughout this book, I've referred to the writing of other experts who have written in various places and ways about the art of the picture book. Complete references to these other sources are included, as well as a listing of all the picture books discussed the book. You'll notice that, for accuracy, the indication of children's books publishers give the name as it appeared on the title page when the book was first published, not as the name may have changed since publication.

Finally, I'd like to thank Don Sager who first saw the potential in this book, and to Nancy Wilcox, who over endless hours attended to details, bringing it to completion. My gratitude goes to publishers who for many years have brought me into contact with picture book creators and their works so I could learn from them. And, as always, thanks to R.D.B., for understanding how consuming a task writing a book becomes.

J. W. STEWIG

Overview

… once or twice she had peeped into the book her sister was reading, but it had no pictures…in it, "and what is the use of a book," thought Alice, "without pictures …?"

Many children since Alice have echoed her sentiments. To meet their demands, the picture storybook was developed and has proliferated. In fact, Kiefer traces the roots of this form back to prehistoric cave paintings. In a chapter on using picture books with all ages, she provides a helpful history of the genre. Today the picture storybook is a recognized genre, and there are awards to honor the best examples. More of these books are published each year than most teachers and librarians can become familiar with. Because picture storybooks are such a pervasive part of children's early education, it is important to consider what they are, the purposes they serve, and the nature of children's responses to them.

How do we help children learn to appreciate picture books fully? These books are ubiquitous: they form a major part of classroom, school, and public libraries. Because they are so commonplace, we may tend to overlook their full potential. Lechner has written about using picture books to make children more aware of the fine art qualities inherent in the illustration in children's books. In her article, she calls picture books, "portable art galleries." And indeed, this combination of carefully chosen words, and skillfully crafted art, is as aesthetically satisfying as the art in museums.

Yet, both adults and children often don't look as carefully as they might at these apparently simple combinations of words and pictures. As Egoff points out, because picture books "deploy …

About the book

There are numerous versions of Alice in Wonderland, *with illustration by artists working in a variety of styles. You might, for example, compare the art by Justin Todd with that by S. Michelle Wiggins.*

two art forms, the pictorial and the literary, to engage two audiences (child and adult)," they are as a result the "most complex" of literary genres.[1]

These books for children present an astoundingly wide spectrum of visual stimulation. Choices range from the bright, full-color illustrations in *Morris's Disappearing Bag*, by Rosemary Wells, to the effective use of a single color with black and white in *The Lace Snail*, by Betsy Byars, to books in which the artist simply uses the contrast of black and white, as in *The Owl-Scatterer* by Howard Norman. In addition to the variety in color use, there is an almost infinite array of styles (from realistic to abstract) and designs (from highly patterned to restrained and understated). Sutherland, in a comment made some years ago but still appropriate today, said: "Sharing such books with children, adults will find themselves as charmed with the pictures as are the children… a wonderful way to teach art appreciation would be through children's picture books which run the whole gamut of styles and techniques."[2] Feeney and Moravcik would agree, given their suggestions about how to talk with children about fine art and book art, in developing the aesthetic sensibilities of young children.

Our purpose here is to help teachers and librarians understand, and respond to, this complex genre as a visual and verbal experience. A related purpose is to suggest how those working with children can more effectively bring the art and language of picture books to young readers and listeners.

Figure 1.1: The Owl-Scatterer

There is interesting variation of depth in this illustration. Our eyes move from the old man, striding across the very front of the picture plane, back into the store, which is in the middle ground, and then to the house, set even further back on the left. What contributes to this sense of space is the overlapping. The owl scatterer's elbow is in front of the scarf-wearer's legs, establishing a relation in space. The grocer is behind the post, but his hand is in front of the display, also establishing depth.

A variety of types

To study the range of illustrations in children's picture books as well as the media and methods used by the illustrators, some authors recommend distinguishing among picture books, picture storybooks, and illustrated books.

Picture books

In these kinds of books, different objects or ideas appear on each page, linked by the artist's style but not necessarily by a sequential story line. Authors like Huck, et al., say that in picture books, the pictures carry the entire message. This category includes:

Alphabet books

There are alphabet books for all ages, although we usually consider these to be for beginning readers. *Ben's ABC Day*, by Terry Berger, features almost full-page color photographs, by Alice Kandell, showing a boy and his family and friends engaged in a variety of activities throughout the day. It is a book for beginners; most children will be familiar with the commonplace activities portrayed. In contrast, *The Museum of Modern Art ABC*, by Florence Cassen Mayers, is clearly intended for a more sophisticated audience; much of the art included is highly abstract.

Alphabet book
Alphabet Annie Announces an All-American Album *by Susan Purviance and Marcia O'Shell.*

Counting books

Counting books are plentiful. *Up to Ten and Down Again*, by Lisa Campbell Ernst, opens with a solitary duck floating in its pond and continues on to a page packed with picnickers, who begin to disappear when rain threatens. Large, full-color, bordered illustrations on facing pages provide much to look at. Brown rather than black line focuses the details in the pictures. Some counting books are appropriate for the youngest viewer. *In Night Counting*, by Ann Morris and Maureen Roffey, the young children are plainly drawn, and what is to be counted is quite evident. In contrast, in *When Sheep Cannot Sleep*, by Satoshi Kitamura, the author/illustrator was obviously aiming at an older audience; the complex, unrealistic pictures require a more developed eye and counting skills.

Counting book
12 Ways to Get to 11 *by Eve Merriam and illustrated by Bernie Karlin.*

Concept book

Nice or Nasty. A Book of
Opposites *by Nick Butterworth
and Mick Inkpen.*

Concept books

An example of a very simple concept book in board book format is *Garden Animals* by Lucy Cousins. In a small, nearly square format, the artist shows purposely unrefined pictures of only ten garden creatures set against solid-color backgrounds, with equally crude lettering for the name of each. It is part of a series of concept books which help preschool children begin to understand animal groupings, as in *Country Animals, Pet Animals,* and *Farm Animals.*

Margaret Wise Brown's *The Important Book* is an example of a concept picture book for older readers. She identifies an object, notes its most salient characteristic, lists several of its other qualities, and at the bottom of the page repeats the first-mentioned characteristic. Brown describes in poetic fashion a spoon, the rain, an apple, shoes, and at the end of the book, the reader. Illustrations by Leonard Weisgard alternate black and white double-page spreads with full-color ones. The large, full-page, simple pictures are bled to the page edge, and are done in opaque watercolor. They remain fresh, despite the fact that this book was first published in 1949.

Picture storybooks

In picture storybooks as Sutherland and Arbuthnot (1991) point out, there is a plot which tells a story, which a picture book may not have. The author tells this in words, while the illustrator tells this in pictures. The form is thus a combination in which each half is equally important. The artist must show characters, settings, and actions in a way that will relate to and advance a plot. The current examples of this genre are modern-day descendents of the work of a British illustrator, Randolph Caldecott (1846-1886), who established a reputation for sprightly picture books depicting rural life in England. As they were published, Caldecott's books set a new standard in illustrating for children, providing art full of action and fun. The award given annually by the Association for Library Service to Children, a division of the American Library Association, is named for Caldecott, and recognizes the most distinguished picture book by an American illustrator published that year.

Figure 1.2: John Gilpin and Other Stories
The artist arranged this flurry of runaway activity on a diagonal from lower left to upper right. All of the subsidiary characters look at the main one, to further establish the center of action. Notice that in this illustration, the buildings are simply background, a lesser role than in art by Allen Say for *Tree of Cranes* or Anthony Browne for *Zoo*, in which they are essential to the composition. (*See captions for these illustrations for further explanation.*)

In the following section, we'll look at a number of books which exemplify, in varying ways, the kind of strong balance between text and pictures, which is possible in effective picture storybooks. An example is James Skofield's *All Wet! All Wet!*, illustrated by Diane Stanley. On each page, meticulously executed, detailed pictures are indeed integral to the story. The story is stronger because of the pictures, and in the same way the pictures benefit from the author's words. The words focus on the main objects and events in the picture; the picture then elaborates on the words.

Besides showing in visuals what the words say, illustrators develop ideas, giving additional details, and sometimes show more than the words tell, or give contradictory information which the reader/viewer must then make sense of.

For example, in *Hetty and Harriet*, author-illustrator Grahame Oakley tells two related, but different stories which provide different kinds of information. On the seventh opening, the words tell us simply that the two run-away hens "tried a change of diet. But they really weren't given time to find out whether they liked it or not." In the picture, we see a fully detailed view of the inside of a department store, with the hens scratching and eating in the confectionery department, kicking candies to delighted, small children, watching the antics, while an upset clerk complains to

For further information
Shulevitz discusses in further detail the illustrator's role in picture storybooks in Writing with Pictures: How to Write and Illustrate Children's Books.

Figure 1.3: Hetty and Harriet
The bird's eye view makes the traffic confusion more apparent than had the artist shown the same action from the side, at eye level. From above, we see the panoramic stoppage, hemmed in by buildings in the four corners of the picture. The cause of the chaos, the two hens, is shown very small, and off to one side, not in the center. To help children respond to Oakley's manipulation of viewpoint, look with your class at *The Church Mice and The Ring* in which the artist continually presents the art from below, at, and above eye level.

the floorwalker. None of that is described in words. On the facing page for the minimal text, "So after that they were reduced to looking for scraps in the tree…," we get an exaggerated bird's-eye view, looking directly down on a traffic circle clogged with cars stopped while the two hens, shown so small that viewers have to search for them, continue to scratch for food. The humor of the additional events, shown visually but not described in the words, is what makes this such a delightful picture storybook. Throughout this and other of his books, Oakley makes us attend carefully to the pictures since they carry such a heavy load of additional, related information.

Oakley has talked in an interview about this aspect of his work, saying: "I've always thought of pictures as being something which you have to look into and see new things… apart from the main story in (a) painting in the background there is another story going on." He continues, saying, "I'm a great believer in never using words and pictures to do the same thing."[3]

Helen Cooper, in *The Bear Under the Stairs*, has provided two interesting examples of how the pictures are as important as the words because they provide information not given in the text itself. At two places in the story the text stops, and the intervening page shows what a character does. Young William is frightened of the bear his imagination has conjured up. The text tells us that he didn't actually see it "under the stairs…" and the following picture shows us that William has drawn a picture of the bear to exorcise his fear. Somewhat later in the story, "while William dreamed…" the interleaved double-page spread shows both the bear at a table, and also his drawing of William.

The most interesting example occurs at the end of this picture storybook, however. The words simply assure readers that because his mother helped him with his fear, William was never scared of bears or the place under the stairs again. But there's an entire small coda in pictures at the end, which shows the bear putting up a sign, "Gone away," on William's door, picking up a valise and umbrella, walking to a small, red single-prop airplane and finally parachuting, baggage in hand, toward a bucolic-looking, small house in the country. Cooper extends the story: having told us in words the end of William's part of the tale, she shows us in pictures the end of the bear's part of the encounter.

Because they combine words and pictures, picture storybooks present an interesting evaluation problem: those who select books for children must make both a visual and a verbal judgment.

Illustrated books

Illustrated books have fewer illustrations than picture storybooks and what they do have are often printed in limited color or just black and white. The illustrations are extensions of the text and may add to the interpretation of the story but are not necessary for understanding it. These books are intended for children who have developed fluent reading skills. An example is *The Ghost of Windy Hill* by Clyde Robert Bulla, which contains ink-wash and line drawings by Don Bolognese. These drawings accompany the strange and exciting adventure of a family that is not sure whether its house is haunted. A more recent example is Martin Waddell's *Harriet and the Haunted School*. The black-and-white illustrations by Mark Burgess break up the text, for the most part paralleling rather than expanding on the story. The hilarious adventures of Harriet, the troublemaker of her elementary school, are conveyed effectively through the words.

Book illustration today

Book illustration today differs significantly from that in earlier children's books for several reasons. First, production techniques are highly developed: new laser technology and computer-set type are only two examples. One cannot but marvel, when watching the paper for the sheets of a book being propelled through four-color presses at an astounding speed, at the advances that make such production possible. As Evans says, the printing industry can "reproduce all manner of surface and color tonality, with an accuracy that is simply miraculous."[4] Many effects are achieved that were not even considered just a few years ago. Second, the field of book illustration attracts immensely talented artists, because of the growing number of picture books published each year. Whereas at one time illustration of children's books was a backwater into which the professional artist did not venture, the same isn't true today. Impressive recognition from various professional groups which give awards is accorded the artist who successfully illustrates children's books. In addition, a fair percentage of the selling price is passed on to the illustrator; in view of the large print runs common today, the financial remuneration a talented and recognized artist receives makes illustrating books worthwhile.

Teachers and librarians should consciously study the illustrator's art so that they can introduce children to the wealth of inventive, imaginative pictures in books today. Adults can help children study illustrations as independent visual artifacts, created by someone, reproduced by some means, designed to create some specific effect on the intended audience. Any work of art, whether it is the most delicate of watercolors or the most dramatic of woodcuts, uses at least one, or several visual elements: shape, line, color, proportion, detail, and space (Harlan, 1970). These will be examined more fully in chapter two.

A book with pictures

Picture storybook
A book in which the story and pictures are of equal importance.

Having described three categories of books with pictures, we'll now focus primarily on picture storybooks. For simplicity sake, the term picture books will be used generically throughout. It will be apparent which of the books described do indeed contain a coherent story with a beginning, middle, and end. In the process of examining this genre, we'll also incidentally look at some books, like alphabet, number, and concept books, which don't include a narrative.

A picture storybook is a book in which the story and pictures are of equal importance. The two elements together form an artistic unit that is stronger than either of them would be alone.

Sometimes such books have few words because they are designed for the very youngest readers, as in the Caldecott Award winner, *Drummer Hoff*, by Barbara Emberley. This is an adaptation of a Mother Goose rhyme, illustrated by Ed Emberley with solid woodcuts in bright colors. The cumulative, rhyming story contains only 30 words, but the highly complex pictures, which culminate in a vibrant red, pink, and purple double-page explosion of "kahbahbloom," are intriguing.

Other picture books are more complex than these and are obviously intended for intermediate-grade readers. *Brave Janet Reachfar*, by Jane Duncan, is the story of a girl's attempts to rescue sheep from an unexpected spring snow. The characters, the animals, and the environment in the Scottish Highlands are realistically depicted. The author uses a sophisticated vocabulary and lengthy sentences (one sentence has 54 words, more than in all of *Drummer Hoff*). However, this impressive story of courage and ingenuity is well worth the demands it makes on the reader/listener. Pictures in this book occur less frequently than in *Drummer Hoff*; the text is pleasantly augmented by the pictures but does not rely on them. The watercolor art is by Mairi Hedderwick, whose more recent work is described in chapter five.

For more information
See Barbara Bader's article "Picture Books, Art and Illustration" (in Newberry and Caldecott Medal Books, *1966-1975), Boston: The Horn Book, 1975, pp. 276-289). Bader is not impressed with* Drummer Hoff *as an award winner, and she offers acerbic comments on most of the others. Her educated eye prompts her to plead for more discrimination in making the awards.*

Collaboration

Some picture books represent a collaboration between an author and an illustrator. Adrienne Kennaway did the striking, full-page pictures, bled to the page edge, for *Hot Hippo*, by Mwenye Hadithi. This *pourquoi* (tell-me-why) tale recounts how the hippo finds its special place in nature. The simple language is augmented by the intense and varied watercolors, which do not add much factual detail but do provide a pleasant accompaniment.

Subsequently this picture book team collaborated on *Crafty Chameleon*, which won the Kate Greenaway Award, the British equivalent of the Caldecott Medal. On plate *1* in the color section, we can see the kind of soft edge to shapes which indicates they

Plate 1: Crafty Chameleon

It is the intensity of the color contrasts which makes the design qualities of this illustration so apparent. For example, we see the spots of the leopard, its whiskers against the tree leaves, and the designs on the chameleon's back so clearly because artist Kennaway chose such very different colors for these objects than the colors chosen for what the objects are shown against. Hadithi and Kennaway collaborated again on *Hungry Hyena* in which the jungle foliage is particularly lushly painted. There are some interesting color and shape similarities between this art, and the pictures done by Judith Riches for *Rooster Crows* by Ragnhild Scamell.

(See full illustration in color plates following page 174.)

About the artist

A. Silvey, an editor, has commented at length about Robert McCloskey and his Make Way for Ducklings, *in the context of the currently burgeoning picture book market in the* Horn Book Magazine *(1991).*

were painted using a lot of water, and on paper which was itself still wet. The apparent repeated patterning decorates the page and is less concerned with realistic representation of detail than with creating a rhythm which will delight the eye. Here, as in most of the other pictures, the wide range of tonalities adds considerable interest. This isn't, for example, just green. Rather, it is a wide variety of shades of green. Notice also how the tree branch forms a very strong diagonal cutting from lower left to upper right. This bisection of the page allows Kennaway to balance the weight of Leopard on top of the branch with the much smaller visual weight of Chameleon. The balance is achieved because Chameleon is so much brighter than Leopard. These collaborators continued their work in *Tricky Tortoise*. All of the books exemplify the non-literal representation, a "symbolic depiction of animals and plants," marked by "subtle changes in shades and tints of the basic color scheme...."[5]

Other picture books are written and illustrated by just one person. An example is *Burt Dow Deep-Water Man*, written and illustrated by Robert McCloskey, a two-time winner of the Caldecott Medal. Burt sets out to sea one day in his leaky old double-ender. McCloskey's pictures show Burt's encounter with a huge whale, who saves him from a storm only to get him into more trouble in a school of whales. The opaque watercolor illustrations bleed off the edges of the pages, resulting in large, bright images that clarify and extend the text. *(See illustration on page 78.)*

Black and white vs. color

Picture books may be illustrated in black and white, in a few colors, or in many hues. Leonard Everett Fisher demonstrates the expressiveness of simple black and white in *The Great Wall of China*. His monumental acrylic paintings use applied white to achieve an array of grey tones that further contrast with the stark white of the page itself. He used the same visual approach in *Pyramid of the Sun, Pyramid of the Moon (See illustration on the next page)*, and a similar large format, to tell the story of the Aztecs, which shows so effectively the mighty structures of the religious center of this civilization at Teotihuacan, Mexico. The illustrator received the Washington Post/Children's Book Guild Nonfiction Award in 1989, given for a substantial body of consistently high-quality works.

Figure 1.4: Pyramid of the Sun, Pyramid of the Moon
Notice what a tight triangle composition Fisher has created here. Follow an imaginary line from the top of the left Indian's headdress, down to the right Indian's left shoulder, down his arms to the victim's head, and back up the strong vertical to the standing Indian. The emotional center of the picture is thus tightly constrained, intensified even more by the heads of the two watching Indians, whose bodies do not show.

One of the most talented illustrators using black and white is Chris Van Allsburg. In *The Garden of Abdul Gasazi*, Van Allsburg creates a surreal world where illusion blends into reality. *(See illustration on p. 42)* The pencil illustrations are realistic, but he uses intensified light, shadow, and perspective to create unusual impressions of space and density. This book, his first, marked the beginning of an impressive succession of high-quality picture books.

Just a few colors are used by Peter Parnall in *Winter Barn*. This book features more realistically detailed drawings with less undesigned space than is usual in Parnall's work. Faint touches of brown and red direct the eye in these drawings. Another example of effective use of a few colors is found in Mary Calhoun's *The Witch Who Lost Her Shadow*. With three colors, artist Trinka

Noble defines the village and the characters. This simple story is about a good witch whose constant companion, her "silent-sipping wisp of a cat," disappears. The book is an admirable combination of low-keyed art and graceful, unobtrusive writing.

Unlike artists who work with few colors, Eric Carle utilizes many hues, both primary and pastel, in his collage pictures for *Why Noah Chose the Dove*. This Bible story was retold from the animals' viewpoint by Isaac Bashevis Singer. The animals, bragging about their good qualities, are depicted in blocky, page-filling shapes, cut from paper and streaked with paint. More than a decade later, perennially popular Carle again used the same technique in *The Foolish Tortoise*, by Richard Buckley. In this case, the artist's considerable talent perhaps overmatches the rather slight fable, but his pictures are as appealing and as "readable" as ever.

Realism vs. fantasy

Picture book stories may be realistic or fantastic. In spare prose, often no more than a sentence or two per page, Donald Carrick tells the poignant story of *The Deer in the Pasture* who "adopted" a human but later had to be returned to the wild. The author provides pleasantly casual watercolor paintings in many subtle shades of brown, green, gold, and orange. The open ending is also realistic; children will wonder what happens to the deer, and hope.

In contrast to Carrick's kind of realism, picture books often feature fantastical tales about either animals or people. Barbara Lucas's *Sleeping Over* is the story of a bear and a frog, which ends happily when the frog finds a comfortable place to sleep (a toothbrush glass full of water). Stella Ormai's watercolor and ink paintings convincingly depict the frog's trouble and the resolution.

A pleasant fantasy about a human is Jenny Thorne's *My Uncle*, featuring a round-faced gentleman nattily attired in black and yellow checked knickers. His desire to go mountain climbing first gets him into trouble with a big-billed bird; later he gets lost in a forest inhabited by strange creatures and finally barely escapes an octopus in the water. The dry, pragmatic language is an interesting contrast to the highly patterned fantasy of the drawings.

Two equally strong components

It is a happy occurrence when both the pictures and words are equally distinguished. The language used in *Wildfire*, by Evans G. Valens, is as impressive as the pictures:

> The heat of the long western summer lay stagnant on the forest when the first raindrops tumbled from the sky. They rattled the dry needles and spanked hot rocks on the ridge above. A chipmunk scuttling for shelter left a wisp of red dust hanging in the drowsy air.
>
> The sky cracked open, a quick electric slit of light running from a cloud to a towering fir. The crack was mended with a clump of thunder, and the echo rolled and ricocheted.
>
> In the clearing dead brush lay dry and hot. The manzanita leaves were ripe with oil. When the flames reached them, the bushes withered. Then they blossomed in a wave of yellow flame. A sound like loud breathing mingled with the snapping and whistling of separate leaves.

Wildfire is among the books recommended by Cianciolo in *Picture Books for Children* (1990). She includes this title in the third edition of her text, despite its being out of print, because it still exemplifies the best possible in picture books.

The language in *Little Silk*, by Jacqueline Ayer, shows what language-sensitive authors can achieve:

> *Deep back in a night-black closet,*
> *hidden behind a tumble of boxes,*
> *boots and bundles,*
> *a faded silk doll*
> *sits and dreams and waits for the closet door to open.*

Note the choice of words "deep back" instead of the more common "way back" or "far back." "Night-black" is a fine choice, since it intensifies the darkness of a closet in a particularly effective way. The doll is hidden in a "tumble" of boxes, an unusual word choice that unconsciously attracts a reader's notice. The alliteration of boxes, boots, and bundles is natural. From among all the objects that might be in a closet, the writer has chosen three beginning with the same sound. The triplet construction "sits and dreams and waits" parallels the three words beginning with *b*. Ayer uses lines of varying lengths to tell the story, until the point at which the family reaches the market, where she changes the style somewhat, creating a heavily accented, shorter, and more regular line, with near rhymes at the ends of lines two and four:

> *Cabbages and kumquats,*
> *Chestnuts on the fire,*
> *"Virtuous and Prosperous,"*
> *Fried squid, rubber tires,*
> *Peppered eels and crab claws,*
> *Chicken-noodle hot pot.*
> *"Constant Joy Harmonious,"*
> *Wong Lee Barber Shop.*

The rhythmic difference of these lines sets apart the market scene very effectively. The book is an example of one editor's contention about the importance of text. Lurie asserts that "A well-written text is the difference between a flash-in-the pan and a title of lasting value."[6]

Introduced by dramatic, dark blue endpapers with a stylized floral design, the illustrations by Jacqueline Ayer combine flat blocks of intense orange, blue, and black paint with softer, contrasting areas of pencil, sharpened in places with ink line of delicate, unvarying thickness. The pictures are in perfect harmony with the words.

Functions of picture books

To understand why picture books need to be a pervasive part of the environment for young children, it is important to identify some purposes these books serve. Like other categories of books, picture storybooks are valuable because they allow children to experience environments unlike their own, to travel to another time, to confront situations unlike their own, or to empathize with a character who shares a common problem. There are, in addition, three unique functions of picture storybooks.

Picture storybooks provide language input for children.

Because of the vocabulary and the syntax they include, picture books provide models that can influence children's language. Authors of picture storybooks use the words necessary to deal with their topics. Writers usually do not limit their word choices, knowing that children's listening comprehension is more exten-

On the other hand

Another type of picture book that has become very common is the type specifically designed to be read by beginning readers themselves. Called by various titles (the "Ready-to-Read" series of Macmillan, the "I Can Read" series of HarperCollins), these series are valuable for children who are eager to read because they have just mastered beginning reading skills. In these books, both vocabulary and syntax are stringently controlled.

sive than their speaking and reading vocabularies. The context often provides clues to word meanings; a child can figure out what a word means by listening to the sentence in which the word occurs:

> Hoarfrost coated their eyebrows as they set out on the slow, wobbly ride homeward.

> John would undo the stanchions in late afternoon and chase the whole herd into the bitter cold outside.

In both these sentences, children can determine at least the approximate meanings for the unfamiliar words because of the context.

Authors also use whatever syntax is necessary to create a desired effect. The following sentence, which is in inverted form (main clause following a subordinate clause) and is longer (22 words) than is usual in picture books, is a model of mature, adult language:

> On the frozen sea of snow that stretched across farmlands broken only by barbed-wire fences, prairie boys would find jack-rabbit trails.

A Prairie Boy's Winter, from which these examples come, is told in third-person narrative, despite the fact that author William Kurelek is relating events from his own boyhood. Although each section can be read independently, the short episodes about different aspects of winter are roughly sequential. Each episode is arranged on one page, with a full-color painting facing it. The author also used this format in *A Prairie Boy's Summer*.

Students need to experience language more complex than what they generally use if their own language is to develop. The influence adult language has on children's language is commented on in an article describing the uses of books. Schmidt warns that teachers must beware of attempting to "protect the child from the frustration of a too rich language environment, a language too different for him (sic) to fully understand."[7]

Picture storybooks provide visual input for children.

Picture storybooks can heighten visual sensitivity by exposing students to fine illustrations on a regular basis. In contrast to the indifferent visual quality of much of the television for children and the banal art found in the thin books sold in supermar-

Activity
It would be interesting for children to compare William Kurelek's descriptions of the seasons with Laura Ingalls Wilder's accounts in her Little House *books.*

Figure 1.5: Maria Theresa

There's nothing idealized here: Signora Rinaldo isn't pretty, the wall phone and coffeemaker in the kitchen aren't elegant, and the tank vacuum cleaner, circa 1955, suggests clutter. Yet it is precisely this ordinariness which so effectively sets off the imaginative fantasy of the story itself. To examine Mathers' art for other authors, see her illustrations for *The Block Book* by Susan Arkin Couture, for younger readers, or see *I'm Flying* by Alan Wade, with a longer text for older readers.

About the artist

In Sophie and Lou, *Petra Mathers developed a timid mouse heroine who overcomes her diffidence. Mathers writes about creating this book in an article about her work in the* Horn Book Magazine *(1991).*

kets and drugstores, the illustrations in quality children's books are a feast for the eyes.[8]

This exceptional art is available in a variety of styles. Some of it is realistic, for example, that in *The Mare on the Hill*, by Thomas Locker. These full-page alkyd and oil paintings are full of three-dimensional details, which combine to create a lifelike effect seldom presented in children's books.

Some of this impressive artwork is surrealistic, such as in *Maria Theresa*, by Petra Mathers. Despite its picture book format, this book is for third- through sixth-grade readers; the theme and some of the Italian referents are clearly beyond very young children. Richard and MacCann, two of the most insightful reviewers of children's books working today, comment on the flat, primitive style that produces "a consistently engaging, otherworldly quality."[9]

Picture storybooks stimulate the visual and verbal fluency of children.

Picture books can serve as a source for the language development of children if they are carefully used. As librarians and teachers use picture books with classes, they can encourage students to notice and comment on the following things:

- *What* the illustrator includes in the picture: the people, objects, and settings.
- *Where* things are in the picture: the location of objects can illustrate, among other things, their relative importance.
- *How* things are made: the medium used and the style employed.

Evaluating picture books

Not all picture books embody the necessary balance between vigorous, evocative language and imaginative pictures. When one or the other of these elements is weak or missing, the book may not be worth sharing with children. Teachers and librarians selecting picture books will do well to examine the candidates carefully, to weed out books that do not combine effective words with effective pictures. Despite the bright colors, John Stadler's cartoon characters in *Snail Saves the Day* are devoid of appeal. The words are written for beginning readers but do not have the wry charm of Arnold Lobel's books. For example, *Owl at Home* and *Frog and Toad are Friends* are also for beginning readers. But as

Figure 1.6: Frog and Toad Are Friends
Another of the cozy, small animal other-worldly habitats so common in children's literature. Notice that this, compared with the Sendak *Pleasant Fieldmouse*, is set indoors rather than outside. Because everything is exactly the right size for these two small animals, Lobel was able to create a world particularly their own. This contrasts with the effect in *Borrowers Aloft* by Mary Norton with illustrations by Beth and Joe Krush. In this longer story, the tiny creatures must make adaptive use of conventional, human-sized objects.

Lobel explores the foibles of these humanized animals, the work achieves captivating, wry charm which is lacking in Stadler's book. Similarly, Denys Cazet's rabbits, in *December 24th*, frolic and cavort but never manage to make real magic. The bespectacled grandfather rabbit entertains his grandchildren, and some child readers may find this funny. But there's nothing to recommend the pedestrian language or the overly bright pictures, which are cute without being appealing and are predictable in their humor.

Often a picture book is unsuccessful because the topic is one that has been treated so many times before. It is difficult, for example, to come up with an imaginative treatment of monsters. Despite his recognized success as one of the key innovators in picture books, Maurice Sendak turned out a book that is undistinguished when he tried his hand at monsters in *Seven Little Monsters*, which is distinctly inferior to his universally known, and critically lauded *Where the Wild Things Are*.

Another major consideration when evaluating picture storybooks is how well the words and the pictures mesh. There may be such distinct contradictions between the text and the illustrations that it becomes doubtful that children will accept the book. Though an artist should be free to interpret words imaginatively, pictures that contradict the words only confuse child readers. An unfortunate example comes from the drawing board of a talented illustrator, Susan Jeffers, whose pictures for *Cinderella* don't bear out the words of translator Amy Ehrlich. The text asserts that "he became a fat coachman with a most imposing beard." The beard Jeffers shows seems rather unremarkable, and the young man is clearly thin, without a trace of extra poundage on him. Further, Jeffers's predilection for drawing beautiful people has here led her astray. The text states that Cinderella is "yet a hundred times more beautiful than her stepsisters." However, the sisters aren't ugly! They may not be as beautiful as Cinderella is, but they are definitely not just plain; they are in fact very comely.

Another element we consider in thinking about the effectiveness of children's picture storybooks is the relation between the pictures and the words. In a helpful section of a longer work, Poltarnees identifies some relationships that are as important today as when he first asked us to think about them. He points out that some pictures:

1. Show things described in the words.

For more information

Stewig has written more about the topic of monsters in picture books in an article entitled "Still Another Monster/ Talking Animal Book?" in the Wisconsin English Journal.

2. Show things mentioned, but not described in words.

3. Show things neither mentioned, nor described.

He gives examples from books which fall into each of these three categories. As we look at books mentioned in this text, we might examine them to see which category they belong in. For example, Nodelman (1992) uses Margot Zemach's pictures for *Jake and Honeybunch Go to Heaven* as representative of the second kind of pictures. The words tell us only that "there were angels everywhere," but as Nodelman points out, Zemach's pictures give us a very detailed—and in some ways unexpected—manifestation of those words.

Criteria to use

Because any teacher or librarian is limited in two ways—by limited budgets and by limited amounts of time to share books with children—decisions must always be made about quality in picture books. For that reason, it is important to develop your own critical facilities, to be able to make decisions about books, beyond the limited number which are described here. To that end, try using some of the ideas examined earlier in thinking about other books you encounter.

Here are some questions which can help you to evaluate the effectiveness of language in picture books:

1. Is there a variety of words—both familiar and unfamiliar—which will stretch children's understanding, providing the assurance of the known and the challenge of the unknown?

2. Is there a variety of sentence structures, including statements, questions, commands and requests? Linguists have long known that all children use these varying sentence types long before they know about them consciously. Because of this, and also because of the intrinsic interest it adds, the best literature incorporates a variety of sentences.

3. Does the author make use of such literary devices as repetition to intrigue the reader/listener? For example, in some books a repeated word, phrase or complete sentence provides a pleasant anticipation.

Some questions which can help you to evaluate the effectiveness of the art in picture books:

1. Does the artist make us see something we've not seen before, or see something familiar in a new way? Perhaps the artist is showing us a place, objects or people we've never experienced firsthand. Or, perhaps the illustrator is, through the use of the visual elements described in chapter 2, making us notice familiar objects depicted in an unfamiliar way.

2. Does the art intrigue us because of where it is placed, the sequence in which it is presented or perhaps because of the medium which is used?

3. How does the art enhance, or extend the words? Perhaps the artist gives us a fuller understanding of the words because of the completeness with which the text is shown through images. Or, perhaps the artist shows many additional details which aren't given in the words at all.

Choose some new book and, without looking for reviews of it to see what critics have said, examine it to identify your own reactions. You might use, for example, Noni Lichtveld's *I Lost My Arrow in a Kankan Tree*. As with any picture book, it is often helpful to simply go through it a first time, examining the art without reading the text. This gives some sense of the flow of the pictures. This procedure will alert you to where the continuity from one picture to the following one is particularly apparent and where there appears to be a discontinuity (probably accounted for in the words). As you are doing this first holistic look through the book, you undoubtedly are unconsciously focusing on how this art relates to, or is different from, the art in other picture books you're familiar with.

A next step would be to go through the book again, reading just the text, to focus on those aspects of the writing which catch and hold your attention. If you have read it silently the first time, go back through and read the text aloud so you can hear how it functions, not as a sequence of words on a page, but rather as a flow of speech sound through time. Then you have reached a stage where it would be useful to consider consciously some of the questions suggested above.

Visual Analysis

This section describes the impressions I gleaned in beginning to get acquainted with *I Lost My Arrow in a Kankan Tree*. Opening to the endpapers, it was immediately apparent that the people shown were closely interrelated with each other and with the natural elements like trees, plants, water, and animals that surround them. The title page illustration called attention to the fact that apparently two males, one larger and older than the other, will figure significantly in the story. The first opening introduces the concept of many, many people, both children and adults, so the story is apparently not going to be about just a few characters. As I continue to turn pages, it becomes apparent that the patterning evident on the endpapers is proceeding very consistently through every picture. By the third opening, I'm noticing some stylistic similarity in the faces of people with and the proportions in the art of Andrew Glass, as in *Professor Popkin's Prodigious Polish* or in *Spooky and the Ghost Cat*. Far more apparent, however, is the color and design similarity with the art of Ashley Bryan; I need to go look at this book in the context of books Bryan has done to see if that impression holds up.

By the fifth opening, it is apparent that the story will be set primarily outside. Though there is a small house shown in the distance in the third opening, so far all the action has taken place outside. The very blue cow in the fifth opening tells me, even without the words, that the story being presented isn't a realistic one. On the sixth opening, I notice that the text is on top of, not integrated with, the pictures. The intensity of the colors in the art is diminished as the words are applied—what is underneath the block of the words still shows through but with the color significantly diminished. On the sixth and seventh opening, the strong diagonal movement from the lower left corner to the top right corner becomes apparent. That causes me to go back and look again at preceding pages to see if that movement carries throughout. It doesn't. On the fifth opening, there is a strong vertical division of the pages caused by the cluster of trees in the middle.

It is on the tenth opening that the jungle setting finally gives way to a cluster of buildings, so I make the guess that the setting has changed, and I will look for that when I read the words. On the 11th opening, we finally have a scene set entirely inside a building, and the adults here are more formally dressed than before. One is in a uniform, the first time we've seen that. On the

11th and 12th openings, the artist uses the architecture as an organizing element. On the 13th opening, the page format changes for the first time. Prior to this, all of the openings have been double-page spreads with small blocks of words set in varying positions around the opening. Here, we discover a single-page picture on the left with no words, facing a page on which many lines of text are set on a pale green background. The 14th opening reverts to a double-page spread which is here wordless. Now that I have done an initial look through, it is time to go back and examine just the words. First, I read silently, to get an idea of the flow of the story.

Textual Analysis

There are several features which distinguish the text of this story about young Jakono's journey, a typical chaining tale or cumulative tale in which, the refrain gets longer with each repetition. Jakono manages to trade something he doesn't particularly need for something which will benefit the person he meets. In return, he is given something which will be useful for the next person he encounters, and so it goes, until he considerably betters not only his own lot, but that of his entire, extended family. Set in Suriname, this includes several distinctive language uses. There are interesting contrasts in sentence structure. For example, the forest gets "smaller and smaller," while his family gets "larger and larger." There is a repetition of sounds, for example, the repeated / th / sound in "he sets off then and there." The author also repeats words effectively, on Jakono's journey, "He walks and he walks and he walks." This repeated refrain comes through like a chant one might call out while walking. Finally, there is interesting use of unfamiliar words, like "Odi odi—good morning" which add to the distinctive character of the text, especially when read aloud.

As I read the text aloud for the first time, several other aspects of it become apparent. First, the sentences vary greatly in length, from short ones of only five words to long ones of as many as 22 words. I'll need to practice this so I can read it to children effectively, making sure to breathe deeply enough to sustain the meaning contour throughout the longer sentences. Second, this reading alerts me to the prevalence of dialogue in the text. Because there are many different people speaking, but only one at a time, not in a group of speakers, I probably don't need to develop individual voices for each of the characters. I will need to work on how the characters say things, however. For example, the old man screams one of his comments, but wails another one, calling for a different oral interpretation of the words. There are unfamiliar words which I'll need to say often enough so they come easily to the tongue: *Granmise*, for example, is not an easy word to pronounce at sight. Finally, there are syntactic arrangements which need careful attention. For example, "Only this pumpkin can I give you," is an uncommon word order which needs to be preserved. More commonly, we might expect to see "I can only give you this pumpkin." Maintaining carefully the exact syntax is important in reading many texts like this one. Noting the number of characters with speaking parts—nine—reminds me that this story has possibilities for readers theatre, which I can develop with a group of children if they seem interested.

Multicultural considerations

In planning an entire program of picture book sharing with youngsters, one factor librarians and classroom teachers must keep in mind is the representation of ethnicity. Recently more and more picture books have become available that show us a wide variety of ethnic groups.

Writers now depict a range of black experiences in picture book format; notable among them is Angela Johnson. Johnson was the 1991 winner of the Ezra Jack Keats Bookwriter's Award, given to a promising young writer whose books represent the multicultural nature of the world, "extending children's awareness and understanding of other cultural and ethnic groups."[10] *Tell Me a Story, Mama*, with pictures by David Soman, is told in two voices, the mother and her five-year-old daughter, recalling details from earlier times which they have ritualized into a shared story. Soman's largely backgroundless illustrations are in softly fluid watercolors, enclosed in a thin black rule. In Johnson's *Do Like Kyla*, the warm story of affection between an older and younger sister is enhanced with full-color, full-page paintings by the black artist James E. Ransome, whose heavy brush strokes add texture to the art.

Sometimes these are books of historic fiction, as in *Sweet Clara and the Freedom Quilt* by Deborah Hopkinson. The fully painted, full-page pictures bled to the page edge, are by black illustrator James Ransome. The story told by Clara, not yet 12,

Activity
It would be interesting to compare Sweet Clara *with Jeanette Winter's* Follow the Drinking Gourd, *which also deals with the railroad, and features paintings that are strongly expressionistic.*

recounts her experiences first as a field slave, and then as a house slave. She uses her needlework skills to create a quilt depicting the route to freedom along the underground railway.

Arone Raymond Meeks, an Aboriginal Australian, used design motifs from his culture to illustrate a tale from the Kokoimudji tribe, in *Enora and the Black Crane*. Full-page, unbordered illustrations done primarily in a strong brick red, and shades of orange and yellow, are heavily overlaid with both black and white line, to create patterned, flat pictures. In the end, because of his curiosity, Enora becomes a crane and joins the rest of the birds.

Hispanic tales are becoming more available than previously, but they are still not plentiful. Friso Henstra, twice winner of the prestigious Golden Apple Award at the Biennale of Illustrations in Bratislava, did watercolor and pen line drawings for *Pedro & the Padre* by Verna Aardema. Though not herself Hispanic, Aardema has, over a long career, won acclaim for the scholarly care of her adaptations from many different cultures. In this case, she is presenting a tale from Jalisco, Mexico, of wily Pedro, whose laziness gets him into a variety of trouble, as he bilks several gullible people. Finally he returns to his adopted home with the Padre, glad to have discovered the virtues of truth-telling. Henstra's illustrations, in a variety of page placements and sizes, make much use of overlaid crosshatching with pen to modify the underlying watercolors.

Material from Asian cultures is also now more accessible. *The Moles and the Mireuk* is retold from her culture by the Korean author, Holly Hyeshik Kwon. This presents a whimsical tale of Papa Mole, who sets out to find a powerful husband for his perfect daughter. Woodleigh Hubbard did full-color, full- and double-page spreads which rely, interestingly, on very little line to define shapes. Rather, she frequently sharpens her abstract forms by creating a very definite edge, and uses strongly contrasting colors to further clarify where one shape ends and another begins. The swirl of recurring circular shapes is seen in the grasses as shown on the fourth opening, or the rays of the sun on the seventh opening, and the breath of the wind on the tenth opening.

American Indian tales are also now available, though some concerns about these are expressed, as pointed out later. Barbara Juster Esbensen, a poet, did extensive research which led to *Ladder to the Sky*, an Ojibway legend she retold. Helen K. Davie's art incorporates stylized representations of flowers and plants into

Activity

This same story of the father mole and his daughter has been identified as a Japanese folktale in the The Greatest of All, *retold by Eric Kimmel. In this book Biora Carmi has created a more realistic presentation which you might help the children compare with* The Moles and the Mireuk.

the borders surrounding the pictures. Her richly varied watercolors are close in tonality. Durga Bernhard used even more abstracted, higher intensity, flat shapes in her art for *Spotted Eagle & Black Crow*, a Lakota legend retold by Emery Bernhard; the author and illustrator are described as "longtime students of traditional shamanism and tribal art."

Shonto Begay, a Navajo, used subdued colors and a variety of textures in the art for his retelling of *Ma'ii and Cousin Horned Toad*, a tale from the Navajo culture. Tricky Ma'ii, the coyote, takes advantage of patient Horned Toad, who eventually has to teach Ma'ii a lesson, using his own rough skin from within Ma'ii's tender insides! The lines stroked over these watercolors provide additional texture and definition to the natural shapes. The book concludes with a page of information about the role of these two characters in Navajo tradition and about the pronunciation and meaning of the vocabulary words used.

As we look at such books, we must keep in mind the issue of authenticity. As pointed out by MacCann and Richard, what appears at first glance to be a welcome new addition to a list of multicultural books, sometimes turns out to be very inauthentic. These writers interviewed the president of the American Indian Library Association, who commented on a paradox: quantitatively books about Native Americans are numerous, but qualitatively they "are mostly inauthentic."[11]

The problem is that sometimes we don't know enough about the ethnic group involved to determine authenticity. For example, when I first looked at *Chin Yu Min and the Ginger Cat* with illustrations by Mary Grandpre, I found it an agreeable picture story about a proud and haughty wife whose idleness and luxury come to an abrupt end. The double-page spreads show the small, rural village near Kunming in China. When I asked a Chinese graduate student to look at the book, she found several troubling historic inaccuracies. The woman, wife of a prosperous government official, has very long feet, which would have been uncommon in that social class before the revolution when foot binding was common. The student pointed out that though the hat shown on the second opening seems to be from the Ching Dynasty (of 1644-1911), the money with a square hole shown on the third opening was in fact in use until 1920. The student felt that Chin Yu Min's clothing throughout is more modern and Western-influenced than clothing from the time period of the money would have been. She commented that neither the rice jar nor its cover on the third opening are very typical shapes. No one of these matters of detail is important of itself: rather what they point out is the need for an artist, when choosing a particular time period, to research it thoroughly enough so that someone from the culture doesn't find visual discrepancies.

More important, perhaps, is a behavior described in the book. The Chinese student pointed out that it wouldn't be logical that each person in the village asked the widow to pay for looking in their baskets for her missing cat. Even a beggar in a small village, where everyone knows everyone else, would have let her look without charging her. That's an example of something of which I, as a non-Asian, wasn't aware.

Publishers are beginning to tell us more about the origins of the materials appearing in picture books and about the backgrounds of the authors and illustrators involved in creating them. For example, Murv Jacob has done elegantly stylized, full-color art for *How Rabbit Tricked Otter and Other Cherokee Trickster Stories* by Gayle Ross. The full-page pictures facing pages of text are surrounded by borders of many different designs, mostly created through multicolored lines. Within the illustration itself, Jacob uses many other colored lines to create patterns and evoke textures, like that of the turkey feathers on page 42, for instance. A small repeated design is placed above and below the text, enclosed with a thin black rule. The 15 tales included here show that Rabbit sometimes tricks and is sometimes tricked; sometimes he is lazy and mean and sometimes he is kind and caring. In all, we meet a hero of many dimensions in stories which will acquaint children with a culture unfamiliar to most of them.

The publisher has provided detailed information on the back jacket about "The Parabola Storytime Series," of which this book is a part, where we learn, among other things, that the stories are appearing in written form for the first time, "with the permission of tribal elders...." In addition, the flap copy identifies the lineage and storytelling background of the author and the ethnicity and art background of the artist. This is particularly helpful in assuring readers of the authenticity of the material.

Gender representation

There is another factor we must consider in selecting picture books to share with children—the issue of gender representation.

For more information
Hearne (1993) dealt helpfully and at length with the problems inherent in presenting folk material from other cultures to young children in the United States.

Do these books present an equitable balance of male and female characters? Stewig and Knipfel (1975) found that picture books featured male characters far more often than was necessary to reflect their actual representation in life. Noting the widely accepted contention that "picture books probably play a part in early sex-role development," Engle (1981) concluded that, even though there was a slight shift toward gender equality in the 1976-1980 period covered in her study of 19 Caldecott Medal and honor books, "greater change is needed." It may be perfectly logical, within the fictional context set up by an individual author, for a boy to be the main character in a particular book and for girls to be nonexistent or relegated to a minor role. (See, for example, *The Chocolate Chip Cookie Contest*, by Barbara Douglas.) In the same way, it is logical in some books for a girl to be the main character and for there to be no boys or for boys to be relegated to minor roles. (See, for example, *Battle Day at Camp Delmont*, by Nicki Weiss.) An observation of gender bias may obscure how well a particular book intrinsically meets the other criteria for a fine picture book. Nonetheless, in considering the total array of picture books to be shared, teachers and librarians will want to keep this issue in mind.

Ethnicity and gender representation are factors to consider in planning a complete picture book program. Another factor is the balance between familiar, by-now-classic books and those new books by as-yet-unfamiliar artists and authors.

Books known and unknown

Clearly one of the special joys of children's literature is the body of well-loved "classics," books which have won the hearts of children across several generations of readers and listeners. We plan a program of sharing picture books which have endeared themselves to generations of children: *Goodnight Moon* by Margaret Wise Brown, *Blueberries for Sal* by Robert McCloskey, *Swimmy* by Leo Lionni, and *The Little House* by Virginia Lee Burton. The newest of these was published over 30 years ago, yet all of them remain in print, ready to speak to today's children. What is there about these books and others like them, in theme, in text, in pictures or in arrangement, which have made them last far longer than most picture books?

Interspersed with such well-known classics are the brand new books, whose authors and illustrators have yet to establish reputations. We consciously seek out such books, searching for the new talents, to acquaint children with as wide a variety of authors, illustrators and titles as is possible. For example, will children 50 years from now, in 2045, still be: 1) delighting in the panoramic sweep of the world of dinosaurs in *Time Flies*, a wordless book by Eric Rohmann; 2) enjoying the imaginatively patterned jungle lushness in pictures by Ed Young for *Bitter Bananas* by Isaac Olaleye; 3) responding to the motifs derived from Huichol yarn paintings in Emery and Durga Bernhard's *The Tree that Rains*?; or 4) talking excitedly about the expressionist illustrations in Katya Arnold's *Baba Yaga and the Little Girl*? No one knows. The history of children's literature criticism is full of two kinds of books: 1) Those which were reviewed very positively when first published, which have subsequently lapsed into obscurity, and 2) Those which didn't attract the attention they deserved, but which have gone on to remain in print for far longer than most other books. So as teachers and librarians, we read reviews widely, for suggestions about new books to incorporate into our picture books programs, but we don't depend solely on those, knowing that space limitations prevent reviews from dealing with more than a small percentage of the total number of books published each year.

With this introduction to picture books, and to some considerations in planning a program to involve children with pictures, we can move on to examining the components of picture books. In the next chapter, we'll focus on the visual elements, the components of pictures.

Recommended children's books

Please note: Publisher's names and locations are given as they originally appeared on the title page, not as they may have changed in the interval since publication. For example, Harper and Row also appears as HarperCollins. Differences in this information are not inconsistencies, but rather an attempt to provide accurate, original publication information.

Arnold, Katya. *Baba Yaga and the Little Girl*. New York: North-South Books, 1994.

Ayer, Jacqueline. *Little Silk*. New York: Harcourt Brace, 1970.

Begay, Shonto. *Mai'ii and Cousin Horned Toad*. New York: Scholastic Hardcover, 1992.

Berger, Terry. *Ben's ABC Day*. New York: Lothrop, Lee and Shepard, 1982.

Bernhard, Durga (Ill.). *Spotted Eagle & Black Crow* by Emery Bernhard. New York: Holiday House, 1993.

————— (Ill.). *The Tree That Rains* by Emery Bernhard. New York: Holiday House, 1994.

Bolognese, Don (Ill.). *The Ghost of Windy Hill* by Clyde Robert Bulla. New York: Thomas Y. Crowell, 1964.

Brown, Margaret Wise. *Goodnight Moon*. New York: Harper & Row, 1947.

Burgess, Mark (Ill.). *Harriet and the Haunted School* by Martin Waddell. Boston: Atlantic Monthly Press, 1984.

Burton, Virginia Lee. *The Little House*. Boston: Houghton Mifflin, 1942.

Butterworth, Nick and Mick Inkpen. *Nice or Nasty. A Book of Opposites*. Boston: Little, Brown and Co., 1987.

Byars, Betsy. *The Lace Snail*. New York: Viking, 1975.

Carle, Eric (Ill.). *Why Noah Chose the Dove* by Isaac Bashevis Singer. New York: Farrar, Straus and Giroux, 1974.

————— (Ill.). *The Foolish Tortoise* by Richard Buckley. Natick, MA: Picture Book Studios, 1985.

Carmi, Giora (Ill.). *The Greatest of All* by Eric A. Kimmel. New York: Holiday House, 1991.

Carrick, Donald. *The Deer in the Pasture*. New York: Greenwillow, 1976.

Cazet, Denys. *December 24*. New York: Bradbury, 1986.

Cooper, Helen. *The Bear Under the Stairs*. New York: Dial Books for Young Readers, 1993.

Cousins, Lucy. *Garden Animals (and Country..., Farm..., and Pet...)* All: New York: Tambourine Books, 1991.

Crews, Donald. *Shortcut*. New York: Greenwillow, 1992.

Davie, Helen K. (Ill.). *Ladder to the Sky* by Barbara Juster Esbensen. Boston: Little, Brown and Co., 1989.

Douglas, Barbara. *The Chocolate Chip Cookie Contest*. New York: Lothrop, Lee and Shepard, 1985.

Emberley, Barbara. *Drummer Hoff*. Englewood Cliffs, N.J.: Prentice-Hall, 1967.

Ernst, Lisa Campbell. *Up to Ten and Down Again*. New York: Lothrop, Lee and Shepard, 1986.

Fisher, Leonard Everett. *The Great Wall of China*. New York: Macmillan, 1986.

—————. *Pyramid of the Sun, Pyramid of the Moon*. New York: Macmillan, 1988.

Glass, Andrew (Ill.). *Professor Popkin's Prodigious Polish* by Bill Brittain. New York: HarperCollins, 1991.

————— (Ill.). *Spooky and the Ghost Cat* by Natalie S. Carlson. New York: Lothrop, Lee & Shepard, 1985.

Grandpre, Mary (Ill.). *Chin Yu Min and the Ginger Cat* by Jennifer Armstrong. New York: Crown Publishers, Inc., 1993.

Henstra, Friso (Ill.). *Pedro & the Padre* by Verna Aardema. New York: Dial Books for Young Readers, 1991.

Hubbard, Woodleigh (Ill.). *The Moles and the Mireuk* by Holly Hyeshik Kwon. Boston: Houghton Mifflin, 1993.

Jacob, Murv (Ill.). *How Rabbit Tricked Otter and Other Cherokee Trickster Stories* by Gayle Ross. New York: HarperCollins, 1994.

Jeffers, Susan. *Cinderella* translated by Amy Ehrlich. New York: Dial, 1985.

Karlin, Bernie (Ill.). *12 Ways to Get to 11* by Eve Merriam. New York: Simon and Schuster, 1993.

Kennaway, Adrienne (Ill.). *Crafty Chameleon* by Mwenye Hadithi. Boston: Little, Brown & Co., 1987.

———— (Ill.). *Hot Hippo* by Mwenye Hadithi. Boston: Little, Brown & Co., 1986.

———— (Ill.). *Hungry Hyena* by Mwenye Hadithi. Boston: Little, Brown, 1994.

———— (Ill.). *Tricky Tortoise*. Boston: Little, Brown & Co., 1988.

Kitamura, Satoshi. *When Sheep Cannot Sleep*. New York: Farrar, Straus and Giroux, 1986.

Krush, Beth and Joe (Ill.). *Borrowers Aloft* by Mary Norton. New York: Harcourt, 1989.

Kurelek, William. *A Prairie Boy's Summer*. Boston; Houghton Mifflin, 1975.

————. *A Prairie Boy's Winter*. Boston: Houghton Mifflin, 1973.

Lichtveld, Noni. *I Lost My Arrow in a Kankan Tree*. New York: Lothrop, Lee & Shepard Books, 1993.

Lionni, Leo. *Swimmy*. New York: Pantheon, 1963.

Lobel, Arnold. *Frog and Toad are Friends*. New York: Harper and Row, 1970.

————. *Owl at Home*. New York: Harper & Row, 1975.

Locker, Thomas. *The Mare on the Hill*. New York: Dial, 1985.

Mathers, Petra (Ill.). *The Block Book* by Susan Arkin Couture. New York: Harper and Row, 1990

———— (Ill.). *I'm Flying* by Alan Wade. New York: Alfred A. Knopf, 1990.

————. *Maria Theresa*. New York: Harper & Row, 1985.

————. *Sophie and Lou*. New York: HarperCollins, 1991.

Mayers, Florence Cassen. *The Museum of Modern Art ABC*. New York: Abrams, 1986.

McCloskey, Robert. *Blueberries for Sal*. New York: The Viking Press, 1963.

————. *Burt Dow Deep Water Man*. New York: Viking, 1963.

Meeks, Arone Raymond. *Enora and the Black Crane*. New York: Scholastic, 1991.

Morris, Ann, and Maureen Roffey. *Night Counting*. New York: Harper and Row, 1986.

Noble, Trinka (Ill.). *The Witch Who Lost Her Shadow* by Mary Calhoun. New York: Harper and Row, 1979.

Norman, Howard. *The Owl-Scatterer*. Boston: Little, Brown, 1986.

Norton, Mary. *The Borrowers Aloft*. New York: Harcourt Brace, 1961.

Oakley, Grahame. *The Church Mice and The Ring*. New York: Atheneum, 1992.

————. *Hetty and Harriet*. New York: Atheneum, 1981.

Ormai, Stella (Ill.). *Sleeping Over* by Barbara Lucas. New York: Macmillian, 1986.

Parnall, Peter. *Winter Barn*. New York: Macmillan, 1986.

Purviance, Susan & Marcia O'Shell. *Alphabet Annie Announces an All-American Album,* illustrated by Ruth Brunner-Strosser. Boston: Houghton Mifflin, 1988.

Ransome, James E. (Ill.). *Do Like Kyla* by Angela Johnson. New York: Orchard Books, 1990.

——— (Ill.). *Sweet Clara and the Freedom Quilt* by Deborah Hopkinson. New York: Alfred A. Knopf, 1993.

Rohmann, Eric. *Time Flies.* New York: Crown Publishers, 1994.

Scammer, Ragnid (Ill.). *Rooster Crows* by Judith Riches. New York: Tambourine Books, 1994).

Sendak, Maurice. *Seven Little Monsters.* New York: Harper and Row, 1975.

Soman, David (Ill.). *Tell Me a Story, Mama* by Angela Johnson. New York: Orchard Books, 1989.

Stadler, John. *Snail Saves the Day.* New York: Thomas Y. Crowell, 1985.

Stanley, Diane (Ill.). *All Wet! All Wet!* by James Skofield. New York: Harper and Row, 1984.

Thorne, Jenny. *My Uncle.* New York: Atheneum, 1982, now o.p.

Todd, Justin (Ill.). Alice's *Adventures in Wonderland* by Lewis Carroll. London: Victor Gollancz Ltd., 1984.

Valens, Evans G. *Wildfire.* Cleveland: World Publishing, 1963.

Van Allsburg, Chris. *The Garden of Abdul Gasazi.* Boston: Houghton Mifflin, 1979.

Weisgard, Leonard (Ill.). *The Important Book* by Margaret Wise Brown. New York: Harper and Row, 1949.

Weiss, Nicki. *Battle Day at Camp Delmont.* New York: Greenwillow, 1985.

Wells, Rosemary. *Morris's Disappearing Bag.* New York: Dial Press, 1975.

Wiggins, S. Michelle (Ill.). *Alice's Adventures in Wonderland* by Lewis Carroll. New York: Ariel Books/Knopf, 1983.

Winter, Jeanette. *Follow the Drinking Gourd.* New York: Alfred A. Knopf, 1988.

Young, Ed. (Ill.). *Bitter Bananas* by Isaac Olaleye. Honesdale, PA: Boyd's Mills Press, 1994.

Zemach, Margot. *Jake and Honeybunch Go to Heaven.* New York: Farrar, Straus & Giroux, 1982.

Professional references

Cianciolo, P. (1990). *Picture Books for Children* (3rd ed.). Chicago: American Library Association.

Cullinan, B. (1991). Ezra Jack Keats Bookwriting Award. USBBY Newsletter, 16(2), 14-15.

Egoff, S. A. (1981). *Thursday's Child. Trends and Patterns in Contemporary Children's Literature.* Chicago: American Library Association.

Engle, R. E. (1981, March). "Is Unequal Treatment of Females Diminishing In Children's Picture Books?" *The Reading Teacher,* pp. 647-652.

Evans, D. (1991, November/December). "An Extraordinary Vision." *The Horn Book Magazine,* pp. 712-715.

Feeney, S., & Moravcik, E. (1987). "A Thing of Beauty: Aesthetic Development in Young Children." *Young Children*, 42(6), 7-15.

Harlan, C. (1970). *Vision and Invention.* Englewood Cliffs, NJ: Prentice Hall.

Hearne, B. (1993, July, August). "Cite the Source." *School Library Journal*, pp. 22-27.

———(1993, July, August). "Respect the Source." *School Library Journal*, pp. 33-37.

Huck, C., Hepler, S., & Hickman, J. (1993). *Children's Literature in the Elementary School.* Fort Worth: Harcourt Brace Jovanovich.

Kiefer, B. (1989). "Picture Books for All the Ages." In J. Hickman & B. E. Cullinan (eds.), *Children's Literature in the Classroom. Weaving Charlotte's Web.* Needham Heights, MA: Christopher-Gordon, 1989, pp. 75-88.

Lacy L. (1988). "1988—A Caldecott year." *Journal of Youth Services in Libraries*, 1(2), 194-197.

Lechner, J. V. (1993). "Picture Books as Portable Art Galleries." *Art Education*, 46(2), 34-40.

Lurie, S. (1991). "First the Word: An Editor's View of Picture Book Texts." *School Library Journal*, 37(10), 50-51.

MacCann, D., & Richard, O. (1993). "Picture Books and Native Americans: An Interview with Naomi. Caldwell-Wood." *Wilson Library Bulletin*, 67(6), 30-34+.

Mathers, P. (1992). "The Artist At Work." *The Hornbook*, 68(2), 171-177.

Nodelman, P. (1992). *The Pleasures of Children's Literature.* New York: Longman.

Poltarnees, W. (1971). *All Mirrors Are Magic Mirrors. Reflections on Pictures Found in Children's Books.* La Jolla, CA: The Green Tiger Press.

Oakley, G. (1992). "Graham Oakley." In S. Marantz & K. Marantz (eds.), *Artists of the page. Interviews with children's book illustrators* (pp. 161-186). Jefferson, NC: McFarland & Co., Inc., Publishers.

Richard, O., & MacCann, D. (1984, September). "Picture Books for Children." *Wilson Library Bulletin*, pp. 50-51.

Schmidt. S. (1977, March). "Language Development And Children's Books In Intermediate Classrooms." *Insights Into Open Education*, pp. 2-10.

Shannon, G. (1994, January). "The Wolf and the Seven Little Kids." *Book Links*, pp. 50-52.

Silvey, A. (1991, July/August). "A Love Letter to Robert McCloskey." *The Horn Book Magazine*, pp. 389-390.

Stewig, J. W. (1977, April). "Still Another Monster/Talking Animal Book?" *Wisconsin English Journal*, pp. 37-38.

———(1992). "Ten from the Decade: Visually Significant Picture Books and Why." *The Dragon Lode*, 10(1), 1-9.

———, & Knipfel, M. L. (1975, December). "Sexism in Picture Books: What progress?" *Elementary School Journal*, 151-155.

Sutherland, Z. (1977). *Children and Books.* Glenview, IL: Scott, Foresman.

———, & Arbuthnot, M. H. (1991). *Children and Books.* New York: Harper Collins.

Pictorial Elements

2

What contributes to the particular distinctive visual style of a picture? Or, what elements does an artist use to affect the overall look of an entire picture book?

In this chapter, we'll examine the individual components an artist works with in creating illustrations. In chapter 3, we'll explore the compositional principles that artists use in organizing the elements of an illustration. Chapter 4 describes the media artists use to deal with the visual elements and compositional principles in creating pictures. In chapter 5, we explore the idea of the book as a visual artifact, or object, with elements like size, shape, heft, binding, and page design—all of which affect the overall look of a book. Chapter 6 suggests ways in which librarians and teachers can help children make links between various art movements, like impressionism and expressionism, and the art in children's books, which often reflects the influence of such art movements.

All picture book artists, no matter what materials they use, or what visual style they work in, have several visual elements that they work with. Decisions made about these elements can result in very different looks in the final art. It's helpful, thus, to be aware of the areas in which artists make decisions. These include shape, line, color, proportion, detail, and space.

Shape

Any artist will pay attention, either consciously or subconsciously, to the possibilities inherent in shape. Shapes may be flat and two-dimensional, giving no impression of thickness or substance, as in *Curl Up Small* by Sandol Stoddard Warburg. This is

Shape
The outline or configuration of a two-dimensional object; the definite external form of something an artist depicts; *form* is the term used for a three-dimensional object.

About the artist

Trina Schart Hyman comments on her working style, and about children's books in general, in an engaging, fey article in The Zena Sutherland Lectures 1983-1992.

Activity

You can find suggestions about how to help children study Hyman's use of three-dimensional shapes and their arrangement in space in Reading Pictures, *J. W. Stewig.*

Activity

Children might enjoy comparing the horses in Anderson's Complete Book of Horses *with* The Mare on the Hill *by Thomas Locker, described in chapter 1.*

Figure 2.1: What Game Shall We Play?

The folk art patterns, i.e., the heart shapes on the fox's body and the leaf-like veining on the duck's feathers, firmly establish this as playful fantasy. The illustration establishes this as imaginary, yet without clothing the animals, as is more commonly done (i.e., see illustrations by Sendak and Lobel). If children enjoy these illustrations, share with them *Tidy Titch* which presents human main characters in a more realistic setting. Or, see *Little Pink Pig* painted in bright gouache colors.

a pleasant rhymed account of mothers relating to their babies. A prolific illustrator and Caldecott Medal winner, Trina Schart Hyman, painted the shapes in soft watercolors—browns and greens with some yellow accents. Even though they are two-dimensional, the shapes of the pointy mother bird, the blocky mother bear, and the rounded human mother are effective.

In *Clocks and More Clocks*, Pat Hutchins provides the same type of flat shapes, but dressed in brighter colors and decorated with black line. Befuddled Mr. Higgins, whose determination to know the right time leads him into a frenzy, inhabits a flat world of orange, green, yellow, and brown shades. The decorative patterns enhance the essentially two-dimensional landscape. Hutchins used a similar approach in her *What Game Shall We Play?*, full of delightfully flat-patterned, two-dimension animals and their rural environment.

In contrast, an artist might create fully rounded shapes, which give an impression of three-dimensional substance and weight, usually accomplished through the use of shading. C. W. Anderson provides very realistic horse drawings in his *Complete Book of Horses and Horsemanship*. Many different kinds of horses, seen from a variety of angles and in various positions, are meticulously drawn and defined with line. This artist, who completely understands the body structure of horses, creates shading through

a buildup of small strokes. We see the lift of an ear, the droop of an eyelid, and the ripple of a cord in a neck because of the artist's skill. All of these details, however, are successfully subordinated to the total impression.

Realistic human shapes are found in the illustrations Trina Schart Hyman did for *Rapunzel*. Because of her thorough understanding of the underlying anatomy of the human figure, Hyman's people here are convincingly three-dimensional. They come to life on the two-dimensional page as they move through the deep space in which she places them. We sense, for example, the depth of a built-in bedchamber because of the realism of the two people she shows inhabiting this space.

Line

Line is another element artists employ in various ways to achieve a final effect. Line may be a thin, barely perceived whisper to enhance subtle color. Or it may be a heavy, dark stroke to boldly define forms and create shapes. Line may be regular, maintaining

For more information
A helpful book for introducing the concept of shapes—what they are and where they are found in nature—is Ed Emberley's The Wing on a Flea. *Two other useful books are Karen Gundersheimer's* Shapes to Show, *a small, mice-inhabited volume with just a word on each page, and Leonard Everett Fisher's* Look Around!, *which has the kind of full-color paintings this artist has been doing recently.*

Line

A mark which continues from one place to another, made by a pen, pencil or other object applied to a surface; line is used to define shapes, or to create textures.

the same form throughout a book, without variation. Or it may be flexible and fluid, varying from thick to thin.

An unvaryingly thin line may have an elegant quality, and a precise yet flowing line can not only outline form but also create mass without the use of color. In *The Aeneid for Boys and Girls*, artist Eugene Karlin provides a detailed, self-assured line that creates shapes with the precision of an etching.

Steven Kellogg uses a spidery, black line with a variety of cross-hatchings and dots to evoke the unreal, the bizarre, and the eccentric in *Gwot! Horribly Funny Hairticklers*. Kellogg's drawings of the scrawny farmer with fiendish eyes, the squatty old lady with a voracious appetite, and cross-eyed, taloned Gumberoo echo the macabre short stories.

Edward Gorey uses another kind of thin line to create his easily recognizable drawings in *The House with a Clock in Its Walls* by John Bellairs. This fantasy features a haunted house with a ticking clock counting the hours to doomsday. Crosshatched black line creates placid, fusty creatures who seem unaware of what may happen to them. The artist presents assorted textures and patterns of light and dark, and a shallow sense of space. Gorey continued to use this characteristic juxtaposition of pattern and line in a series of three books about a boy and his befuddled parents, written by Florence Parry Heide, the latest of which is *Treehorn's Wish*.

Ann Grifalconi used a fluid, contour line which seems to be smoothly connected, and yet which conveys a sense of movement and energy, in *Everett Anderson's Friend* by Lucille Clifton. Originally published over 15 years ago, it has recently been reis-

Figure 2.3: Everett Anderson's Friend
The simple, unornamented, but expressively moving line here can be compared to a melody played unaccompanied by a single musical instrument. There is noting unnecessary here; in fact Ann Cameron leaves out many details other artists might have thought essential. There is as little to concentrate on here as in some of the line etchings by Pablo Picasso; in each case the art is stronger because of its simplicity. For an example of more recent art by Grifalconi, see her double-page spreads showing Trinidad in *Jasmine's Parlour Day* by Lynn Joseph, with lustrous pastel colors reminiscent of the French painter, Auguste Renoir.

sued. The minimal nature of the backgrounds focus our attention on the fluidity of the line, which varies in width, depending on how heavily the pen was pressed. There are also spots, at the ends of line, where the ink spreads a bit, also due to some extra pressure on the pen. Small, accurate details aren't as important in this style of drawing as is the sweep of the movement shown. Everett, a young black boy of an age when girls are anathema, discovers that he can learn something new from Maria, his neighbor. Clifton's poetic text tells a story as engaging today as it was when originally written.

A very energetic line often pervades the work of James Stevenson. A good example is *Worse Than Willy.* It is part of a series of books about Grandpa, both in his current form as an elderly man and in his amusing childhood personification (also replete with mustache!). Stevenson's line is everywhere, leading to a "super-charged, frenetic cartoon-like" quality, recommended by Richard and MacCann (1984) as a particularly effective example of an energetic line. Because it is rather unlike his usual work, you might compare *Higher on the Door* with more typical Stevenson titles. In this book, he used watercolor and brush to create quite impressionistic small sketches; in these, almost none of the shapes are outlined. It is the forms of the objects themselves, casually brushed on, that show us his intent. These illustrations are quite similar in technique to those Chris L. Demarest created for *Today I'm Going Fishing with My Dad*, discussed later in this chapter.

In *The Two Reds*, a Caldecott Honor Book by William Lipkind, Nicholas Mordinoff's robust line crams the page with energetic detail. The pictures spill off the edges of the pages in this story of a small boy and a cat named Mr. Furpatto Purrcatto. Intense reds and yellow are splashed here and there; sometimes the color defines a form, and at other times it only lands generally in the area of the character. This use of color, only generally contained within the lines, is similar to the French painter Raoul Dufy's technique.

Far less pervasive than the line in the Lipkind and Mordinoff book is the line used by Catharine O'Neill for *Mr. and Mrs. Muddle.* Here Mary Ann Hoberman tells of two happily married equines who disagree on only one thing. The eccentric couple, shown in richly varied watercolor paintings of varying sizes placed in varying locations, eventually solve their disagreement

About the artist

Roberston and Underwood (1984) provide a catalogue of a retrospective exhibit of Dufy's work, which shows in large, full-color reproductions not only his paintings, but also the variety of other forms, like ceramics, in which this artist worked.

and paddle home to lunch. O'Neill's line is here, there and everywhere, but it starts and stops at will, underlining a shape, providing a bit of texture, but not lingering long enough anywhere to become pervasive. It is just a hint of a line which does not dominate the color.

John Burningham uses extensive, though not aggressive line, in *Mr. Grumpy's Outing*, a story in which the main character's good-hearted nature, despite his name, results in all of the characters getting wet in the end! Throughout, Burningham lays down soft pastel washes of watercolor and then overlays them with many thin pen lines, hatched and crosshatched to create interesting textures. What makes the book particularly effective is that though the line is black on some pages, in many places it is other colors. For example, on the first opening, we see that Burningham is going to use green, brown, red, yellow, and blue inks to define his shapes. The pleasantly scratchy effect he obtains is enhanced, for example, on the seventh opening, by the wide variety of different-colored brown inks he uses to depict the pig. On the eighth opening, the sheep is shown with soft grey and white

Figure 2.4: Mr. Grumpy's Outing
A light and frothy souffle of a story is illustrated in an equally airy way. Compare the crosshatching here with that done by Sendak for *Pleasant Fieldmouse*. If you have copies of both books, notice the difference in effect when crosshatching is done in shades of one color (in the Sendak) compared to many different pastel shades (as in this Burningham). More recently, Burningham has used watercolor washes, and darker shades of crosshatching, to show the story of *Aldo*, an imaginary friend.

lines, on a background with blue lines. Throughout, this alternating of the color of the lines keeps our interest. This book was included in the Biennale of Illustrations, Bratislava, a prestigious international exhibition of children's book art (Urblikova, 1975).

The line varies from thick to thin in Leo and Diane Dillon's art for *The Tale of the Mandarin Ducks*. In a *Horn Book* article the artists described their process for creating this art. It was derived from extensive study of the Japanese ukiyo-e style, which was actually done in woodcut. As the Dillons point out, though the art from which their book illustration descends was cut into wood, it wasn't the kind of angular, European approach most often identified with woodblock art (described later in chapter 4). Rather, the Japanese prints had the "character of a brush line."[1] So, using brushes, inks, watercolors, sponges, and even an ink eraser (to texture the paper for a grainy effect like woodcut), the artists made full-page illustrations.

Sometimes an artist upsets our expectation, for example, by providing white, instead of black or other dark-colored line. In *Happy Baby*, a board book from the "Dial Very First Book"

Activity
You might have children look at the line in The Tale of the Mandarin Ducks *and compare it with the line used in* Why Mosquitoes Buzz in People's Ears *by Verna Aardema, a Caldecott Medal winner, also with art by the Dillons.*

For more information
Preiss (1981) gives a very complete examination of the Dillons' early work, including art in various other formats (like posters and record sleeves) not widely known among those interested in children's books.

Figure 2.5: Go Away, Stay Away
Haley created a buoyantly "noisy" picture by showing a lot going on, and using many lines to include many different objects. This visual effect, present in the art throughout the book, emphasizes the nervous energy of the story itself, which features not a single main character, but rather a variety of scary beings. Compare this with her use of black line in *Jack and the Fire Dragon*, in which the sheen is intensified because of the high-gloss paper used.

series, Angie and Chris Sage outline the simple, backgroundless forms with a white, intermittent line. The roundfaced baby shows up against the solid color backgrounds because the line, sometimes appearing as dots in a sequence, defines the shapes.

In *Go Away, Stay Away (See illustration on previous page)*, Gail E. Haley effectively uses pervasive black line which defines and encompasses the shapes of Mother, Father, and Peter in their daily life. But this contrasts with the white line she uses to show the *Spinnikins*, "imps who fly in through open windows," hide, and cause all manner of small-scale mischief. Haley also uses white line to show us the *Bunshees*, who steal food from people's plates when they're not looking; the *Kicklebucket*, who lurks around the cowshed, waiting to cause trouble, and the *Hobble Goblins*, who trouble unwary travelers. In the double-page spread toward the book's end, we see the white-lined flurry of pesky creatures being ousted from the village, as the villagers can then settle down to enjoy spring dancing, free of bother.

An even more pervasive use of white line is apparent in *Mother Crocodile by* John Steptoe, a book for older readers presenting an Ouolof folktale from Senegal, West Africa. The paintings won a Coretta Scott King Award for Steptoe when the book was published. In this translation by Rosa Guy, we hear and see the story of Golo-the-Monkey, who torments Mother because she has snapped at him. In the richly complex illustrations, full of subtle shades of blues and greens, Steptoe has used white line to create patterns (like the skin of the crocodile on the ninth opening) and to outline shapes (like the bodies of the men shooting on the 11th opening). This is art which revels in complexity that compels our attention, rather than representing objects realistically. The endpapers are particularly noteworthy for the rhythmic patterns they present.

Line color is also unexpected in Erica Rutherford's illustrations for *The Owl and the Pussycat* by Edward Lear. This flat, decorative, and minimalist art uses line of many different colors, but never black. In places the line is a vibrant red, on others pages an electric blue, and in other places a neon green. These outline, persistently, the few shapes she uses to show the essence of the words in this nonsense poem, published over 140 years ago, about the improbable characters and events Lear described.

For more information

For a further discussion of line, see the article by Moebius (1986), which considers a variety of the visual codes found in picture books.

Edge

Some artists stop a shape, not by using line, but rather by creating an edge. This means that instead of encircling a shape with an added line, the artist uses another technique to show us where the object ends and the background begins. By making the edge of the shape so precise, and the color of the object so different from what it is next to, we can see clearly the separation. In *Erni Cabat's Magical World of Monsters*, by Daniel Cohen, we have an illustration of a griffin. It faces, as do all the pictures of imaginative, fanciful, and fearsome creatures, a brief page of text, telling interesting facts about these animals. We are introduced to the chimera, the basilisk, and the cerberus, among others. Throughout the book, Cabat doesn't encircle his forms with added lines. Rather, he relies on the sharpness of the edge, the clarity of the distinction between colors, to show us where parts of the animal begin and end, and how this contrasts with the plain color of the background. The unequivocal edges and the distinctive color differences show us the nature of the shapes Cabat is depicting.

Doonan sees this visual element as especially critical, when we guide children to look at pictures. She says:

> The systematic search always…begins with looking at lines of all kinds. The line gets me closest to the artist, which is where I want to be at this stage. The drawn (or painted) line is a direct record of the movement of the artist's hand, describing objects and events… reveal(ing) at the same time something of the personality of the picture-maker and how he [sic] thinks and feels about what he is doing.[2]

Color

Some artists prefer to work within the range offered by black and white including the many intermediate shades of gray. In *The Garden of Abdul Gasazi (See illustration on the next page)*, a Caldecott honor book by Chris Van Allsburg, we see this subtle palette used to impressive effect. When asked by Miss Hunter to care for her incorrigible dog, Alan tries his best, but only the retired magician Abdul Gasazi is able to outwit the small, peevish creature, who bites everything. Van Allsburg creates a surreal world where illusion blends into reality. His pencil illustrations are realistic, and he uses light, shadow, and perspective to evoke strong impressions of space and density.

Color

Pigments are dry materials often extended in a wet base used by artists which absorb, transmit, or reflect light in different ways so we see them differently; an artist uses *hue* (pure color) as a basis for mixing *shades* (by adding black) or *tints* (by adding white).

Figure 2.6: The Garden of Abdul Gasazi

Notice the repetition with variation Van Allsburg uses. The three figures—two statues and one child —are all looking away from us, and are about the same size. Our eye moves from the top of the left statue's head downward to the child's head and back up to the top of the right statue, inscribing a "v" shape, which is the opposite of the stone garden entrance itself, which makes an inverted "v." Having studied this artist's use of monochrome in black and white, you could direct children's looking at *The Sweetest Fig* in which he uses a different kind of monochrome scheme, dominated by shades of brown.

Many artists work with a broader spectrum of color than just the shades available from black and white. An artist may use just one or two subtle hues to underlie or understate an idea. This is apparent in the ink-line illustrations done by William Wiesner for *The Gunniwolf*. Wiesner's simple aqua and orange washes modestly complement his ink drawings for this tale of a little girl living next to a dense jungle.

Donald Crews's *Parade*, which won an International Reading Association Children's Choice Award, shows how effective high-intensity, saturated color can be when printed on a shiny, clay-coated paper. Crews provides flat, decorative shapes that serve as symbols for the people and objects he is portraying. The complete array of colors he uses is more effective than words would be in capturing the excitement of this outdoor, public event — the *parade*.

Another example of color use is the restrained, highly sophisticated technique of concentrating on two or more unusual shades. Barbara Cooney uses color this way in her illustrations for William Wise's humorous, rhymed account titled *The Lazy Young Duke of Dundee*. Cooney uses shades of blue-green for the duke and his family and magenta for the attacking MacClane and

Figure 2.7: Parade

A picture as brash as the sound of the brass band Crews creates; this sings with flat color and repeated patterns. There's no attempt here to evoke in-depth responses to a particular character as in the Trina Schart Hyman illustration for *Rapunzel*. Rather the artist asks us to simply enjoy the loud fun this surface display of action calls forth.

In *Shortcut*, Crews uses a softer edge to his shapes, less repeated flat symbols, and more realistic details. Throughout, the use of airbrush softens the art. The endpapers, featuring designed type, are elegant.

his horde. To complete her palette, she adds grey and some small accents of yellow. Even more restricted color use appears in the illustrations for Joseph Jacobs's retelling of an old tale, *The Buried Moon*. Susan Jeffers limited her palette to purple, lavender, beige, and black to illustrate this complex fantasy in which the moon is trapped by the Quicks and Bogles and Things that dwell in the bog. The evil qualities of these beings are well depicted, and the flowing black line augments the somber pages.

Fionna French, author/illustrator of *The Blue Bird*, places figures and other elements formally in her pictures, balancing areas of pattern with large plain areas. The only color other than blue is the peach and yellow of the main character's gown. After the denouement, the pictures burst into color. The pattern becomes more enveloping and the illustration on the last page is reminiscent of the pattern-packed paintings of the French painter Henri Matisse (1869-1954).

You might look at French's use of color and pattern in this book with a more recent book, *King of Another Country*. In it, this winner of the Kate Greenaway Award tells the story of the African King of the Forest, who offers to make Ojo, a young man, king of another land. In the process, Ojo learns that it is wise to say both "Yes" and "No." The endpapers, which vibrate

About the artist

For another comment about Fionna French's work see S. Hannabuss, 1981.

The Greenaway Award

Has been given annually since 1955 by the British Library Association, to the "most distinguished work in the illustration of children's books first published in the UK in the preceding year."

with repeated patterns of highly saturated colors applied in small lines and circles, introduce a set of illustrations which juxtapose various patterns one against another. On many of the pages, wide borders accompany the segmented pictures. The pervading tonality changes from page to page. For example, on the first opening, brown tones are dominant, while on the third opening shades of green and blue predominate. This highly decorative, flat art shows how pattern can enrich a surface.

The use of color may be highly realistic when the artist wants to create a natural effect. Master watercolorist Robert McCloskey used color this way in pictures for *Time of Wonder*, his Caldecott Medal-winning book depicting weather changes. McCloskey's color varies from the crisply contrasting blues and greens of a bright, early morning through the deep-hued blacks, blues, and purples of a storm at its height. Although the shapes themselves are not clearly defined and the brush line adds few details, the color creates the desired realism.

An artist may make use of arbitrary color that does not depict objects naturally. In *The Christmas Birthday Story*, by Helen Lucas, for example, abstract line drawings are highlighted with large, simplified blocks of color, which divide the page into segments, rather than coloring in particular parts of the drawing. The handsome result in this nativity story is art as surely as is any literal representation. Still, you might want to read Dressel's (1984) remarks about the appropriateness of abstraction in illustration for children.

Greenberg and Jordan provide a helpful discussion of color in *The Painter's Eye. Learning to Look at Contemporary American Art*, describing how different contemporary artists make it work for them in quite different ways. They make, for instance, effective contrast between the pure hues used by Ellsworth Kelly in which "the edges between each color glow" and the abstract images done in wash by Mark Rothko (1903-1970), which provide "an ever shifting relationship between the shapes."[3]

Proportion

Proportion in illustrations may be highly realistic: parts of bodies are shown in correct relation to the whole body, and objects are kept in accurate scale relative to the environment. Charles Mikolaycak was one artist whose work is stronger because of the absolute accuracy of his proportions, yet the imagination in his

Activity

A teacher might help children study paintings by Kelly and Rothko, and then look for a children's book illustrator whose color parallels the way these two artists use color.

Proportion

Makes comparison possible between objects in a composition; proportion may be *realistic* (parts as they usually are in our real world), or *exaggerated* (distorted in some way unlike our real world).

illustrations far transcends simple accuracy. Several of his books have been honored by the American Institute of Graphic Artists. His pictures for *The Cobbler's Reward* are typical of his draftsmanship. Whether portraying the handsome, young cobbler or the fat, old peasant woman, Mikolaycak was equally at home, using realistic proportions to create scenes we find believable despite the fantasy elements in the story itself.

More recently, this artist used the same carefully accurate proportions to show the male and female characters in the Greco-Roman myth of *Orpheus*. His draftsmanship in illustrations arranged in a variety of page placements, goes beyond simple attention to accuracy, however. Working in an elegantly large vertical format (9" x 12"), Mikolaycak showed us how important all aspects of design become when the intent is to produce a book which is, in addition, a beautiful art object.

In contrast to realistic proportions, artists may exaggerate proportion to create funny or fantastic effects. An example is the exaggerated forms created by Dennis Lyall for a modern tall tale, *So You Shouldn't Waste a Rhinoceros*. Lyall exaggerates the amount of hair on the characters' heads, the roundness of their body shapes, and the bend in their spines. He also exaggerates size—a huge, green telephone sprawls across a double-page spread, a soap-bubble pipe stretches to the size of a head, and a soap bubble with one of the characters inside becomes as big as a standing police officer.

Dr. Seuss, a favorite with children, often used exaggerated proportions to create humor in his drawings. Seuss's color is unexceptional, and his line is for the most part uninteresting. As can be seen in *One fish two fish red fish blue fish*, Seuss took proportions beyond realism in the convoluted horns of the Gack, the funny roundness of Joe's body, or the comical swayback of the cow.

For more information

An extended analysis of Seuss's work is available from Marshall (1987).

Detail

Artists may also vary the amount of detail to create desired effects. A cluttered illustration, straining against its borders, with objects literally packed in, can be used to reflect the state of mind of one of the characters or to comment on a crowded plot. The illustrations for Mary Norton's *Borrowers Aloft* were created by artists Beth and Joe Krush to evoke the tiny world of the Clock family. The detail-packed drawings executed in thin black line

Detail

Comprised of the separate components of an object or objects in an illustration; an artist may choose to show many details resulting in art of great complexity, or purposely show only a few details, resulting in a simpler style.

Plate 2: Seven Blind Mice
The art here has an understated quality (i.e., a few simple, distinct visual images with no background details to clutter up the pages). That is a particularly effective showcase for this fable, a literary form characterized by bare-bones language honed to the essentials. Talk with children about why this simple sans serif lettering was such an appropriate choice for this book. There are other examples of this style of lettering included in *The Letter Jesters* by Cathryn Falwell (See chapter 5).

Look at Young's art in the context of illustrations he did for *Bitter Bananas* by Isaac Olaleye. In this, he allows his luxuriant patterning to overtake the entire page, appropriate for this tale of a family living in the verdant African rainforest. Beginning to end this sings with dense color. *See full illustration in color plates following page 174.)*

Space

The distance from one point to another; in an illustration an artist may choose to show shallow space (little or no depth) or may create the illusion of very deep space.

show every shingle on the roof, every brick in the chimney, and every leaf on the tree.

In contrast, illustrations with relatively few details are appropriate for characters who lead a calm life or for peaceful, ordered environments. Horizontal bands in soft shades of blue and green lead the reader on in Uri Shulevitz's *Dawn*. The artist begins the story with a soft-edged oval shape that increases in size and includes more and more objects until finally becoming a verdant image of the world turning green as sunrise strikes a lake.

Where an artist places the detail may also be of interest, such as in *The Girl Who Loved the Wind* by Jane Yolen. Ed Young, a native of China, uses watercolor and collage, arranging the details in various places. Pages that have much detail alternate with pages that have large plain spaces to provide needed balance. Even on the title page, space is broken up geometrically and pattern is relegated to only one part of the design. The formal placement of the text and illustrations within a wide gold band emphasizes the story's formal nature.

Part of the appeal of Young's Caldecott Honor Book, *Seven Blind Mice*, is the contrast between the detail of the mouse shapes, set against the large black empty spaces. Because of how the mice are grouped, the empty space is different on each page. The cut-paper figures are presented in intense color, printed on a high-gloss, coated paper.

Sometimes the amount of detail increases gradually to add emphasis to the story line, as in *An Invitation to the Butterfly Ball*, a counting rhyme by Jane Yolen. The artist, Jane Breskin Zalben, adds objects and animals page by page, from one mouse looking for a floor-length dress to 10 porcupines disagreeing over a velvet evening jacket, until on last page, all the animals arrive at the ball.

Space

Finally, artists may manipulate space in a variety of ways. Some artists use a flat plane in their pictures, providing no sense of a third dimension. Janet McCaffery's imaginative two-dimensional illustrations in *The Witch of Hissing Hill* combined cut and torn paper shapes, crayon lines, and overlapping transparent papers to establish a two-dimensional environment for Sizzle, a wicked old witch. On the other hand, some artists arrange three-dimensional objects in perspective, one behind another, to give the impression of deep space. In *The Brook*, by Carol and Donald Carrick, watercolor, ink-line, and charcoal drawings encourage the reader to wander visually among the trees, all the way back toward high rocks in the distance.

Most artists probably do not sit down to think consciously about these six elements—shape, line, color, proportion, detail, and space—before planning and executing illustrations. However, examining each of these elements separately can help children appreciate the artist's skill in creating a final effect.

Combining elements

In the previous sections, individual books served as exemplars of the separate visual elements. Each was chosen because it in some way was a particularly effective example of the element. However, these elements seldom if ever function completely alone. Rather, an artist combines most or all of them into unified compositions to make a whole which is more effective than the individual parts might be.

What can we discover when we look at all the elements in one book? For an answer to that question, let's examine what Don Wood did in creating the art for *King Bidgood's in the Bathtub*, a Caldecott Honor book by Audrey Wood.

Shape: We see that the shapes he creates are all toward the most realistic end of a continuum from realistic to abstract. It is easy to see what everything is, because the shapes are rendered in three dimensions, as they appear in the real world. They are shown clearly enough throughout the book so that nothing is indistinct. Even the decorative moldings on the columns (see fourth opening, for example), are shown with enough clarity so that it is apparent what they are. The shapes are, perhaps especially in the clothing details, more rounded in outline than they would really be, but that doesn't in any way interfere with determining what they are. When we look at these shapes, in the context of the two-dimensional shapes in Olga Zharkova's *We Three Kings*, we find Wood's shapes easier to understand. The degree of abstraction involved in Zharkova's work requires a more sophisticated viewer than does Wood's work.

Line: There is only minimal use of line in Wood's illustrations. There is some use of colored line, for instance, in the fish scale mask, in the suit of armor, and in the neck ruffs shown in the 12th opening. But far more often, Wood relies on juxtaposing one colored edge against another, so that the color differences show us where one shape stops and another begins. For instance, in the same illustration, we can see the edge of the skirt worn by the lady in blue, not because it is outlined, but rather because the color is so different from what is behind it. Similarly, we see both of the king's arms quite clearly, not because they are outlined, but rather because they are such a distinctly different color than what they are in front of. Throughout the entire book, Wood uses edges created by contrasting colors to create clear shapes, rather than an all-encompassing line. When we compare *King Bidgood's in the Bathtub* with *This Little Pig* by Leonard B. Lubin, we can see the contrast. In Lubin's work, each shape is so clearly defined because of the pervasive thin, black ink line which surrounds it.

Color: We can observe Wood's use of color in the pervasiveness of two different tonalities, a mauve/gold/brown and an intense blue, throughout the book. On many openings, the mauve/gold/brown predominates, though there is an underlying blue tonality. This color scheme is introduced on the dedication page and is apparent on the second, eighth, ninth, and other openings. In contrast, the blue tonality is introduced on the fourth opening and is also apparent on the fifth, the tenth, and 11th openings. On the sixth opening, we see Wood's other use of color, a widening of the spectrum, to incorporate many more colors than are used on the openings where a single tonality pervades. This opening up of the color range is also apparent on the ninth opening.

In contrast to this use of dark, intense colors with many different shades of the same color, like the blues, we can look at this set of pictures in the context of those by Chris L. Demarest for *Today I'm Going Fishing with My Dad*. Two different aspects of color are readily apparent. One, the colors in Demarest's pictures incorporate, in every opening, a wider range of hues than do Wood's. Or, in other words, there isn't the purposeful, limited color palette in Demarest's art that we see in Wood's work. Two, there is a difference in the space the paintings use. Wood paints fully to the edge, using the whole page for his painting, without leaving any of the original paper color for contrast purposes. Unlike this, in Demarest's art, the watercolor is splashed on casually, so that the white of the paper intensifies the colors. This is carried further: in addition to leaving most of the backgrounds primarily white paper, within the shapes themselves Demarest often leaves white spaces, which again has the effect of sharpening his colors.

Proportion: Proportion is the fourth element, and we can always examine book art to see if the proportions are realistic or exaggerated. In *King Bidgood's in the Bathtub*, Wood uses mild exaggeration throughout the book, for decorative reasons. For example, on the 12th opening, there's a pleasant, rhythmic pattern of arms and legs above the bathtub, created by the slight stretching of these limbs. On the left half of the eighth opening, both of the courtier's legs are thinner than they would really be, and the exaggeration is comical. However, overall, it is easy to recognize what everything is in these illustrations, because sizes of objects and parts of objects in relation to other things are shown the way they would actually be.

In contrast to this art, look at the exaggerated proportions which pervade *The Clock Shop* by Simon Henwood. We see on the cover the attenuated nose and sharp chin of the clockmaker, and on nearly every page we see people, and objects, which are thinner and longer, or fatter and wider than in real life. Because Henwood is creating a fantasy environment, this exaggeration of shapes is particularly appropriate.

Detail: We can examine Wood's illustrations to determine how much detail he has included, and where it is placed. On nearly every page, this artist has accumulated an incredible amount of detail, of costume, of architecture, and of other objects, to create art children will return to again and again, to savor the information Wood presents visually. He obviously delights in, and compels his viewers to examine, the patterns, construction details, and ornamental frills of the men's and women's costumes. But there are architectural details as well: valances on curtains, decorative detailing on columns, and moldings around windows—all add interesting clutter to the pictures. And yet, these areas of intense accumulated details are contrasted with large, quite plain areas which provide visual resting places for our eyes. For example, on the second opening, notice how most of the detail is concentrated to the left of the center pillar. Yet the pillars themselves, the hallway of arches on the left, the walls behind the columns are mostly devoid of detail. Notice on the tenth opening, how the detail is massed in two places: in the archway on the left, and to the right of the center column. In each of these places there is much to be examined, and yet the areas between and around these focal points are primarily devoid of detail, which provides a pleasant contrast. Without such resting places, the art would be overly busy.

You could look at *King Bidgood's in the Bathtub* in the context of another artist, Steven Kellogg, whose approach to detail is different. Kellogg has for some time worked from the principle that if there's an empty space on a page, it ought to be filled. The art for *Engelbert the Elephant* by Tom Paxton is an example: this rambunctious story is crammed nearly to the page edges with an accumulation of detail. The small spaces where the text is set are usually the only plain areas on a page. There are no resting places for the eye in these illustrations.

Space: Finally, we can examine the use Don Wood made of space in his illustrations. His art here is an example of how an artist creates the impression of deep space on a flat piece of paper, through the use of both rounded shapes, and perspective. By overlapping shapes, an artist can lead our eye to objects that appear to be farther away because they are behind each other. For example on the title page, it appears that we could walk from one building to another, because their placement from low on the page to higher up, overlapping buildings behind others, gives the impression of deep space. Throughout the book, Wood uses this device of placing shapes in front of and behind other shapes, and placing them farther up on the page, to indicate a progression through space. In addition, he uses the device of the arches, shown on openings one and two as well as elsewhere, to give the impression of space farther away from the viewer. On the dedication page, he uses another device artists have used for hundreds of years: the window on the back wall shows an outside view which is clearly farther away than the action taking place in the stairway.

This kind of evocation of deep space is far different from the impression of a two-dimensional world with shallow or no depth, as shown in the work of Claire Henley, in *Farm Day*. Though the artist juxtaposes one object in front of another and places some objects at the bottom and others farther up on the page, the final outcome is a flat, two-dimensional world. The color in this charming, simple story of rural life is done in solid shades with

Here, the artist uses white line to create her flat shapes arranged from top to bottom of the page, in two dimensional space. Some objects overlap others, but she didn't try to create a sense that some of these are really in front of, or behind others. This rural illustration is different in style from Donald Crews' urban *Parade*, and yet they are really quite alike in the purposeful flatness apparent in each. In *Stormy Day*, Henley continued her use of white line; the endpapers decorated with umbrellas and leaves are particularly exuberant.

no modeling of tones to indicate roundness of shape. As a result a patterned world is created in which it is quite clear everything shown exists at the front of the picture plane. We're not tempted to try to walk, visually, into the picture, simply because its two-dimensional quality is so apparent.

Involving children in studying pictorial elements

It is natural for students to talk about the illustrations in books. Some examples of picture books used to stimulate verbal language will illustrate the potential that they have.

One teacher shared an old favorite, *Animal Babies*, by Arthur Gregor (now fortunately available in an inexpensive paperback reprint), which has clear black-and-white, close-up photographs of animals. The teacher showed the book to children and invited them to give their reaction to one of the pictures in the book. Two kindergartners contributed the following:

> I like the elephants. They are big animals. They have long legs, a trunk and big ears. The baby elephants are small. They are going to grow up into big elephants. **Michael**

> Polar bears are my favorite animals. I like polar bears because my uncle has one. Polar bears are one of my favorite animals

because they swim in the water. Polar bears are my favorite because they splash and because they sit funny. **Heather**

These represent the kind of beginning story dictation that results when children study an illustration and comment on it. When this activity is repeated with other books at intervals over an extended period of time, it can sharpen children's observations of what artists portray on the page and their ability to respond verbally to it. Three other books by Gregor, more specifically focused on one kind of animal, include *The Sleepy Little Lion*, *Two Little Bears*, and *The Little Elephant*. Each book features the same large format and clear, appealing black-and-white photographs by Ylla as in *Animal Babies*.

Story variants stimulate language

For more information

Shannon (1994) describes at length what he sees in three editions of the Grimms' "The Wolf and the Seven Little Kids." As we read such articles as these, we learn to see more deeply.

Comparing and contrasting illustrated versions of the same folktale can reveal how differently artists perceive and represent tales that are the same or nearly the same. Broadening our own perception as adults who work with children is an important first step before we try to help them see with more clarity. Then, we can work with boys and girls, beginning very simply with primary children.

Two teachers of first-graders presented traditional literature in picture book format, sharing more than one version of the same story and asking children to comment on the illustrations. They asked children to respond to pictures in versions of *Little Red Riding Hood*. Some commented on the Bernadette version:

The colors made things look real. They looked like they were made with Craypas. **Mikaela**

I don't like this wolf, because he looks like a dirty mouse. No one would be afraid of him, but he doesn't look right. **Drew**

About the Paul Galdone version, other children commented:

There were lots of interesting patterns, like in the quilt and in the flowers in the grass. **Jodie**

In this one the grandmother looks more like a grandmother, because she's dressed the way they should dress. **Alex**

Two other versions of this story that librarians and teachers might use in doing a comparison/contrast activity with children include Lisbeth Zwerger's version, *Little Red Cap,* which has soft-edged watercolors that make effective use of negative space. She focuses our attention on character detail by eliminating almost all extraneous background detail. Entirely different in effect are the black-and-white, superrealistic, contemporary photographs by Sarah Moon in an edition of *Little Red Riding Hood* that won the grand prize at the Bologna International Book Fair. Moon's book differs from Zwerger's in more than just the illustrations; the completely different emotional tone of the former is also due to the fact that the text is based on the French version by Charles Perrault rather than on the German version by the Brothers Grimm. More recently, Christopher Coady's version of the tale was presented in elegantly textured double-page spreads which are filled with more foreboding than some versions. The edition by the Caldecott Medal-winner Beni Montresor is problematic for many adults. In going back to the original story by Charles Perrault, illustrated in pale colors with heavy black overlays, Montresor shows us Little Red in the wolf's stomach, a wordless spread perhaps purposely designed to shock. It certainly accomplishes the purpose of making us rethink the story. No matter which version one uses, there are notable differences in shape, size, binding, endpapers, paper, typeface, and page layout, design elements discussed at greater length in chapter 5.

Working with third-grade children, one teacher read two versions of the Hans Christian Andersen tale *The Nightingale (plate 3)*, introducing them by saying they were different but not pointing out how. She encouraged the children to study the illustrations as she was reading but did not comment on the art herself. She then made the books available in the classroom for the rest of the week and asked the children to write descriptions of the books. One student wrote the following response to the version illustrated by Nancy Burkert:

> The picture of the castle and garden looks more Chinese and the colors are much softer and more delicate. It looks more like the story itself. The porcelain castle looks realistic with its gardens and forest and the ocean rushing in on the beach. The people look more Chinese and more like real people. The outfits of the people are so delicate and the people stand out. The artificial bird is pretty with its diamonds and rubies, and the real nightingale looks very beautiful, even though it is not so colorful as the artificial bird.   **Michelle**

Plate 3: The Nightingale
The softly flowing curves of the people's body shapes, of the clothing they wear, and even of architectural details (i.e., the rounded corners of the door opening and the building seen through it) evoke tranquility. Compare the detail in this, for example, in the faces, with the abstracted, simplified treatment of people in Donald Crews's *Parade*. *See full illustration in color plates following page 174.*)

About the artist

For a reviewer's comments on the Burkert edition of The Nightingale *(and three others not described here), see Burns (1986). Burkert (1991) has also written about her work.*

Dooley has described Burkert's work as "notable for its precision and delicacy," though she goes on to say that Burkert's "intricacy never looks forced or dry."[4] Another student described the illustrations by Fulvio Testa:

> The garden and the castle don't look very real and around the picture is just white. There is no real background for the picture. The pictures aren't as soft and delicate as in the other book. The castle looks fake as does its surrounding. The people don't look Chinese, and they don't really fit into the Chinese story. The pictures look like any American pictures would. The real bird looks artificial just as the artificial bird really does, and the pictures of the birds don't really catch someone's eye with all the white showing around and in it.
>
> **Liz**

Looking to solve problems

In addition to the kind of comparing/contrasting activities suggested, an art educator has described her use of the art in picture books to provide possible solutions to the problems children encounter in creating their own art works. Gainer says that often children have difficulty representing something in an art work and are frustrated by this. She finds that, by systematically having children study and talk about how artists of picture books have solved their problems, children become more adept at "structuring visual forms,"[5] Focusing for example on line, she has children observe many different kinds of line and encourages them to use some of these in their own artwork, when they feel it is appropriate. She does this with each of the art elements, and helps children see picture books as a resource to which they can turn when they are perplexed about how to make something turn out the way they want it to. In the article, she mentions several specific book titles to which children have responded positively.

In this chapter, we have looked at the potential visual vocabulary from which an artist can choose as separate, discrete elements. In actuality, however, these seldom, if ever, function in isolation. Rather, choices the artist makes interact with other choices in an integral way. In the next chapter we will look at the organizational structures within which these separate visual elements function to make a whole composition.

Recommended children's books

Anderson, C. W. *C. W. Anderson's Complete Book of Horses and Horsemanship.* New York: Macmillan, 1963.

Anderson, Hans Christian. *The Nightingale* illustrated by Fulvio Testa. New York: Abelard-Schuman, 1974.

Bernadette. *Little Red Riding Hood.* Cleveland: World Publishing, 1969.

Burkert, Nancy. *The Nightingale*, translated by Eva Le Gallienne. New York: Harper and Row, Publishers, 1965.

Burningham, John. *Aldo.* New York: Crown Publishers, Inc., 1991.

———. *Mr. Grumpy's Outing.* New York: Holt, Rinehart and Winston, 1970.

Cabat, Erni (Ill.). *Erni Cabat's Magical World of Monsters* by Daniel Cohen. New York: Cobblehill/Cutton, 1992.

Carrick, Carol, and Donald Carrick. *The Brook.* New York: Macmillan, 1967.

Coady, Christopher. *Little Red Riding Hood.* New York: Dutton Children's Books, 1991.

Cooney, Barbara (Ill.). *The Lazy Young Duke of Dundee* by William Wise. Chicago: Rand McNally, 1970.

Crews, Donald. *Parade.* New York: Greenwillow, 1983.

Demarest, Chris L. (Ill.). *Today I'm Going Fishing with My Dad* by N. L. Sharp. Honesdale, PA: Boyd's Mills Press, 1993.

Dillon, Leo and Diane (Ills.). *The Tale of the Mandarin Ducks* by Katherine Paterson. New York: Lodestar Books, 1990.

——— (Ills.). *Why Mosquitoes Buzz in People's Ears* by Verna Aardema (reteller). New York: The Dial Press, 1975.

French, Fiona. *The Blue Bird.* New York: Henry Z. Walck, 1972.

———. *King of Another Country.* New York: Scholastic Inc., 1992.

Gorey, Edward (Ill.). *The House with a Clock in Its Walls* by John Bellairs. New York: Alfred A. Knopf, 1964.

———(Ill.). *Treehorn's Wish* by Florence Parry Heide. New York: Holiday House, 1984.

Greenberg, Jan and Sandra Jordan. *The Painter's Eye. Learning to Look at Contemporary American Art.* New York: Delacorte Press, 1991.

Gregor, Arthur. *Animal Babies.* New York: Harper and Row, 1959.

———. *The Sleepy Little Lion.* New York: Harper and Row, 1975.

———. *Two Little Bears.* New York: Harper and Row, 1954.

———. *The Little Elephant.* New York: Harper and Row, 1956.

Grifalconi, Ann (Ill.). *Everett Anderon's Friend.* New York: Henry Holt, 1992.

——— (Ill.). *Jasmine's Parlour Day* by Lynn Joseph. New York: Lothrop, Lee and Shepard, 1994.

Haley, Gail E. *Go Away, Stay Away.* Blowing Rock, NC: New River Publishing Co., 1988.

———. *Jack and the Fire Dragon.* New York: Crown Publishers, 1988.

Henley, Claire. *Farm Day.* New York: Dial Books for Young Readers, 1991.

———. *Stormy Day.* New York: Hyperion Books for Children, 1993.

Henwood, Simon. *The Clock Shop.* New York: Farrar, Straus & Giroux, 1989.

Hutchins, Pat. *Clocks and More Clocks.* New York: Macmillan, 1970.

———. *Little Pink Pig.* New York: Greenwillow Books, 1994.

———. *Tidy Titch.* New York: Greenwillow Books, 1991.

———. *What Game Shall We Play?* New York: Greenwillow Books, 1990.

Hyman, Trina Schart (Ill.). *Curl Up Small* by Sandol Stoddard Warburg. Boston: Houghton Mifflin, 1964.

———(Ill.). *Rapunzel* by Barbara Rogasky. New York: Holiday House, 1982.

Jeffers, Susan (Ill.). *The Buried Moon* by Joseph Jacobs. Englewood Cliffs, NJ: Bradbury, 1969.

———. *Cinderella* translated by Amy Ehrlich. New York: Dial, 1985.

Karlin, Eugene (Ill.). *The Aeneid for Boys and Girls* by Alfred Church. New York: Macmillan, 1962.

Kellogg, Steven (Ill.). *Engelbert the Elephant* by Tom Paxton. New York: Morrow Junior Books, 1990.

———(Ill.). *Gwot! Horribly Funny Hairticklers* by George Mendoza. New York: Harper and Row, 1967.

Krush, Beth and Joe (Ill.). *The Borrowers Aloft* by Mary Norton. New York: Harcourt Brace, 1961.

Lipkind, William, and Nicholas Mordinoff. *The Two Reds.* New York: Harcourt Brace, 1950.

Locker, Thomas. *The Mare on the Hill.* New York: Dial, 1985.

Lucas, Helen. *The Christmas Birthday Story.* New York: Alfred A. Knopf, 1980.

Lyall, Dennis (Ill.). *So You Shouldn't Waste a Rhinoceros* by Nathan Zimmelman. Austin: Steck-Vaughn, 1970.

McCaffery, Janet (Ill.). *The Witch of Hissing Hill* by Mary Calhoun. New York: William Morrow, 1964.

McCloskey, Robert. *Time of Wonder.* New York: Viking Press, 1957.

Mikolaycak, Charles. *Orpheus.* San Diego: Harcourt Brace Jovanovich, 1992.

———(Ill.). *The Cobbler's Reward* by Barbara and Ewa Reid. New York: Macmillan, 1978.

Montressor, Beni. *Little Red Riding Hood.* New York: Doubleday, 1991.

Moon, Sarah (Ill.). *Little Red Riding Hood* by Charles Perrault. Mankoto, MN: Creative Education, 1983.

Norton, Mary. *The Borrowers Aloft.* New York: Harcourt Brace, 1961.

O'Neill, Catharine. *Mr. and Mrs. Muddle* by Mary Ann Hoberman. Boston: Joy Street Books/Little, Brown and Co., 1988.

Ormai, Stella (Ill.). *Sleeping Over* by Barbara Lucas. New York: Macmillan, 1986.

Perham, Molly. *King Arthur and the Legends of Camelot.* New York: Viking, 1993.

Rutherford, Erica (Ill.). *The Owl and the Pussycat* by Edward Lear. Montreal, Quebec: Tundra Books, 1986.

Sage, Angie and Chris Sage. *Happy Baby*. New York: Dial Books for Young Readers, 1990.

Seuss, *Dr. One fish two fish red fish blue fish*. New York: Random House, 1960.

Steptoe, John (Ill.). *Mother Crocodile*, translated by Rosa Guy. New York: A Doubleday Book for Young Readers, 1981.

Stevenson, James. *Higher on the Door*. New York: Greenwillow Books, 1987.

———. *Worse Than Willy*. New York: Greenwillow, 1984.

Testa, Fluvio (Ill.). *The Nightingale*. New York: Abelard-Schuman, 1974, now o.p.

Van Allsburg, Chris. *The Garden of Abdul Gasazi*. Boston: Houghton Mifflin, 1979.

———. *The Sweetest Fig*. Boston: Houghton Mifflin, 1993.

Wiesner, William (Ill.). *The Gunniwolf* by Wilhelmina Harper. New York: E. P. Dutton, 1967.

Wood, Don (Ill.). *King Bidgood's in the Bathtub* by Audrey Wood. San Diego: Harcourt Brace Jovanovich, 1985.

Young, Ed (Ill.). *Bitter Bananas* by Isaac Olaleye. Honesdale, PA: Boyds Press, 1994.

———(Ill.). *The Girls Who Loved the Wind* by Jane Yolen. New York: Thomas Y. Crowell, 1972.

———. *Seven Blind Mice*. New York: Philomel, 1992.

Zalben, Jane Breskin (Ill.). *An Invitation to the Butterfly Ball, A Counting Rhyme* by Jane Yolen. New York: Parents' Magazine Press, 1976.

Zemach, Margot. *Jake and Honeybunch Go to Heaven*. New York: Farrar, Straus & Giroux, 1982.

Zharkova, Olga. *We Three Kings*. New York: Scholastic Hardcover, 1993.

Zwerger, Lizabeth. *Little Red Cap*. New York: Morrow, 1983.

Professional references

Burns, M. (1986). "Anderson's Nightingale." *The Hornbook Magazine*, 62(1), 78-79.

Burkert, N. E. (1991, January/February). "Valentine and Orson." *The Horn Book Magazine*, 45-47.

Dillon, L., & Dillon, D. (1992). "The Tale of the Mandarin Ducks." *The Horn Book*, 68(1), 35-37.

Dooley, P. (1989). "Contemporary Illustrators: Tomorrow's Classics?" *Touchstones*, ed. by P. Nodelman, 3, 153-163.

Doonan, J. (1993). *Looking At Pictures in Picture Books*. Stroud, Glos., U.K.: Thimble Press.

Dressel, J. H. (1984). "Abstraction in Illustration: Is It Appropriate for Children?" *Children's Literature in Education*, 15, 103-112.

Gainer, R. S. (1982). "Beyond Illustration: Information About Art in Children's Picture Books." *Art Education*, 35, 16-19.

Hannabuss, S. (1981). "Sources of Information for Children's Book Illustration." *Journal of Librarianship*, 13, 154-171.

Hyman, T. S. (1993). "Zen and the Art of Children's Book Illustration." In B. Hearne (ed.), *The Zena Sutherland Lectures 1983-1992* (183-205). New York: Clarion Books.

Marshall, R. (1987). *The Tough Coughs As He Ploughs the Dough.* New York: William Morrow and Co., Inc.

Moebius, W. (1986). "Introduction to Picturebook Codes." *Word and Image*, 2, 141-158.

Preiss, B. (ed.). (1981). *The Art of Leo and Diane Dillon.* New York: Ballentine Books.

Richard, O., and D. MacCann. (1984, September). "Picture Books for Children." *Wilson Library Bulletin*, pp. 50-51.

Schmidt. S. (1977, March). "Language Development And Children's Books In Intermediate Classrooms." *Insights Into Open Education*, pp. 2-10.

Shannon, G. (1994, January). "The Wolf and the Seven Little Kids." *Book Links*, pp. 50-52.

Stewig, J. W. (1991). *Reading Pictures. Trina Schart Hyman.* Hilton Head Island, SC: Child Graphics Press.

Urblikova, A. (1975). *Bienale Ilustracii, Bratislava.* Bratislava: Mlade leta.

Composition

In the second chapter we examined the separate visual elements, the pictorial "vocabulary" from which an artist can choose. These elements like proportion, detail, and color, are similar to individual words that a writer uses. But writers arrange individual words into an order, sentence syntax, so that this organization conveys a message. Often times how the words are arranged causes us to notice, not only the message, but also the way the message is conveyed. So, too, in visuals. Certain of the elements are chosen, others are largely ignored. The individual elements; line, shape, or space, are put together in a particular relation to other elements.

In helping children think about the composition of pictures, we are asking them to examine two questions:

1. What has the artist put where?

2. Why might the artist have arranged the composition in a particular way?

It's important, before going on to look at compositional devices, to point out that the answer to the first question is usually finite. We can indeed identify what objects the artist has included in a painting, and where they were put.

The answer to the second question is often more problematic. Thinking about what they have seen in order to speculate about why the artist may have organized a composition in a particular way is difficult. In fact, since artists often don't talk about their reasons for doing something a particular way, we may not have a clear idea what the intent was. Nonetheless, encouraging children to think about what they have observed is always a useful experience.

We can lead children through a planned set of experiences which will help them understand such compositional principles as: 1) unity, 2) proximity, 3) similarity, 4) continuation, 5) variety, 6) dominance, 7) rhythm and movement, and 8) balance. These are the names for the compositional principles described by Hobbs and Salome in *The Visual Experience* (1991). As with the visual elements described in the second chapter, you should be aware that different books on composition talk about these ideas in different ways. If you looked at several books, you'd find that the terminology varied, and that not every book talked about all of these principles. For example, Miller and Ragans, in *Exploring Art* (1992), use slightly different terms to talk about the same basic ideas.

In the following section, using the ideas about composition proposed by Hobbs and Salome, we'll look at specific examples from picture books which exemplify these principles.

Unity

Unity

The techniques an artist uses to relate the various parts of a picture to each other, resulting in an integrated whole; this can be achieved through visual elements like color, through physical properties like scale, or by consciously using such other compositional techniques as repetition.

The analogy that Hobbs and Salome make is that unity can be compared with teamwork in sports. Each member of a team must work together with the others in order to win the game. So, too, in a piece of art in a book. The separate visual elements discussed in chapter 2 must work together, enhancing the total overall effect, and not eclipsing the others in importance. As one star does not a team make, so, too, one stunning visual element does not make an effective composition. All the elements need to work together to create unity.

We can look at one of the large watercolor illustrations which Allen Say did for *Tree of Cranes* to notice the unity he has created. On the second opening of the book, the unnamed young boy "not yet old enough to wear long pants," is coming home from playing at the neighbor's pond, knowing his mother will be angry with him for catching a chill. He pauses at the entryway to their Japanese home, and Say shows viewers a tranquil scene, unified by the encompassing lines of the house's architecture. There are the strong verticals of the wooden wall paneling, of the sliding wooden door, and of the rough hewn post supporting the door lintel. The lintel, plus the cement step leading into the walled courtyard are the strong horizontal elements, though above the little boy's head we can see another horizontal, the small lintel over the glass door into the house itself. All of these vertical and hori-

Figure 3.1: Tree of Cranes
The size of the illustrations
(8¹/2" X 9¹/2") and the severe
elimination of any extraneous
detail leads to a tranquil feeling
reflective of the culture
depicted. The modulation of
solid color from one shade to
another within the same object
(i.e., a garment, or a pillow) is
subtle, and also contributes to
the tranquility. The line is
smooth and connected, another
device used to avoid anything
abrupt or jerky in movement.
In *Grandfather's Journey*, for
which Say won the Caldecott
Award, he uses architecture in
less organizing ways. Notice
in that book the interesting use
of impressionistic color
application techniques in the
mountains and the trees (pp.14-
15) as well as in the fields
(p.20).

About the artist

*Say has talked at greater
length about his work, in an
interview (Marcus, 1991) and
in an article he wrote himself
(1991).*

zontal elements work together to direct our attention to the boy, peering apprehensively into the dark house. We really can look only there, because of the way the architecture contains our viewing. Say uses color to further direct our attention: the bright orange of the boy's scarf is the most intense color in the composition, and it draws our eye because of the tonality.

In *We Keep a Pig in the Parlor*, artist Suzanne Bloom has given us several examples of unity. In the illustration reproduced here, we notice right away how tightly constrained our attention is on the pig itself, because of the way Bloom has hemmed it into the doorway space. She surrounds the pig on both sides and on top by the structure of the barn, the bare bones of posts and beams. These create strong verticals on either side of the pig, and the blue sky showing through the door is stopped by the beam over the opening. Our eye doesn't travel further down on the page because the broad swath of hay forms a strong vertical stop. We

Figure 3.2: We Keep a Pig in the Parlor

The textures in this illustration are created by stroking one color over another, not covering completely but letting the underneath color show through. Look at the original to see how this enriches the colors. If your children enjoy the idea of pigs as main characters, use with them *Oink Oink* by Arthur Geisert in which the very pink porcine creatures are shown through this artist's etching technique.

can pause to notice the rhythm formed by the v-shape of the roof beams, repeated several times over. But in all, every element of the background Bloom includes works together to focus our attention on the falling pig. These other visual elements aren't important in themselves. Rather, they serve the purpose of highlighting the center of attention, the pig, which isn't in the center of the picture at all.

Color leads to unity

Another kind of unity is created when an artist controls the tonality of the palette she or he uses. The artist chooses colors which are very much alike, in either the hues selected (i.e., using many different tints and shades of a single color, like blue), or in the intensity of the colors (i.e., using all very bright, medium range, or soft colors). Floyd Cooper's illustrations for *Brown Honey in Broomwheat Tea*, poems by Joyce Carol Thomas, exemplify both kinds of unity. These softly glowing, full-page pictures bled to the page edge are enhanced by the rich cream matte paper on the facing text pages. Throughout this art, we see a wide variety of colors, i.e., the warm golds and oranges in the picture for "Cherish Me," as well as cool greens and blues in the illustration for "Brown Honey." Nonetheless, Cooper provides unity through the golden browns which suffuse the art, providing the shading for example, in the cool green and blue clothing in "Cherish Me." In addition, the intensity of the color range is close: the pictures don't include very light, or very dark tonalities, but rather remain in the mid-range. This, also, unifies the paintings.

Proximity

Hobbs and Salome point out that separate objects can be unified by placing them close to other objects, by grouping them. We see syllables in words because we perceive certain letters together. They "clump" into clusters. The same is true in paintings. Our eye moves from one group of objects to another because of the closeness of the objects.

In his illustrations for *The Gold Coin*, a story set in Central America, by Alma Flor Ada, artist Neil Waldman makes effective use of proximity throughout the book. On the 13th opening, the

Proximity
How near or how far from each other various objects in a picture are placed.

Figure 3.3: The Gold Coin
Neil Waldman's art for this story exudes tranquility, through the use of two devices. First, the largely pastel hues fall within a very narrow range; there are no abrupt color transitions. Second, extraneous detail is largely eliminated; there is seldom any interesting but distracting detail to divert attention from the main action of the picture. If children enjoy Waldman's art, share with them the full-page pictures, with decorative side panels for *Nessa's Fish* by Nancy Luenn. Depicting life in an extremely different culture (that of the Arctic) the pictures are nevertheless similarly tranquil.

thief Juan is reassuring Doña Josefa that she can indeed go with the young child to her mother, now that the baby is due any moment. Waldman has grouped the figures together in the bottom half of the picture and further unified them by placing Juan's arm directly around Doña Josefa's shoulder. But even the little girl is part of the clump of figures, because she is standing so close to the other two. We "read" this group as a visual unit because of their proximity. It is only after we have examined this cluster of figures that we notice the curvilinear design in the repeated cloud forms which occupy the entire top half of the composition.

Another effective example of the use of proximity is apparent in *My Day* by Heide Goennel (fourth opening). Notice the placement of the group of three children, unified by how close together they and their chairs are placed. There is dual reinforcement of the proximity here: the children's bodies are close, but the four legs of each chair also reinforce that closeness. In contrast, the child printing at the chalkboard—set apart because she is standing rather than sitting—is far enough away so that we see her as a separate visual element. Despite this, she is contained within the group, because her legs extend far enough down so as to be placed between two of the children's heads.

Throughout the book there are several examples of effective use of proximity. For example, on the seventh opening, the two children and the dog on the left page are grouped closely together to enhance the feeling of unity, and together they make a mass which balances the house in the upper right corner of the facing, right page. On the eighth opening, the two children at the bottom of the page are linked because of proximity, while at the top of the basketball standard, the backboard, hoop, and ball are placed tightly together to maximize proximity.

This artist's consistently spare style emphasizes the juxtaposition of large, hard-edged, simplified shapes in flat colors, with an almost complete absence of line. The flatness of the shapes is reminiscent of the two dimensional shapes used by Ezra Jack Keats early in his career, for example in *The Snowy Day*, a Caldecott Award winner. Goennel continues using this style in other of her books, including *If I Were a Penguin....*

Eve Rice's pictures for *Benny Bakes a Cake,* the simple story of a preschooler helping on his birthday, provide many examples of the effective use of proximity. In this reissue of a book published earlier, the story line about a happy ending to a potentially disastrous birthday is set in a thin sans serif typeface. On several of the pages we can see how Eve Rice uses proximity to direct our attention. For example, on the fourth opening, we have two separate spreads on facing pages. On the left, the dog Ralph is positioned so he's nearly touching Benny; the dog's leg and paw are extended to the boy, and Benny's arm reaches out to the dog. The position of the window curtain further unifies this composition. On the right page, Ralph's tail curls in front of the leg of Benny's high chair, his head is in front of the stove, and his paws nearly touch Mother's leg. This tight knit composition is further unified because of the placement of the bowl containing cooking utensils: positioned between Mother and Benny, it ties the two together visually.

On the 12th opening, also two separate scenes on facing pages, notice how the use of overlapping forms enhances the proximity of the compositions. On the left, Mother's leg is in front of the stool, while the corner of her elbow overlaps the corner of the wall telephone. The placement of the telephone cord further connects the composition. On the right, the way Mother cuddles Benny, while the dog's paws rest on her leg, is another example of proximity.

Similarity

Another means of achieving unity in a picture is to make several objects the same color, texture, shape, or size as other objects. For example, if an artist uses a particularly vibrant shade of blue on one object, we're likely to notice other objects of that same color throughout the illustration. Or, our eyes may notice a recurring shape. Is the hat a person is wearing basically a triangle shape? If so, our eye is likely to instinctively search for a repetition of that shape in other places.

Louise Brierley, in *The Twelve Days of Christmas (See illustration on the next page)*, provides many examples of the effective use of similar shapes. In the illustration for the ninth day, notice how effective a pattern she creates by making all the drummers' elbows similarly attenuated, sharply pointed triangles. The points of those elbows are echoed in the pointed elbows of the narrator, who wears a different garment, in the points of his collar, and in the triangular shape of the clusters of grapes, and the points on the bananas and the pear. Even the tiny apple leaf is the same shape.

For more information

Uri Shulevitz (1985) has talked at length, in both words and in many accompanying small sketches to illustrate his ideas, of the importance of where things are located in a picture. He emphasizes how often he moves objects around in succeeding sketches, before settling on a location which suits his purposes. Another of Shulevitz's quotes about his own work is included by Cummins (1992) in her large, elegantly-designed collection of appreciations of 80 artists.

Similarity

How alike or unalike the various objects in a picture are; objects can be similar in separate visual elements like color or proportion. We tend to notice things because they are dissimilar in some way from other objects which are near them.

Activity

To see how differently artists interpret the same text, you might look with children at John O'Brien's version of The Twelve Days of Christmas.

Figure 3.4: The Twelve Days of Christmas

Notice how this artist uses the table top as an organizing element, arranging her drummers around it. Everything moves in from the outside toward the center of the table top, and the two plates placed there. In showing just part of the figures, Brierly is visually akin to the French artists Edgar Degas and Henri de Toulouse-Lautrec, who often showed only part of the people in their paintings. This is commented on by Richard Muhlberger, in *What Makes a Degas a Degas?*, a helpful reference for expanding you understanding of this artist.

Plate 4: Zoo

Compare the architecture here with that shown by Allen Say in *Tree of Cranes*. Though the buildings shown come from different cultures, in each case the artists use the building shapes (and the window and door openings) to constrain and direct where we look. The architecture is an organizing structure within which the action takes place.

Throughout the book she uses the device of similar shapes. In the illustration for the second day, the bird cage, the stair rail balusters, and the foliage urn are all basically the same shape. What makes the illustration humorous is that the characters' heads are slightly convex, echoing the shape of the rest of the objects!

Anthony Browne, in his illustrations for *Zoo (color plate 4)*, has used the principle of similarity in effective ways. Browne's story is about a thoroughly obnoxious father, his obsequious wife, and their two distressing boy children, bound on an outing to stare at the animals. Browne's surrealist style is apparent early in the book: on the second opening the driver of the truck with pictures of bananas on its side is remarkably ape-like. On the right side, several of the characters waiting in line at the ticket booth have animal characteristics. On the right page of each opening, the pictures of the animals themselves have the kind of peculiar emptiness characteristic of surrealist art. Notice in this plate, for example, how the color of the giraffes is so close to the color of the brick wall in front of which they stand, that they almost disappear into the wall. There's striking similarity of size and shape in the dead tree and the restraining fence at the bottom of the picture. The blackness of the fence at the bottom is similar to the blackness of the interior of the building into which the left giraffe puts its head; this echoes the blackness of the supporting members apparent beyond the building roof in the upper right corner of the picture. The tree itself is interesting because the bark isn't really bark-like at all: rather it is sinewy and almost seems as if it could be an animal limb. In this way, the tree is reminiscent of the human quality Arthur Rackham gave his trees in art done much earlier in this century.

Faith Ringgold's art for *Dinner at Aunt Connie's House* provides another effective example of similarity, here accomplished through the repeated use of pattern: squiggly lines, small dabs of color, and flowery wallpapers present an intensified surface that vibrates with activity. This book is based on a painted story quilt she did earlier. In addition to telling a warm family anecdote, it also incorporates portraits of 12 African American women, including Mary McCleod Bethune and Bessie Smith, who become characters in the story. The line quality throughout the book is similar: most often it moves energetically in short, rounded (not angular or straight) lines. For example, on the first opening, notice how the tree leaves are indicated, in the same "scribbly" lines used to show the waves in the ocean on the right side of the opening. These aren't long, smooth, gently curving lines, but rather the shorter kind of lines also found outlining the flowers on the wallpaper (second opening). Though the pattern in the wallpaper (third and following openings) is in straight lines, even these aren't smooth, but rather zig-zag tightly up the wall. Some of this patterning is also apparent in Ringgold's *Tar Beach*, a Caldecott Honor Award winner.

Continuation

How does the illustrator direct our eyes from one place to another? Hobbs and Salome point out that often this is done by a strong line, or by an equally strong edge of a shape.

Stephen Gammell, in his illustrations for *The Relatives Came*, often uses line overtly to show viewers where to look. For example, in the illustration on the third opening, we follow from point to point because he uses the device of the road on which the relatives are driving in their rattletrap car as a way to encourage us to follow along. Gammell's colored-pencil illustrations show a

About the artist
Martin (1989) pointed out other ways in which Browne's work is significant in The Telling Line, *which includes essays on 15 contemporary illustrators.*

Activity
If you want to engage children in further considering the art in quilt making, Mary E. Lyons's Stitching Stars *would be a useful extension. This tells of the life and story quilt art of Harriet Powers, born into slavery in 1837. The full-color reproductions show many of the 299 appliqued panels making up Powers's Bible quilt, a monumental work of visual storytelling.*

About the artist
To learn more about Ringgold, you could read a short article by Krull (1991) or the children's books which feature her work (Sills, 1989; Turner, 1993).

For more information
A further explanation of the use of color similarity, including examples from specific books is given in Stewig (1992).

Continuation
The concept that an idea extends from one place in a picture to another; a character's arm, for example, may direct us to notice the object being pointed at.

particularly scruffy looking collection of many relatives who exude a delicious delight in being together.

In his *Bear Hunt*, British illustrator Anthony Browne directs our eye through the use of many different lines. The two trees on either side of the composition in the seventh opening, for example, serve as walls, keeping our attention focused on the center part of the picture. The hunter leans slightly forward, but the most obvious direction comes from the gun barrel, pointed directly at the bear. Browne reinforces where we should look by inscribing a triangle formed when the hunter's arm, bent at the elbow, also directs us to follow along the gun barrel, at the tiny bear. Browne won the Kate Greenaway Award, the British equivalent of the Caldecott Medal, for a later book, *Gorilla*.

At times an illustrator achieves continuation by having the characters look in a particular direction, so we also look at what they are focusing upon. In *Would You Rather…*, John Burningham, who has twice won the Kate Greenaway Medal, poses a series of humorous improbabilities, and asks readers to choose. On the eighth opening, he asks whether it would be worse if Dad danced at school, or if Mom made a fuss at a cafe? In showing the second, equally distasteful probability, all eyes of the customers and even passers-by on the street look at Mother in the midst of the dispute. The lone exception is the red-cheeked, embarrassed little boy. Throughout, Burningham makes use of pleasant pastel watercolors and colored pencils, augmented with a tentative, though effective, darker line to highlight shapes.

The same technique is used by Pat Cummings in her illustration for *My Mama Needs Me* by Mildred Pitts Walter. On the sixth opening, both Mama and Jason, getting used to the idea of having a new baby sister, are looking right at the baby. But in addition to that, undrawn lines encircle the important part of the scene. Notice how the right edge of Mama's robe, the curve of her two arms, and the connecting curve of the blanket frill and Jason's head, all serve to make a circle keeping our attention where the artist wants it. The two dimensional illustrations, which make use of repeated, flat patterns, are done with a thin brown (not black) line.

Niki Daly's illustrations for *All the Magic in the World* by Wendy Hartmann provide other examples of continuation. This affirming, slight story of young Lena and her friends tells of the "magic" old Joseph, the odd-job man shows them. Notice the

Figure 3.5: My Mama Needs Me
As often in her art, Pat Cummings develops symbolic representations rather than the sort of particular realities we see in Trina Schart Hyman's art, as in *Rapunzel.* The pattern in the blanket, the lace trim, the rhythmic though unrealistic folds of the baby's blanket, are all juxtaposed for their decorative effect, not to create realism, though what is shown, is realistic. More recently, Cummings used four-color illustration for her own story, *Clean Your Room, Harvey Moon!*

tight, circular composition on the third opening. The arms and legs of the children in the tree point in a sweep of motion toward Lena. The chain-link fence which cuts across the bottom left corner directs our eye up to old Joseph, and his head, tilted forward toward the center of the circle, directs our eye across the opening above Anna to complete the circle back at the three children again. On the right side of the seventh opening, the direction the characters are looking guides our eyes to the most important part of the composition, the soft-drink pop-tops. In addition, the children bend forward to Joseph, making a tight circle around him, while his arms form strong vertical lines toward the pop-tops. The conscious use of continuation as a composition device is apparent throughout this book.

Variety

Any artist considers ways to unify a composition, but too much unity can make an illustration dull. We wouldn't notice and comment upon a kitchen floor in which all of the tiles were exactly the same size, shape, and color. Because any illustrator wants viewers to notice the artwork, s/he varies elements to attract our attention. The variety may come through differences in materials, for example in a collage, when a particularly interesting texture is set against a very different material. Or, an artist may vary size.

Variety

Can be apparent in any one of the visual elements described in chapter 2; in one picture, for example, the lines used may be both thick and thin, straight and curved, continuous and interrupted.

We notice a very large figure (nearer the viewer), because of the contrast with a very small one (much further from the viewer).

Notice the amount of variety in an illustration for *All Night, All Day* by Ashley Bryan, the third opening in the book. This collection of African American spirituals with the music included, shows an amazing variety in shapes and lines. There are rounded shapes, as in the flowers in the upper left corner, in the people's bodies, in the moon in the upper right corner, and in the lily pad shapes in the lower center of the right side of the painting. There are sharp, spikey shapes, in the plant forms in the far lower left corner, in the foliage along the right edge of the painting, and in the tree branches themselves. There are outlined shapes as in the flowers in the upper left corner and the leaf shapes in the bottom left. But there are also unoutlined shapes, as in the flowers in the tree on the left side, and in the lily pads. The many curved lines in the painting contrast with the narrow band of straight lines which cross through the middle of the painting. You'll notice that there is also considerable variety in color. The artist has used hot colors, as in the garment the man is wearing, and cool colors, in the garment the woman is wearing. Sometimes the foliage is in reds, yellows and oranges, as in the lower right, while just directly above that, the foliage is done in cool shades of blues and greens.

The previous paragraph focuses on the variety evident in a single illustration from one of Ashley Bryan's books. But looking at the entire body of his work would show children another sort of variety. This winner of the Coretta Scott King Award for Illustration, for *Beat the Story Drum, Pum Pum*, has also illustrated some of his work, like *The Cat's Purr*, by using only soft brown line drawings. Other of his work, like *SH-KO and His Eight Wicked Brothers*, is illustrated by a different artist.

Paul Goble's illustrations for *Crow Chief* exhibit an intriguing mix of treatments of objects, showing variety. This artist won the Caldecott Medal for his 1979 *The Girl Who Loved Wild Horses*. In the Plains Indian story, *Crow Chief*, we have, on the ninth opening, several unoutlined silhouettes, as in the body of the hunter with the feather on the left. In contrast to that, the bodies of the crows are also silhouettes, but they are outlined with a thin black line. In contrast to the silhouettes, the figure with the horned headdress, and the far right figure are completely painted in, with a plethora of costume detail that contrasts pleasantly with the medium brown silhouettes of the other figures. The natural

Activity

One could pull together an array of Bryan's books and use them with children, focusing on the variety they show, in both illustration style and in text.

The *Coretta Scott King* Award

Given annually since 1970 to a black author and since 1974 to a black illustrator, whose books exemplify "outstanding, inspirational, and educational contributions." The award is administered by the Social Responsibilities Roundtable, with the cooperation of the Association for Library Services to Children, both of the American Library Association.

Figure 3.6: Crow Chief
Two dimensional images characterize Goble's work. In this illustration, the small, intensely patterned areas, as in the clothing on the Indian at the right, are effectively balanced with many other areas which are completely without pattern. That is a technique also used by Ed Young in his illustrations for *Seven Blind Mice*, though in other ways the two books are stylistically very different. You might look at this art in the context of a more recent book by Goble, *Dream Wolf*.

forms of the humans and the animals are quite different than the stylized, geometric treatment of the sun. Throughout this book, and others he has done, like *The Great Race of the Birds and Animals*, Goble achieves variety by treating the figures in this way.

Edward Gorey's slightly fusty illustrations for *The Shrinking of Treehorn* by Florence Parry Heide, achieve their variety through the quality of line the artist uses. On the 28th opening, and throughout, Gorey contrasts very slight, thin line, as in the calendar, tablecloth, and cupboards, with a much bolder line in the pattern on the floor, the chair, and the printing on the cereal box. We get contrast through the use of straight lines in the cupboards and the table, as juxtaposed against the curved lines of Treehorn and his mother, as well as the curved chair back.

An artist may achieve variety through the way s/he depicts certain objects or characters. In *Old Henry* by Joan Blos, artist Stephen Gammell lines up a variety of neighbors, concerned over

Henry's indifference to standards of home maintenance. Though five neighbors are lined up in a row, notice the differences: men and women, fat and thin, young and old, front, back and profile views, walking and riding, standing stiffly or gesturing indignantly, closer together and farther apart. You could have children compare this full-color illustration on the seventh opening, and done full-page size, with the quasi-silhouette small monochrome sketch set above the text on the left side of the fifth opening. Again Gammel has used a row of five neighbors, but there's as much variety in this simple row as there is in the full page mentioned earlier.

Other ways we might help children notice variety as a compositional device are apparent in John Collier's *The Backyard*. After enjoying the spare emptiness of these paintings which accompany a reflection of times past, you might help children notice the variety, for instance, of the visual distance the artist uses. In contrast to the physical distance (i.e., how closely we hold the book), artists often manipulate visual distance (i.e., how closely or how far away the artist makes the scene appear to be). On the first opening, we view the scene from middle distance, the second we are closer, while the third presents a panoramic far-distant view. The fourth opening shifts to a dramatic closeup, while the fifth moves to a middle distance. And so it goes throughout the book: the conscious alternation of distances provides a pleasant variety children might not notice unless we work on it with them.

Or, we could help children notice that the positioning of the figures varies greatly as well. On the first opening, the two characters are facing right while on the second, one character faces in each direction. On the fourth opening the character faces left, on the fifth to the right, and on the sixth the character again faces left. This variety in figure position adds to the richness of the composition in the book.

Dominance

We've all been at a party where one person talked a great deal, and because of that, became the center of attention. We may notice and interact with other less verbal guests, but our attention is drawn to the dominant person. Similarly, in any illustration there is a focal, or center point, and we tend to look at that first and to look at it for longer than we study other less-important elements.

Why does something dominate? Among party guests, someone may capture and hold our attention because of their size, their location (near the center of the room) or the distinctive clothing which sets them apart from other guests. In looking at a book illustration, we notice that an object catches our attention, perhaps because of its size, color, unusual shape or texture, or some other feature.

On the fourth opening of Lane Smith's *The Big Pets*, we notice the cat immediately because of its size, or scale. It is so much bigger than the tiny child in the lower left corner whose foot it is licking, that we are drawn to the cat, and particularly its tongue. Smith has commanded our concentration, capturing perfectly the feeling of being overwhelmed that small children often have when an animal, seeming to be so large, shows affection. The words for this picture are very pragmatic: it is the visual that shows the affect, or feeling of the child. Smith has written about his work and particularly of the unexpectedness of much of his illustration, saying that he delights in "playing with all the conventions and really turning them upside down..."which gives us an insight into how to approach his work.[1] In each of the illustrations in *The Big Pets* and other of his books, there is something to catch viewers by surprise.

Figure 3.7: The Big Pets

Notice the pebbly texture Smith achieves here, by stroking one color over others. Our eyes follow the v-shape composition, an invisible line down from the top of the child's head to its foot, connected to the cat's tongue (lowest point of the "v") and then back up to the cat's nose and out the top of the illustration. There are other vaguely scary images throughout Smith's art for *Halloween ABC*, a collection of poems by Eve Merriam. In *Glasses, Who Needs 'Em*, Smith provides illustrations on every page for a strange encounter between a young boy and an optometrist.

There's a different kind of emphasis in Peter Parnall's *Feet!* which comes from positioning of objects. Notice on the 12th opening, for webbed feet, that we see on the left page a tight closeup of the bird's feet, drawn with subtle hatching and cross-hatching to indicate both texture and shading, underlaid with a subtle, blue watercolor wash. Right away we know this is what the illustrator wants us to attend to. Our eye follows back into the picture, past the roosting pelican and still further back to the palm trees on the far distant island on the right page. All of this is done in the kind of masterfully understated drawing for which Parnall has justly become known. The simple, abstract quality of the background, done in flat washes of color, carves the space into sections, leaving ample white space showing to intensify the limited range of colors used. Throughout this book he uses the same technique: a variety of different kinds of feet are shown close up (and often to one side of the opening). Then for contrast, a simplified, abstracted background done in an elegantly thin pen line shows the entire animal.

Earlier in his career, Parnall did illustrations for a series of books by the southwestern writer, Byrd Baylor, and it was in this context that many first became aware of this talented illustrator. In *If You Are a Hunter of Fossils*, for example, Parnall showed that he could sculpt flat shapes on the page using as few visual elements in his art as Baylor used words in her poetry-like texts. We always understand what is the dominant part of the illustration, because most of the color is there. On the tenth opening, we clearly see how the main idea, "sharp-toothed monsters," those lizards 40 ft. long who swim, is shown—once again far over to one side of the double-page spread. The visual weight of the illustration is there, because that's where the most intense color is, and most of the design. On the rest of the spread, details are few and lines are simple, subordinated to the drama of the large lizard. In the way that musicians understand that silence intensifies sound, and thus they build rests into their music, so Parnall understands that emptiness intensifies design. So frequently in these earlier works, we see him using the blank areas in the page as a foil for his spare designs.

On the 12th opening of *Desert Voices*, we continue reading Baylor's text written as if the coyote were speaking, and we see how the coyote's head is dominant. Other details, like the small plant and animal scene in the background, are less important.

Figure 3.8: Jason Goes to Show-and-Tell

It's the inanimate character (the teddy bear) which faces viewers; Jason is too busy tromping through the snow to turn around. The two are firmly held in the triangular composition. Follow an imaginary line from the lower left at the fire plug, up to the crotch of the tree, down to the highest fence post on the right, and back across to the fire plug. Compare this treatment of the topic with the cartoon-style art done in mixed media, by Barney Saltzberg for *Show-and-Tell*.

Because of Parnell's placement of the circular sky form above the miniature scene (less than an inch wide and a half inch high), we sense the immenseness of the desert.

Another example of dominance is apparent in Linda Weller's illustrations for Colleen Sutherland's *Jason Goes to Show-and-Tell*. In the watercolor illustration on the ninth opening, we notice Jason, as he runs through the cold, for two reasons. First, our eye is drawn into the picture by the snow-capped fire hydrant which occupies the lower left corner (indeed extending beyond the frame). Then we move to the tall anchor of the tree, which because of its width draws us to Jason, and because of its blocky trunk, keeps our eye from wandering to the left. The brown color is such a contrast with the brightly colored outdoor clothes he is wearing that it causes us to look directly at Jason. Our eye stays on him, the dominant figure in the illustration, because to the right, the fence and the bush are done without any color to distract us from the focal point.

The dominance of intense color is readily apparent in John Burningham's illustrations for *Harvey Slumfenburger's Christmas Present*. In this whimsical story, frequently the center of the composition isn't in the physical center of the picture nor is it the largest object shown. Nonetheless, because of the use of intense,

For more information

Stewig (1990) reported on children's responses to these images of the Southwest, looking particularly at differences among urban, rural, and suburban children's comments about the Baylor and Parnall books.

bright color, we know right away where the focus is going to be. For example, on the fourth opening, we sense the length of Santa's walk: the tiny figure is only one-inch high set in a vast double-page spread, fully 20" wide and 12" high. Yet Santa dominates this spread, because of the contrast between the bright white of his face, beard, and trim on his coat, and the much more subdued background. On the sixth opening, it is the bright yellow of the airplane which dominates the double spread, most of which is in soft shades of brown. On the 11th opening, notice how the bright red (on Santa) and blue (on the girl) stand out and hold their own against the much larger splash of black representing the ground.

Rhythm and movement

Rhythm and movement
Leads the eye from one place to another, not randomly, but rather predictably, controlled by the way the artist has used techniques like repetition.

Activity
To introduce rhythm and movement to children, you might help them think about repetition in nature, a common feature which children won't necessarily notice. There's a useful section called "Repeating Patterns" in a children's book by Taylor. You could use this with students, then have them look for repeating patterns in nature before beginning a study of this element in illustrations.

Controlled repetition in art is called rhythm. A musical composer repeats a particular chord progression several times throughout a piece of music. The first time we hear it, we notice the beauty of the sounds. At a second repetition, we recognize that we've heard it before. The third time it's repeated, we start actively listening for the series of sounds, because we're aware of the composer's intent.

Similarly in visuals, an artist may consciously repeat a particular kind of line, an alternation of light and dark, or a distinctive shape. This controlled repetition results in a visual rhythm, according to Hobbs and Salome. Where do we see this idea exemplified in children's book illustration?

In the fourth opening of Jan Brett's *Annie and the Wild Animals*, the artist presents viewers with a rhythmic element, a swirl of snow-tipped pine trees, moving from the top left rear of the picture to the bottom right front. The repeated tree shapes, along with the repetition of the clumps of snow on the branches, makes for a rhythmic painting. The horizontal lines indicating the crests of the snow, beginning with the one closest to the bottom of the page and moving in succession toward the back; the final hill we see behind the house is another rhythmic element. In addition to the kind of movement she establishes in the pictures by using repeated elements, Brett also repeats design elements in the heavy frames which encompass all of the illustrations. Children will enjoy studying the myriad small repeated details which characterize this artist's work, drawn to show visually the tale of young Annie, who searches for a substitute pet when her beloved cat Taffy disappears, temporarily.

Figure 3.9: Annie and the Wild Animals

This is an interesting example of a large, calm painting which is mostly landscape, in which there is actually less going on than there is in the wide pictorial borders. After you've enjoyed this book as a visual unit with your students, focus their attention on the borders. Cut a piece of plain construction paper the size of the art, hold it over to block out the picture, and ask children to talk about what they notice in the borders. Compare this art to the pictures for *Town Mouse Country Mouse*. Here, Brett encompasses her minutely detailed vignettes, varying in number on the page, with expected frames (like flowers) and unexpected ones (like broken crockery).

Robert McCloskey, in *Burt Dow Deep-Water Man*, made effective use of repeated shapes to create a sense of movement. Burt, enjoying his tranquil retirement after a life at sea, has an amazing adventure with whales. On the 26th opening of the book, notice the playful repetition of just whales' tails that allows McCloskey to set up a rhythm enhanced by the various colors he used for the tails. The individual details and the surface texture of the whales aren't at all important. Rather, what McCloskey clearly enjoys here, and wants viewers to enjoy, is the way we can follow a progression of tails from the front to the back of the picture plane, because of the overlapping of the simple shapes. On all of the openings showing Burt's encounter with the school of whales, McCloskey sets up one rhythm after another, as he exaggerates the large size of the mammals, in order to delight us

Figure 3.10: Burt Dow Deep-Water Man

McCloskey doesn't need, anywhere in the text of this book, to *tell* us how big the whales are in comparison with the size of his hero, Burt Dow. Rather, he *shows* us in the illustrations, and because of the clear sense of scale established, we can understand the difficulty of Burt's task. Some libraries may still have a copy of *Lentil*, a story featuring a child main character, also illustrated by McCloskey. Look at the two books to see if children can observe some stylistic similarities.

with his repeated shapes. Notice, also, the superb design decision apparent on the 16th opening. After following this character for many brightly-painted pages, the opening "showing" Burt in the whale's belly is complete black, with the text set in white. The stark contrast of going from the previous cheerfully colored pages, into this black page with no illustration at all, makes us feel more intensely the darkness of the whale's interior.

In *The King's Chessboard* by David Birch, illustrator Devis Grebu has in several places established a rhythm through repetition. In this tale about the King of Deccan in India, we read of a ruler who cannot understand the wise man who wants no reward for serving him well. On the tenth opening, notice the repeat of the three horizontal lines, each created, not with a line, per se, but rather through other means. At the bottom of the page, the Grand Superintendent of the King's Granaries' arms reach out to form one horizontal. In the middle ground, the row of oxen pulling the wagons of rice forms a second horizontal. And finally, at the top of the illustration, done only in black pen line with no color used as in the other two horizontals closer to the viewer, we see a group of people making another strong horizontal. Besides these repetitions, the vertical thrust of the superintendent's body is echoed in the vertical towers of the castle, to the top rear.

On the last opening of *Through the Magic Mirror*, illustrated by Anthony Browne, we see several different kinds of repetition that contribute to the movement in this understated illustration. There is, most obviously, the repeated shapes and colors in Toby's sweater. But notice also the repeated horizontal lines indicating the stair treads. To emphasize the design quality here, Browne chose not to depict these realistically, i.e., with weight/thickness that real stairs would have, but rather as simple thin lines with only a bit of pale green shading on one side. There is also the very strong vertical repetition, of the handrail, and the sharp edge of the wall beside the stairs, which serve to focus our attention. We look at Toby because he is so narrowly contained between these two vertical elements. Toby, fed up with everything, walks through a mirror and while inside, passes an invisible man, and an easel holding a painting, both of which are direct visual quotes from paintings by the Belgian Surrealist artist, René Magritte (1898-1967). Children won't know these associations, but you might use Browne's book in conjunction with work about Magritte. Cirlot has described why Magritte is "one of the most representative of surrealist painters."[2] Magritte's work is also featured in *Looking at Paintings. Horses*, by Peggy Roalf. As usual in this fine series, the reproductions are full-page size, in color, and the commentary is accessible.

There's much evidence of rhythm and movement in Tim Vyner's illustrations for *Arctic Spring* by Sue Vyner. Not a story, per se, but rather a simple account of the way various animals wake up in this environment unfamiliar to most readers. The account helps children sense the hopefulness in the seasonal change. On the third opening, notice how the artist sets up a rhythm in the repeated, straight slashing strokes used to show the tundra grass clumps and the way these are similar to the pointed ears of the rabbit. On the left page, we view this close up, while on the right page we are looking from a greater visual distance. The same rhythm is apparent on the more panoramic sixth-opening double spread, in the repeated clumps of vegetation. A different kind of movement is apparent on the seventh opening, where the

For more information
There's a particularly helpful section on rhythm and movement in a children's book by Waters and Harris (1993), using examples of paintings by such disparate artists as Rosa Bonheur and Vincent Van Gogh, to guide us in better understanding this concept. The oversized format (10" x 13") enhances the presentation of such topics as visual elements like color, of compositional devices like pattern, and even artists' techniques, like painting solid forms.

About the artist
This enigmatic painter is well served in the volume by Waldberg (1965), with large, full-color reproductions and a text printed in English.

bird's wings, making a number of different V-shapes (wide to narrow), establish a rhythm of their own. The different-sized chunks of floating ice from near the bottom of the picture plane to much farther away, nearly at the top of the illustration, set up another rhythm.

Balance

Where the artist places objects in an illustration affects the balance achieved, according to Hobbs and Salome. Sometimes the balance is *symmetrical*, that is, what is on one side of an imaginary line through the painting is of equal *visual weight* with what is on the other side. The illustrator has created an illustration in which one part seems to mirror what is in the other part. The question of balance isn't simply related to the size of the objects, or placement, however. It can also be related to such factors as color. For example, a small but very brightly colored object on one side of a painting can indeed balance out a much larger, but more neutrally colored object on the other side. Symmetrical balance can be talked about as balance on either side of a line running from top to bottom. But symmetrical balance can also refer to a composition divided in half horizontally, so that what is above and below an imaginary line is balanced.

Another kind of balance is *asymmetrical*, in which there is more visual weight on one side of a composition than on the other. This is a less formal way of arranging objects in a painting.

In a series of small ($4^3/4$" x $5^3/4$") books, Nicola Bayley often makes use of formal, or symmetrical, balance. On the cover of *Elephant Cat*, the various cats are shown staring straight at the viewers. The design elements of the frame, and surrounding plant

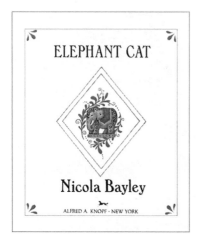

Figure 3.11: Elephant Cat
The lettering here, the border, even the tightness of the diamond shape around the elephant, are all designed to reinforce the tidy, tight, and tiny shape of this book. The elements of the page are entirely consistent with the size the artist chose for the book. Bayley used a similar small format for her equally detailed animal illustrations for Paul Manning's *Fisherman*, a rhymed story about a sea-going weasel. Her attention to tiny detail creates books which are comparable in scale to the small books of Beatrix Potter.

material are also arranged so what is on one side is balanced by what is on the other side of a vertical line dividing the cover. The endpapers continue this predictable balancing of equal elements, as they arrange diamond shapes with cats and other animals in them, in a pattern that is symmetrical both vertically and horizontally. The title page from *Elephant Cat* is also symmetrical. The type face, and the small design within the diamond shape, when divided in half, are mirror images of each other. Notice that within the diamond shapes the swirl of leaves above the elephant on the top left is balanced by the swirl of leaves on the bottom right. Inside the books in this series, the pages are balanced, with each opening featuring a left page with text and above a small drawing of an element from the illustration which takes up the entire right page. Contents of both pages are always contained within a thin black rule, providing further balance.

In black and white, Ann Jonas has bisected her pages horizontally for *Round Trip*. This impressive tour de force is a book

About the artist

Bayley has talked about her work in an interview with Marantz and Marantz (1992), as well as influences on her development as an artist, and the use of actual objects as she develops her illustrations. The book of interviews includes material on over 25 artists currently doing picture books.

Figure 3.12: Round Trip

A hard-edged, unequivocal style was essential to carry out this clever book design idea, pictures which "read" differently when viewed from two different directions. Look at this book in the context of Jonas's *Reflections*, in which the same design idea is employed. Done in four color, there is more to look at, and it is thus more difficult to understand.

"Oops! Sorry!" said the caterpillar as he crawled away.

Then he saw the strange man.

caterpillar. "Where are you?"

said a voice. "You're eating my hair!" "What?" said the

"That looks a bit more juicy," said the caterpillar   as he started to nibble. . . "Ouch! Get off!"

Figure 3.13: If At First You Do Not See

A hand-drawn outline, on some pages breached by objects extending beyond it, separates the richly painted watercolors in the illustration, from the text which moves around all four edges of the page. There are a wide variety of textures to entrance the eye in this slight tale of a caterpillar who sets out to find something more appealing to eat than leaves. Compare the animal main character's adventures with those in Eric Carle's *The Very Hungry Caterpillar.*

to be read in the usual direction from the front, then turned upside down, and reread from the back. Each of the pages can be divided in half with an imaginary line, and what is above the line is balanced with what is below the line, even though it will show something entirely different during a reading in the other direction. The delicate balance is evident in that the illustration "reads" as a complete unit when viewed, but one sees something else entirely when the book is repositioned.

Ruth Brown, in *If At First You Do Not See*, uses a similar page device, that is, designing the paintings so they must be looked at both right side up, and then upside down, to see the two different images being created. Brown's full-color paintings are thickly painted to the edge, and her subtle use of symmetrical and asymmetrical balance help her create the images which "shift" content depending on how the book is held.

Figure 3.14: The World from My Window

In this visual exploration of shapes, the artist creates a resolutely two-dimensional world. The very simple tree trunk and branch shape is varied in five similar but slightly different patterns. After studying this book with children, you might have them cut their tree shapes from colored construction paper. These could be arranged in a composite group mural to emphasize variations within the same basic shape. Samton uses a looser style with less distinct edges, in the double-spreads she did for *Jenny's Journey.*

Some of the illustrations in Mordicai Gerstein's *The Mountains of Tibet* feature round mandala-like paintings, as in the one found on the tenth opening. This tale of the woodcutter who has longed to travel all his life, but never leaves his valley until he dies, is an example of formal balance. In this painting, notice how the river nearly bisects the painting. Each half is balanced. The buildings, top left, balance a similar-sized clump of buildings in the top right. The two islands on either side of the circle balance each other. The cluster of onion-domed buildings on the lower left balances the pagoda-like structures on the lower right. Throughout this intricate painting, the formal balance is quite evident.

Sheila White Samton's brightly decorative illustrations for a counting book, *The World from My Window*, show asymmetrical balance. On the page showing six trees, notice that the two black-trunked trees on the left of the center line balance the three smaller-sized trees with cream colored trunks, shown farther back in the picture on the right. On the following spread, the two cranes to the left of the river face across it to the five on the right side, who are facing left. Though the number is unequal, the way they are grouped balances the composition, but not symmetrically. These brightly colored illustrations are reminiscent of the kind of paper cuttings the French artist Henri Matisse was doing toward the end of his life. You could use Samton's book and then introduce *Meet Matisse* by Nelly Munthe to children, before having them make their own cut paper designs.

For a small, square-shaped book (7¼"), illustrator Victoria Chess provided watercolor and pen line illustrations for Hilaire Belloc's cautionary tale *Jim, Who Ran Away from His Nurse, and Was Eaten By a Lion*. Several of the illustrations are interesting examples of balance in a picture. For example, on the eighth opening, notice how the very round-shaped lion is on the left side of the illustration, placed horizontally, while on the right half of the picture the equally round-shaped animal keeper is placed vertically. The brighter green uniform of the keeper balances the more neutral tan color of the lion, compensating for the lion's rather larger size.

Vladimir Radunsky's illustrations for *The Story of a Boy Named Will, Who Went Sledding Down the Hill* by Daniil Kharms, are completely asymmetrical, beginning with the cover. Kharms, a Russian poet, was involved with a group of avant-garde poets and artists active in Russia during the late 1920s. The cover indicates we're in for an unusual ride. It includes a small figure of Will, set off-center, upper right, as the only thing on the cover except for the lettering. That lettering, done in a crisp serif typeface, includes only *The Story of a Boy Named Will*, with a comma telling viewers we need to open the book to find the remainder of the title. The accumulative tale ends in a wordless double spread of rampant confusion as the crowded sled runs into a bear. On every page there's something unexpected to look at. The contemporary illustrator provides intense closeups, often showing us only part of the people and animals involved, who are so large that they extend off the page in all directions. Clearly, literal representation wasn't intended here.

For another explanation of composition, you might want to read a section called "Structure," in Andrew Pekarik's book for children, *Painting. Behind the Scenes*. Though the terminology he uses in his chapter about composition is different than the terminology used here, he discusses many of the same ideas. The author includes paintings done between 1372 and 1991, all reproduced in full color and large enough to be easily seen. The selection includes such well-known artists as the Spanish painter, Pablo Picasso, and others less familiar, like the American Ad Reinhardt. The works discussed include representational styles like a painting by Jan Vermeer, a Dutch artist; abstract pieces like a painting by the Swiss painter, Paul Klee; and nonobjective works like a painting by the Russian, Wassily Kandinsky. This book, a companion to the PBS series, is intended for middle-school readers, but librarians could easily summarize some of the ideas to help younger children understand the concepts.

Molly Bang is an illustrator who describes composition principles in different terms than those used here. She does, however, remind us of something very important, now that we have examined each of these principles individually. In her book, *Picture This*, she says:

> ... remember that these principles are used not one by one, but always in combination and always in some context. Each of the principles appears quite clear when it is considered individually, but each picture we see uses a combination of principles which makes the interaction of the parts and the overall effect more complex.[3]

Because of this, and to make the interrelationship of these principles overt, at least in one illustration, we will now look more particularly at a single picture and search for these principles in it.

Combining principles

We'll use an illustration by Elisa Kleven from *Abuela* by Arthur Dorros, to illustrate how several of these principles of composition can function in a single picture. The book is discussed in chapter 4, as an example of collage, and the reproduction we'll consider is included in the full-color section, plate 5 *(following p. 174)*.

Unity: As an example of *unity*, this illustration shows how color can work to enhance the total overall effect so that nothing stands out at the expense of the other elements. This picture includes a lot of visual elements, in many different colors. But since the general tonality, which is both light and bright, is so consistent throughout the picture, we get a very unified feeling from looking at it.

Proximity: Notice how the artist achieves proximity, creating an arch from lower left to upper right. Begin with Rosalba's bright red shoes, follow up her body, noticing the way her arm overlaps Abuela's skirt. Continue up to the grandmother's head and notice the way she is so close to Aunt Elisa, even though they are on opposite sides of the counter, that the sweep of the move-

Plate 5: Abuela
Everywhere we look in this illustration there is something new to notice. There's an energy here which results from the busy accumulation of detail. You might look at this interior scene for its kinetic quality, in the context of the exterior cityscapes done by the American painter Dong Kingman, which have a similar quality. Despite the many details, the focus of the composition is clear. Follow with your eyes the imaginary line which inscribes a "C" from the cat at the bottom center to the man at the top right.

ment continues. Elisa overlaps Uncle Pablo, whose arm extends to the upper right edge of the picture. Indeed, his hand is off the edge, leading us to the next page.

Similarity: Our eye naturally looks for similarity of shapes, and the illustration is full of that. The repeated shapes of the boxes, cans, and bottles on the shelves behind the counter form a pleasing pattern. This is echoed in the display of merchandise in the bottom, right-hand corner of the picture. Notice that the accentuated roundness of the people's heads is similar in size to the roundness of the cat's body.

Continuity: There are several examples of continuation in this illustration. Abuela looks at Elisa and Pablo, who themselves look at both Rosalba and her grandmother. The strong vertical of the counter, which extends virtually completely across the upper third of the picture is another example. The squares in the floor form a pattern which directs our eye to the counter, where the three adults stand.

Variety: There's interesting variety in this picture. Notice, for instance, the number of different sizes of rectangles the artist uses. Sometimes these are very small, as in the boxes behind the counter, and in the display at the bottom right corner. Compare these in size with the rectangles of blue and white in the tile floor. Notice that the display posters on the front of the counter are significantly bigger and are a different size than the rectangle shape of the box the cat sits on. The papaya sign in the lower right, which extends off the page, is evidently the largest of all.

Dominance: Dominance is achieved in this illustration through size, not through color. As mentioned earlier, because of the closeness of the tonalities, they contribute to the unity of the picture. So Kleven had to achieve dominance by making the four characters large enough to catch and hold our attention. Even Rosalba is larger than she probably would be if represented realistically. She's a young girl (and that is shown more clearly, interestingly enough, in the first and second illustrations in the book). Here, to help the figures dominate the very busy surroundings, artist Klevin elongates Rosalba's figure, making her nearly as tall as her Abuela.

Rhythm and movement: There are both large and small evidences of rhythm and movement in this illustration. Notice how the repeated shapes of the cans, boxes, and bottles move across the shelves, marching together in more orderly fashion than they would be in real life. Notice the larger, up and down v-shape movement of the arms of Elisa and Pablo: they inscribe a large repeated design across the bodies of the two characters, which is—incidentally—reflected in the v-shaped design around the neck of Pablo's sweater.

Balance: Balance is vertically symmetrical, i.e., the two figures of Abuela and Rosalba on the left half of the picture balance out the two figures of Elisa and Pablo on the right side of the picture. But they are balanced differently when the picture is divided horizontally. Looking at the composition horizontally, Abuela, Elisa, and Pablo, in the top half of the picture, balance out Rosalba, the cat on the box, and the display stand, in the bottom half of the picture.

So we can often find several, or all, of the compositional principles which Hobbs and Salome identify, in this illustration. The principles probably always vary in their importance in a given picture, and sometimes one or more of them may not be important at all. It's also probably true that an accomplished artist never sits down to consciously think about how to incorporate these into an illustration. But thinking about these ideas and how they are manifested in a picture or throughout a book in a set of pictures, will undoubtedly make it easier for us to understand and enjoy more fully what an artist has created.

Page arrangement

Throughout the previous section, the emphasis was on composition principles within a given illustration. Using the terminology and ideas suggested by Hobbs and Salome, we looked at various examples of these principles as exemplified in particular illustrations from children's books. We can also think, however, about organizational ideas evident on a page within a book, and throughout a book. First, let us consider some examples of page arrangement.

Sometimes a consistent page arrangement is set up and continues throughout the book, providing a layout that viewers can anticipate with certainty. For example, in *No Dodos* by Amanda Wallwork, each double-page opening is always arranged exactly the same. On the left page, the geometric design is arranged in two parallel, horizontal lines, above and below the san serif type, giving the number and the endangered animal being counted. On the right, the same geometric design forms a border around the rectangle of color on which the animals, which always extend beyond the edge of the rectangle, are arranged. The artist sets up a predictable rhythm which, because of the security it provides, focuses the viewer's attention on the animals themselves.

At other times, page arrangement varies throughout the book. For example, in Molly Bang's *The Paper Crane*, an American Library Association Notable Book, the artist's collage illustrations are of different sizes, set in different ways on the page. Some are double-page spreads, taking the entire space. Other openings feature different placements. On the sixth opening, there is a large, full-page picture on the left, framed with the text set below the single picture. On the right page there is an interesting composition. Four smaller pictures are arranged, so that a wide horizontal illustration tops three vertical illustrations showing the crane and the boy. This arrangement of sharply defined pictures is quite unlike the following page, on which several small, unbordered and backgroundless vignettes of people are shown. Certainly one of the things we could talk with children about is how the page arrangements in this book vary.

To think about arrangement on the page, we can also return to a book introduced earlier, *The Gold Coin*, illustrated by Neil Waldman. That book was used to discuss the element of proximity, and it is informative to notice how Waldman lays out his individual pages to make use of this compositional principle. The diagram below shows how each of the pages (except the last one) is laid out.

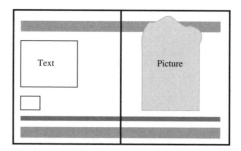

Across the top is a band of solid color, while at the bottom, across both pages are two bands: the upper is narrower while the lower is wider (and the same color as the top band). On the left margin is a small, square watercolor design, repeating an element from the larger illustration on the facing page. The block of text is always in the same relative position, across from the illustration. The large, unbordered illustration on the right page extends up to overlap the band of solid color at the top. Two interesting uses of proximity are apparent here: 1) the smaller square is very close to the color bands, and the two lower color bands are very close to each other; 2) the illustration is so close to the upper color band that in almost every case it overlaps.

Another possibility is to study the composition throughout the book. Pictures are seldom considered as isolated units, but rather are understood in the larger context of the entire book. It is commonly pointed out, for example, that in Maurice Sendak's *Where the Wild Things Are*, the size of the pictures increases from rather small (5¹/2" x 4") on the first opening, to the much larger 20" x 9" double-page spreads showing the height of the action, the rumpus pages (Nodelman, 1988). After the climax, the illustration size shrinks again.

Similarly, several book critics have commented on the tonality change in Margaret Wise Brown's *Goodnight Moon*. It is already night when the story begins, but the tonalities in the picture on the first opening are bright. By the time the story has run its course to the last opening, set in the same room, the tonality has changed entirely, becoming much more muted, and the objects are thus much less distinctly shown.

Another example of composition throughout a book is apparent when we use two editions of *A Child's Good Night Book*, a Caldecott Honor winner by Margaret Wise Brown. You might compare two editions, the 1986 and the 1992, with a class to help children see the differences. This would allow us to notice differences in the composition of individual paintings, since the art, lithographs by the French-Mexican artist, Jean Charlot, is not identical in different editions. The typeface used, and its position on the page also varies. Bader provides an interesting history of the changes in this book, which she calls "the first of the true bedtime stories."[4] The 1986 edition is apparently a reprint of a reconfiguration done during the 1950s, when it was made into a large-size, vertical format. In the 1986 paperback edition, the text is placed on the left page, set in a serif face—opposite an illustration on the right. Bader shows in color the original 1943 edition, and it is this much smaller (5¹/2" x 6¹/2") size which makes it more appropriate, she feels, for a bedtime book. In the 1992 edition, the text is set below the double-page spread, in a san serif face printed in grey, not black. Notice how the illustration varies. In the 1986 edition, we get just the picture of the tree, the birds, and the sheep on the first opening. The sun is to the right of the tree, and the three baby

About the book

Jones's (1989) analysis of Where the Wild Things Are *is helpful in deepening our insight about this classic. Cott's (1983) long and provocative profile of this artist considers this as well as many other Sendak books.*

For more information

Marcus (1991) has described further the historical details surrounding the creation of Goodnight Moon, *now a classic.*

birds are already asleep with beaks closed. Mother, perched on the tree, is also asleep. In the 1992 edition, the double-page illustrations show the baby birds still awake, beaks open to receive the food which Mother, returning to the nest, is bringing. The sun goes down to the left of the tree. The position of the sheep is different, and there is a rabbit in the 1992 edition which is included as the second opening in the 1986 edition. The entire right half of the double-page spread, showing the house, children, and the cat on the roof, is included as the second opening in the 1986 edition. Therefore, viewers get a very different composition when looking at the two editions.

For another description of how to look at the overall composition throughout a book, you might read Doonan's (1993) description of the design of *When Sheep Cannot Sleep*. She provides a particularly helpful analysis of the way in which there is a two-dimensional pattern of light and dark when one looks at the book as a whole. She points out that in the first 14 plates, bands of dark tones in the upper half contrast with bands of light tones in the lower half. The 15th illustration is a pivot, with light tones predominating. Then, the pattern is reversed, and throughout the rest of the book, bands of light tones cross the upper half of the openings, while bands of dark tones predominate in the lower half.

Involving children in studying composition principles

Hewett and Rush (1987) assert that librarians and teachers, even those without formal training in art themselves, can help children learn more about composition, or what they call formal properties of art, using a technique called *aesthetic scanning*. In this process, we lead children through a series of different types of questions, to observe carefully and talk about what they discover as they observe. Viewers think together about:

1. Sensory properties (like line and color, called visual elements in chapter 2 of this book;

2. Formal properties (often called the principles of art, called compositional principles in chapter 3 of this book);

3. Expressive properties (expressing a feeling or idea, like tranquility, or nobility); and

4. Technical properties (the characteristics of the media and how the artist used it).

To help children think about the composition of an illustration, librarians could ask such questions as:

a. Leading questions, i.e., "The balance in this is symmetrical, isn't it?"

b. Selective questions, i.e., "Is this balance symmetrical or asymmetrical?"

c. Parallel questions, i.e., "Is there any kind of balance here other than symmetrical?"

d. Constructive questions, i.e., "What kind of balance do you see here?" and

e. Productive questions, i.e., "Can you describe one of the formal properties in this illustration?"

Hewett and Rush believe that such question-asking strategies encourage children to examine the art carefully and to volunteer information based on their own perceptions. They conclude that the "greater the children's participation, the greater their learning will be."[5]

Viewing art

Finally, we could consider some ideas which Lanier (1985) thinks affect the way in which we view art, in applying these to picture books. This critic talks about the *screens* through which we see a piece of art, as these affect how and what we perceive. Each of these points can also affect how we as adults perceive picture books. In addition, we could to some degree help children think about each item.

As we look to understand art, we are affected by:

1. *What others say about art, and this work in particular.*

   Lanier means that both verbal and written commentary about art influences our perception. Applying this to picture books means that what we, as adults, read of reviews or what we hear other teachers and librarians saying about books affects our own judgements. In group discussion with children, what one child says about a picture book may expand or limit what another child sees in it.

2. *The setting.*

   Lanier means that the context is important. How do children see a particular book we are using in the context of all the other picture books they have viewed and thought about? The more we have seen, the more likely we are to see more.

3. *How we have learned to see.*

   Lanier means that our perception is conditioned by the ways we have been taught to use visuals. If, for instance, children are continually, and only, asked to look at pictures in order to verify text, then they will only use visuals for that purpose. If, in contrast, children have been encouraged to look at illustrations for the sensual pleasure to be derived from them, they will see with greater insight.

4. *How much we know about elements and principles of art.*

   Lanier means here that if children have, in some systematic and continuing ways, been encouraged to look at the visual elements described in chapter 2 and the principles of art described in this chapter, they are more likely to perceive more fully.

5. *What we know about the particular symbols used.*

About the artist

To expand your awareness of Kandinsky, you might look at the book by Roethel and Benjamin (1982), Though this includes many reproductions which are only black and white, there are sufficient full color (and full page) pictures which give a very clear idea of this artist's work.

   Lanier means that any language, like mathematics for instance, uses symbols, and art is a language. In realistic art, the symbols are more easily understandable than in less realistic styles. For example, the geometric forms used in the paintings of the Russian painter, Wassily Kandinsky (1866-1944) convey a less-easily understood meaning.

6. *What the artwork reminds us of.*

   Lanier is here suggesting that helping children make conscious association with other aspects of their lives is important in responding to illustration. For instance, does the color an artist used remind you of seeing that particular shade in an object elsewhere? Is the pattern in a picture similar to a pattern you know?

7. *How much we know about its history.*

   Lanier here suggests that knowing things like the medium which was used, the artist's name, and the date it was created, may enhance response. Talking with children about a medium (either before or after giving them opportunities to work with it), pointing out the illustrator's name (and reminding children they've earlier seen art by the same person), and mentioning a date (which could set the book as a very early, or a more recent one), can enhance response.

8. *How we judge it.*

Lanier is specific in recommending that we need to look at art over a period of time to really see what is there. If we do this, we can go beyond simple critical judgements ("I like, or don't like it") into more sophisticated response, "I like, or don't like it because…"). This means children need opportunities to return to books again and again to re-see the art.

9. *What relationship it has to our lives.*

Lanier here is thinking about encouraging children to make connections, exploring such questions as: "Would you like to own a copy of this book, and if so—why?" Is the art in this book important to us because of the topic, because of the style, or because of some other, perhaps idiosyncratic, reason?

All of these visual screens, to use Lanier's term, affect our adult viewing. Becoming consciously aware of them may help broaden our perception of the art in children's books. Thinking about these as we work with children may in addition help us to enhance children's ability to look at, think about, and respond to the art of picture books.

Recommended children's books

Bang, Molly. *The Paper Crane*. New York: Greenwillow, 1985.

Bayley, Nicola. *Elephant Cat*. New York: Alfred A. Knopf, 1984.

——— (Ill.). *Fisherman* by Paul Manning. New York: Macmillan, 1988.

Bloom Suzanne. *We Keep a Pig in the Parlor*. New York: Clarkson N. Potter, Inc., 1988.

Brett, Jan. *Annie and the Wild Animals*. Boston: Houghton Mifflin, 1985.

———. *Town Mouse Country Mouse*. New York: G.P. Putnam Sons, 1994.Brierley, Louise. *The Twelve Days of Christmas*. New York: Henry Holt, 1986.

Brown, Margaret Wise. *A Child's Good Night Book*. New York: HarperCollins, 1943, 1992.

———. *A Child's Good Night Book*. New York: Harper Trophy, 1986.

———. *Goodnight Moon*. New York: Harper & Row, Publishers, 1947.

Brown, Ruth. *If At First You Do Not See*. New York: Holt Rinehart and Winston, 1982.

Browne, Anthony. *Bear Hunt*. New York: Atheneum, 1979.

————. *Gorilla*. New York: Alfred A. Knopf, 1983.

————. *Through the Magic Mirror*. New York: Greenwillow, 1976.

Bryan, Ashley. *All Night, All Day*. New York: Atheneum, 1991.

————. *Beat the Story Drum, Pum, Pum*. New York: Atheneum, 1987.

————. *The Cat's Purr*. New York: Atheneum, 1985.

————. *SH-KO and His Eight Wicked Brothers*. New York: Atheneum, 1988.

Burningham, John. *Harvey Slumfenburger's Christmas Present*. Cambridge, MA: Candlewick Press, 1983.

————. *Would You Rather ....* New York: Thomas Y. Crowell, 1978.

Carle, Eric. *The Very Hungry Caterpillar*. New York: Philomel, 1969.

Chess, Victoria (Ill.). *Jim, Who Ran Away from His Nurse, and Was Eaten by a Lion* by Hilaire Belloc. Boston: Little, Brown, and Co., 1987.

Collier, John. *The Backyard*. New York: Viking, 1993.

Cooper, Floyd (Ill.). *Brown Honey in Broomwheat Tea* by Joyce Carol Thomas. New York: HarperCollins, 1993.

Cummings, Pat. *Clean Your Room, Harvey Moon!* New York: Bradbury Press, 1991.

———— (Ill.). *My Mama Needs Me* by Mildred Pitts Walter. New York: Lothrop, Lee and Shepard, 1983.

Daly, Niki (Ill.). *All the Magic in the World* by Wendy Hartmann. New York: Dutton Children's Books, 1993.

Gammell, Stephen (Ill.). *Old Henry* by Joan Blos. New York: William Morrow, 1987.

———— (Ill.). *The Relatives Came* by Cynthia Rylant. New York: Bradbury Press, 1985.

Geisert, Arthur. *Oink, Oink*. Boston: Houghton Mifflin, 1993.

Gerstein, Mordicai. *The Mountains of Tibet*. New York: Harper and Row, 1987.

Goble, Paul. *Crow Chief*. New York: Orchard Books, 1992.

————. *Dream Wolf*. New York: Bradbury Press, 1990.

————. *The Girl Who Loved Wild Horses*. New York: Bradbury Press, 1978.

————. *The Great Race of the Birds and Animals*. New York: Bradbury Press, 1985.

Goennel, Heide. *My Day*. Boston: Little, Brown and Company, 1988.

Gorey, Edward (Ill.). *The Shrinking of Treehorn* by Florence Parry Heide. New York: Holiday House, 1971.

Grebu, Devis (Ill.). *The King's Chessboard* by David Birch. New York: Dial Books for Young Readers, 1988.

Hutchins, Pat. *Tidy Titch*. New York: Greenwillow Books, 1991.

Johnson, Crockett. *Harold and the Purple Crayon*. New York: Harper and Row, 1955.

Jonas, Ann. *Reflections*. New York: Greenwillow, 1987.

————. *Round Trip*. New York: Greenwillow, 1983.

Keats, Ezra Jack. *A Snowy Day*. New York: Viking, 1962.

Kleven, Elisa (Ill.). *Abuela* by Arthur Dorros. New York: Dutton Children's Books, 1991.

Lyons, Mary E. *Stitching Stars.* New York: Scribner's, 1993.

McCloskey, Robert. *Burt Dow Deep-Water Man.* New York: The Viking Press, 1963.

————. *Lentil.* New York: Viking Press, 1940.

Muhlberger, Richard. *What Makes a Degas a Degas?* New York: The Metropolitan Museum of Art/Viking, 1993.

Munthe, Nelly. *Meet Matisse.* Boston: Little, Brown and Co., 1983.

O'Brien, John. *The Twelve Days of Christmas.* Honesdale, PA: Caroline House, 1993.

Parnall, Peter (Ill.). *Desert Voices* by Byrd Baylor. New York: Charles Scribner's Sons, 1981.

————. *Feet!* New York: Macmillan, 1988.

————(Ill.). *If You Are a Hunter of Fossils* by Byrd Baylor. New York: Charles Scribner's Sons, 1980.

Pekarik, Andrew. *Painting. Behind the Scenes.* New York: Hyperion Books for Children, 1992.

Radunsky, Vladimir (Ill.). *The Story of a Boy Named Will, Who Went Sledding Down the Hill* by Daniil Kharms. New York: North-South Books, 1993.

Rice, Eve. *Benny Bakes a Cake.* New York: Greenwillow Books, 1981, 1993.

Ringgold, Faith. *Dinner at Aunt Connie's House.* New York: Hyperion Books for Children, 1993.

————. *Tar Beach.* New York: Crown Publishers, Inc., 1991.

Roalf, Peggy. *Looking at Paintings. Horses.* New York: Hyperion Books for Children, 1992.

Saltzberg, Barney. *Show-And-Tell.* New York: Hyperion Books for Children, 1994.

Samton, Sheila White. *Jenny's Journey.* New York: Viking, 1991.

————. *The World From My Window.* New York: Crown publishers, Inc., 1985.

Say, Allen. *Grandfather's Journey.* Boston: Houghton Mifflin, 1993.

————. *Tree of Cranes.* Boston: Houghton Mifflin, 1991.

Sendak, Maurice. *Where the Wild Things Are.* New York: Harper & Row, Publishers, 1963.

Sills, Leslie. *Inspirations. Stories About Women Artists.* Niles, IL: Albert Whitman and Co., 1989.

Smith, Lane. *The Big Pets.* New York: Viking, 1991.

Smith, Lane. *Glasses, Who Needs 'Em?* New York: Viking, 1991.

———— (Ill.). *Halloween ABC* by Eve Merriam. New York: Macmillan, 1987.

Taylor, Kim. *Pattern.* New York: John Wiley and Sons, Inc., 1992.

Turner, Robyn Montana. *Faith Ringgold.* Boston: Little, Brown and Co., 1993.

Vyner, Tim (Ill.). *Arctic Spring* by Sue Vyner. New York: Viking, 1992.

Waldman, Neil (Ill.). *The Gold Coin* by Alma Flor Ada. New York: Atheneum, 1991.

——— (Ill.). *Nessa's Fish* by Nancy Luenn. New York: Atheneum, 1990.

Wallwork, Amanda. *No Dodos. A Counting Book of Endangered Animals.* New York: Scholastic Hardcover, 1993.

Waters, Elizabeth and Annie Harris. *Painting. A Young Artist's Guide.* New York: Dorling Kindersley, 1993.

Weller, Linda (Ill.). *Jason Goes to Show-and-Tell* by Colleen Sutherland. Honesdale, PA: Boyds Mills Press, 1992.

Professional references

Bader, B. (1976). *American Picturebooks from Noah's Ark to the Beast Within.* New York: Macmillan Publishing Co., Inc.

Bang, M. (1991). *Picture This. Perception and Composition.* Boston: Little, Brown and Co.

Bishop, R. S. (1993). "Profile: Pat Cummings, Artist." *Language Arts*, 70(1), 52-59.

Cirlot, L. (1990). *The Key to Modern Art of the Early 20th Century.* Minneapolis: Lerner Publications Company.

Cott, J. (1983). *Pipers at the Gates of Dawn. The Wisdom of Children's Literature.* New York: Random House.

Cummins, J. (ed.). (1992). *Children's Book Illustration and Design.* New York: PBC, Library of Applied Design.

Doonan, J. (1993) *Looking at Pictures in Picture Books.* Stroud, Glos, UK: Thimble Press.

Hewett, C. J., and J. C. Rush (1987). "Finding Buried Treasures: Aesthetic Scanning With Children." *Art Education*, 40(1), 41-43.

Hobbs, J., and R. Salome (1991). *The Visual Experience.* Worcester, MA: Davis Publications, Inc.

Jones, R. E. (1989). "Maurice Sendak's *Where the Wild Things Are*: Picture Book Poetry." In P. Nodelman (ed.), *Touchstones* (Vol. 3) (pp. 122-131). West Lafayette, IN: Children's Literature Association.

Krull, K. (1991, February 15). New textures in children's book art. *Publishers Weekly*, p. 61.

Lanier, V. (1985). *The Visual Arts and the Elementary Child.* New York: Teachers College Press.

Marantz, S., & Marantz, K. (1992). *Artists of the Page. Interviews With Children's Book Illustrators.* Jefferson, NC: McFarland and Co., Inc., Publishers.

Marcus, L. S. (1991, January-June). "Margaret Wise Brown, Clement Hurd, Ursula Nordstrom and *Goodnight Moon.*" *CBC Features*, 44(1), unp.

———. (1991, May/June). "Rearrangement of Memory: An Interview with Allen Say." *The Horn Book Magazine*, pp. 295-303.

Martin, D. (1989). *The Telling Line.* New York: Delacorte Press.

Miller, G. A., and R. Ragans. (1992). *Exploring Art.* Lake Forest, IL: Glencoe Publishing.

Nodelman, P. (1988). *Words About Pictures: The Narrative Art of Picture Books.* Athens: The University of Georgia Press.

Roethel, H.K. and J. K. Benjamin (1982). *Kandinsky.* London: Philip Wilson Publishers Ltd.

Say, A. (1991). "Musings of a Walking Stereotype." *School Library Journal,* 37(12), 45-46.

Shulevitz, U. (1991). *Writing Pictures. How to Write and Illustrate Children's Books.* New York: Watson-Guptil Publications.

Smith, L. (1993). "The Artist at Work*." The Horn Book Magazine,* 69(1), 64-70.

Stewig, J. W. (1990). "Children's Responses to Images of the Southwest." In R. A. Braden (ed.), *Perceptions of Visual Literacy* (pp. 77-88). Conway, AK: International Visual Literacy Association. (ERIC Document Reproduction Service No. 312 607)

———. (1992). "Reading Pictures, Reading Text: Some Similarities." *The New Advocate,* 5(1), 11-22.

Waldberg, P. (1965) *René Magritte.* Brussels, Belgium: André De Rache, Publisher.

Media

4

Whenever a book artist begins a new project, one decision that must be made is which medium or media will be used. Artists choose materials that they think will fit best with the nature of the writing, be it a work of fiction or an information book. The final outcome, i.e., the art in the book, looks very different depending upon which medium has been chosen. The methodical, time-consuming processes involved in producing a woodcut result in art which is dramatically different in final effect than the mercurial, fast-paced technique of watercolor. This chapter will examine how these media vary from each other, and how they affect what an artist can or cannot do to achieve particular desired effects. We will examine several of the most popular media used and describe particularly noteworthy examples in each medium.

Drawing

Almost all artists draw to some degree in preparing artwork which may indeed later appear to be primarily done in paint or some other medium. In many cases, preliminary sketches serve to help the artist clarify their intentions, to work through various possibilities, and to plan when and how various scenes will be shown. In those cases, the drawing is a tool to achieve a different end product.

In other cases the draftsperson uses the drawing as an end in itself, a finished product of great subtlety. The artist whose name comes readily to mind in this category is Chris Van Allsburg, who since the publication in 1979 of *The Garden of Abdul Gasazi*, has been acknowledged as one of the most skilled practitioners working with drawing materials (Heller, 1988). Using "just" black and

Figure 4.1: Jumanji

The intensified patterns of light and dark make for a mysterious picture, in a surrealistic story. Details are purposely few, and become even more important because they are so spare. This isn't a realistic environment, which would be less perfect, and more cluttered. Small areas of much detail (i.e.: the entangled tree branches seen through the open door) contrast with larger plain areas (i.e.: the wall and the door). Look at this art in the context of the black and white art David Wiesner did for *Night of the Gargoyles*.

white, Van Allsburg creates in this book, as well as in *Jumanji*, an array of shades ranging from the palest near-white greys to deeply intense blacks. In the process, he creates a solidity of forms and depth of field that evoke remarkably realistic, yet often surreal, settings into which one feels one could easily walk.

The showcase for *Garden* is an elegantly ample (11¹/₂" x 9¹/₂") rectangle, set with sufficient white space, particularly on the left-side text pages, to enhance the array of tones in the large full-page pictures on the right. These are unbordered, though there is a repeated simple black-and-white border around the text. Using carbon pencil, Van Allsburg has created soundly three-dimensional shapes on the flat paper, both human forms and the architectural elements he depicts so convincingly. Look, for example, at the scene showing Alan running into the garden through the open stone doorway (fourth opening). The range of tones is impressive, varying from the white of the paper showing on the statues' shoulders, through the inky blackness of the trees inside the door opening. In a very formal composition, Van Allsburg has used his palette to create drama that reflects the uncertainty of the text. What will Alan discover when he bolts through this opening? We want to know because of the visual drama Van Allsburg has established.

The same range is used throughout *Jumanji,* as in the illustration showing Peter bolting out of the door (12th opening). The interesting compositional device of Peter being almost insignificant, in size at least, surrounded by all of the architectural detail shown, is typical of this book and others by Van Allsburg. Notice the juxtaposition of the strong black tone of the stair baluster contrasted with the intense white of the open door. The wall behind and the trees outside provide the mid-range tonality. In these two books, Van Allsburg has shown the very outer edges of light and dark to which a medium like pencil can be pushed.

There is a similar array of tones, and a pleasing pebbly texture in *The Widow's Broom*, with the addition of sepia tones. In contrast to the earlier horizontal format Van Allsburg used, this is presented in an elegantly thin vertical rectangle format ($7^{3}/4$" x 13"), clearly a case where the narrow shape accommodates the thin, tall broom effectively. The constant interplay of black and brown enhances the presentation. This begins with the black linen sleeve binding on the cover, in brown paper over boards format with an elegant copper-colored, die-stamped silhouette of the broom. It continues through the intense black endpapers into the body of the book, where the full-page pictures face text pages decorated with a frieze of pumpkins both above and below the words. A typical example of the range of tonality Van Allsburg achieves in these drawings is the eighth opening; notice how dark the shadows under the piano are, compared with the whiteness of the piano keys.

There's a range of tonalities in Carole Byard's chalk drawings for *Africa Dream (See illustration on p.104.)*, by Eloise Greenfield, though the drawings are in general much more loosely controlled than those by Van Allsburg. The author does an impressionistic account of the young girl's dreaming—of cities, the countryside, the small villages of the continent. She "step(s) across countries…" as she sees the people (her long-ago grandaddy), the animals (the donkey on which she rides), the objects (pearls and perfume), and events (dancing a hello dance). All of this is shown in double-page spreads bled to the edge, in which Byard provides vigorous depictions of the action, in an array of tones, tied together with a quick, unifying line.

Another artist who effectively evokes a range of tonalities in a book that depicts a very different time and place, is Ronald

About the artist
Evans (1992) explains in greater depth how Van Allsburg creates his art, in particular pointing out his use of the conte pencil dust in the process.

Blind Stamp
To create a die-stamp color designs or type are stamped under pressure using a brass die. If no ink is used, the sunken image is referred to as a blind-stamp.

Figure 4.2: Africa Dream

There's an impressive sweep across this double spread, from the upper left (where the man is shown farther away) to the lower right where the child's face is shown larger, because she is so much closer to the front of the picture plane. Look at this art in the context of the four-color illustrations Byard did for *The Black Snowman*. Can you see some of the features which identify the two sets of art as by the same illustrator?

Himler, in *Dakota Dugout*. The story, by Ann Turner, is a first-person narration about life a century ago, told by a woman talking to her grandchild long afterwards. The language is as spare as the country was empty. Her comment on seeing the sod house, "I cried when I saw it," is as bleak as the landscape which Himler shows us. In strokes which are crosshatched to create depth and texture, Himler shows us the seasons: winter, when "the ground was iron," and the hope of spring, which "was teasing slow then quick." We know, when the narrative ends, that this woman who lived through those hardships means it when she says, "Sometimes the things we start with are best." There couldn't be a more effective accompaniment to this story: color would have trivialized the impact of the account. In looking at any of these books, we can see the wisdom of Marcia Brown's (1986) remarks:

> We have become so saturated with color in our advertising, in our magazine illustration, and in our motion pictures that we almost lose sight of the fact that children enjoy equally books with little or no color, and books in full color.[1]

In contrast to the many subtle variations of tonality possible in pencil, we can enjoy the airy, understated whisper of line which Ashley Bryan used to illustrate *The Cat's Purr*, a fanciful tale of the time when Cat and Rat were the best of friends, living in huts next to each other, and doing everything together. These small drawings, done in crayon, are placed above, below, and beside the text. They are full of action created by the large number of lines laid down. Some of these are lighter in weight and thus seem almost the preliminary thoughts of the artist, while others are heavier and thus seem more final. No matter how many are included however, in total they are lighter in effect than the darkness apparent in many of Van Allsburg's drawings.

In his pencil drawings for *The Song and Dance Man* by Karen Ackerman, artist Stephen Gammell has provided resolutely cheerful pictures that avoid becoming either saccharine or sentimental. The narrator for this Caldecott Award book is one of three children who listen with rapt attention to Grandpa's stories about his performing on the vaudeville stage. Coming to their grandparents' house to visit, they accompany him to the attic where they try on his costumes, watch while he turns on the "spotlight" (a cast-off lamp), and spur him on while he does his act. This red-nosed grandpa, decidedly thick in the waist by now, tells corny jokes the children have heard before, but the slightly disheveled kids, so typical of Gammell's drawings, applaud anyway. Gammell eschews idealized representations: the youngest boy's sweatshirt is perpetually parted from his pants. These are not beautiful children. Grandpa's hair is askew, and his vest no longer buttons. But they are appealing precisely because they seem so human. Mixing a wide variety of shades of color, Gammell gives viewers just enough background to set the scene, and then focuses our attention on these characters, so obviously happy to be together. In the hands of an artist with less control, this could have turned cloying, but it is a tribute to Gammell's skill that we leave refreshed, not overloaded with sugar.

Figure 4.3: The Cat's Purr
Anthropomorphized animals inhabit this West Indian folktale, with art done in a soft brown pencil line, varying in thickness. This understated art with only minimal backgrounds is very different than the brightly painted, full-color illustrations Bryan did for such books as *Sing to the Sun*, a collection of poems and pictures. Despite the difference in mediums used, can you see some similarities in the two styles?

Watercolor and other paint media

Watercolor is a medium often used by book illustrators. An artist mixes a pigment—either in dry form or bound with gum arabic and glycerine (a water-soluble solution)—with water. The pigment may be mixed with a lot of water and washed onto the paper to create a very fluid, loose effect with flowing forms and undefined edges. Or the pigment may be mixed with very little water and applied with an almost dry brush to create a brilliant, highly controlled effect having precise edges and strong colors.

Another factor determining the final appearance of watercolor painting is the paper. Unlike painters' canvas, which has a minimal texture, or the kind of smooth papers used in finger-painting, watercolor paper usually has a very noticeable *tooth*, or irregularity in the surface texture. High ragged peaks, resulting from the large amount of cloth incorporated in the papermaking process, catch the brush and prevent it from laying down the color smoothly, unless the watercolorist uses a great deal of water or applies the paint in a very determined manner. As a result, some of the surface area of the watercolor paper remains untouched by the brush; small flecks of white paper usually show through the color, increasing what painters call the "sparkle." The whiteness of the paper contrasts with the intensity of the watercolor, increasing the brilliance of the image.

The watercolor illustrations of several artists are well worth studying for what children can learn from them about technique. Berthe Amoss uses watercolor to evoke realistically the shady recesses of the bayou in her book *Old Hasdrubal and the Pirates*. As Billy and Old Hannibal fish, the old man tells about an encounter his adventuresome grandfather Hasdrubal had with Jean Lafitte, a French pirate in the Americas (ca. 1780-1825). Amoss employs the sparkle of watercolor by applying paint so that the white paper shows through. She mixes many subtle shades of color and uses soft brown ink line in a few places to help define shapes.

Watercolor is often used with ink line, which adds definition to the forms. In one watercolor illustration in *Little Tim and the Brave Sea Captain*, Tim and the Captain survey the stormy waters from the ship's bridge just as it seems they are about to go under (18th opening). Author/illustrator Edward Ardizzone uses watercolors to create the wave, the ship, and the figures themselves and ink line to further define the forms. In other illustrations in this book, it is notable how Ardizzone's use of crosshatched ink lines alone gives very sharp, well-defined images.

Sometimes an artist creates illustrations in which the color itself defines the form or the line is so incidental that it goes almost unnoticed. In Aileen Fisher's *Listen, Rabbit!*, Symeon Shimin uses soft, gentle colors to create pictures that shimmer with enchantment and require only minimal addition of line. The straw and the nest, for example, are three-dimensional forms created only with color.

Few art education textbooks recommend using watercolor with children in elementary school, because it can be frustrating to work with. First, it is difficult to control due to the large amount of water in the medium. Second, if misused, watercolor can become very hard-edged and may inhibit children's creativity. Teachers can, however, incorporate watercolor into art experiences for intermediate-grade children.

In contrast with the kind of transparency which most often characterizes watercolor, gouache (pronounced *gwash*) is powdered color, mixed with Chinese white. The result is an opaque surface that sometimes looks like oil painting. Simon Henwood's illustrations for *A Piece of Luck* show the kind of distinctive flatness of finish typical of gouache. What makes these particularly interesting is that the surface colors seem to have been overpainted on a dark blue underpainting. The line which defines shapes is an unusual dark blue, and in places small flecks of the dark blue show through the top surfaces. Large, abstract shapes accompany this morality tale; the double spread (sixth opening) showing the village presents a particularly effective juxtaposition of building shapes.

Illustrators who want a more opaque final effect often choose to use acrylic paints. Frezzolini points out that this medium "can exhibit the strength of oils or the delicacy of watercolors."[2] One advantage this medium offers is that it dries much faster than do oil paints, allowing an artist to go back and repaint sooner than would be possible working in oil. Another advantage is that the opacity of acrylics allows the artist to rework an area, completely covering what lies beneath (Feiser, 1992).

This Night... by the German artist Irmgard Lucht, winner of the Juvenile Literature Prize in 1990, is a gentle mood piece about how different animals react to the coming of night. The art is full of rich deep blues and greens, heavily influenced by black and contrasted with the bright light of moon and stars. A note in the back of the book points out the artist chose acrylics, applied in many layers "to achieve color blends and give depth to the pictures."

Another opaque medium is tempera, a powder color ground in water, and mixed with colloidal, gelatinous, or albuminous medium. It is not only easy to work with, but gives two other advantages: 1) its opacity can be increased or decreased and 2) its brightness and dullness can be controlled. Ashley Bryan used this medium skillfully in *Climbing Jacob's Ladder*, African American spirituals about heroes of the Bible selected by John Langstaff. Throughout, the high-intensity yellows and greens make a very cheerful mood, and the subtle brushstrokes of varying tonalities fill the page with an energy that captures our interest.

Oil paints are a medium not often used by illustrators, perhaps in part because they take a long time to dry. Thomas Locker, in *The Mare on the Hill*, combines oil and alkyd paints for his full-page illustrations set on each right page facing a left-side page of text. These are extremely realistic, panoramic landscapes of a rural area, in which the people are always less important visual elements than is the setting itself. They are reminiscent in tonality of the paintings of the seventeenth century Dutch artist, Jacob Van Ruisdael.

In a longer, illustrated book, *The Moon of the Monarch Butterflies*, artist Kam Mak did oil paintings on masonite board to accompany naturalist Jean Craighead George's journey tale of a migrating butterfly. The paintings, full- and double-page spreads, contrast areas of intense detail with larger, plain spaces. This series of 13 books, named for North American animals, is illustrated by several different artists using different mediums; the reissued series makes available again George's fine nature writing.

Very different than these fully painted oils is the kind of lightly brushed, atmospheric effect which Floyd Cooper achieved in his illustrations for *Be Good to Eddie Lee* by Virginia Fleming. This is a compelling exploration of the relationships between Eddie Lee, a Down's syndrome child, and two others, Christy, and JimBud, who don't want their fun spoiled by Eddie Lee. Soft-edged, double-page spreads are done with only a minimum of line, and the pebbly texture looks very similar to the surface created when an artist uses pastels as a medium. There's impressive gradation of naturalistic colors throughout.

The way in which the refinement of oil painting expanded the color possibilities available to artists is explained in a helpful section of a book by Alison Cole, *Eyewitness Art. Color*. Appropriate for middle graders, this expands teachers' and librarians' background in many different aspects of color, using reproductions of paintings in the collection of the National Gallery of Art.

Robert Bender used a different kind of paint, vinyl animator's paint, usually used by artists painting on the clear acetate sheets from which film art is made. His art for *The Three Billy Goats Gruff* is distinctive both because of the intensity of the highly saturated colors he uses, and also because of the softly-atmospheric edges to his forms. The colors are intensified because of the contrast with the type, set in white. Bender has said that he backs the individual sheets of clear acetate with black paper, which intensifies the colors.

Woodcut

Woodcut and its more recent descendants, linoleum-block printing and cardboard cuts, are media well worth children's study. The Japanese used woodcuts as early as A.D. 800 to make art prints. In addition, woodcut has a long history as a medium for book illustration. As early as 1493, woodcuts were used to produce illustrations for a book entitled *Der Ritter vom Turn*, published in Switzerland. These first black-and-white illustrations contrast sharply with the brilliant full-color reproductions found in current children's books. Working in linoleum is not as formidable as working in wood, which has a hard, resistant grain, so some artists prefer to use linoleum blocks, which give a finished effect very similar to woodcuts. Whether the artist works in wood, linoleum, or cardboard cuts, the finished product has a recognizable "look."

When making a woodcut or linoleum block, the artist works with a surface thick enough to be cut into several different levels. First, the artist draws a design on the surface of the wood or linoleum, in reverse of the desired final effect. Because this is a printing process, the final art reverses direction. For example, an arm to be shown facing right in the final art must be cut into the wood facing left. Using a small sharp gouge, the artist then cuts away everything except what is to be printed. (Small bits of the surface often remain outside the desired areas, giving the characteristic appearance to the print.) After cutting the design, the artist is left with a two-level block. Areas that have been cut away, and will thus not print on the paper, are deeper than the raised portions, which will print. The ink is applied to the top surface of the block with a small roller called a brayer. Because both the brayer and the wood have hard surfaces, the ink does not reach the deeper, cutaway portions. The artist places a piece of paper on the inked

For more information
Michail Rothenstein's Linocuts and Woodcuts *is a book for adult artists that is written clearly enough for the novice to understand. Chapters on materials and processes are liberally illustrated with many black-and-white and a few color photographs. These show details of processes involved; reproduction of linoleum-block prints and woodcuts by such artists as Pablo Picasso and Paul Gauguin are also included. Of direct use to teachers is the chapter titled "Print Methods for Schools."*

Figure 4.4: *Whaling Days*
The strong angularity of the individual strokes of the woodcut gouges are typical of this medium. This quality is modified somewhat by the curves of the line of the rope attaching the harpoon, the curve of the whale's head, and the smaller curves of the waves. Look at this use of woodcut in the context of art for a book on a very different subject, but done in the same medium. *King Wencenslaus* with art by Christopher Manson is done in four color, rather than in the more limited tonalities Carrick uses.

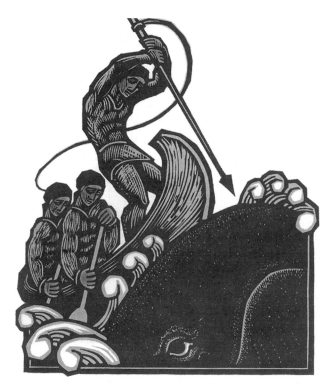

surface and rubs, transferring the ink to the paper. After examining the print, the artist may decide to alter the image by cutting away more of the block's printing portion. Obviously, adding anything at this stage of the process is impossible.

The artist repeats the process of cutting and inking blocks and lifting prints for each color to be included in the print. Only one color, except in instances where two areas are widely separated on the block, can be printed from each block, although the artist may overlap colors to create new colors. Most block-printing inks are opaque, so mixing colors is harder to do than it is with transparent watercolors.

Many illustrators use block printing. Color is a rather incidental element in the strongly patterned woodcuts which David Frampton did for *Whaling Days* by Carol Carrick. The bold, blocky serif letters of the title on the dust jacket are pushed at but not dislodged by the equally strong sweep of the whale's tale, showing us that this will be a book full of energy. The men in the boat are indeed pulling with all their might to steady it against the equally strong, repeated swirls of the waves. Overall, pattern predominates. There are soft shades of blue, yellow, and orange which accompany the dramatic black of this illustration, but they're less important than the black patterns themselves. Inside this large book (8^1/$_2$" x 11^1/$_4$"), Carrick tells the factual account of adventurous men who braved their lives at a time when whales were prized, not protected. Other denizens of the sea are depicted, for example, the octopus on page 11 will give child readers/viewers a much more intense understanding of this sea creature than a realistic photograph would. We delight sensorially in the patterns Frampton creates: curves of the octopus intertwine with the curves of the ocean waves. Color is present, but relatively unimportant as our attention is demanded by the wood block's vigor. The elegant, cream-colored coated paper is an appropriate foil for the gloss of the black ink of the woodcuts themselves.

Nonny Hogrogian, a gifted woodcut artist, uses woodcut in *Hand in Hand We'll Go*, a collection of ten poems by Robert Burns. Using just four colors—brown, black, grey, and mustard yellow—she creates bold silhouette shapes, angular details, and strong patterns to augment the poems. The shapes are essentially two-dimensional, but because of the strong body positions the characters take, there is no lack of movement. Two figures—the old man and woman in "John Anderson My Jo"—for instance, make a powerful visual statement because of the contrast between their sturdy bodies and the empty spaces surrounding them.

Bonnie Mackain did woodcut illustrations for a counting book, *One Hundred Hungry Ants* by Elinor J. Pinczes, using a very limited array of colors that are even more subtle because they are all of about the same intensity. The book is particularly useful for studying the characteristic look of woodcut, i.e., the small pieces of wood which remain when areas are cut away. These tiny scrap areas are often cut away completely, but that in fact reduces the characteristic roughness of woodcut. In this case, the artist left most of the cut marks showing, and so the illustrations have an additional rhythm because these small pieces remain. Children will chuckle over the conclusion, where the ants discover that too much planning can indeed result in not achieving a goal: the many ways to subdivide one hundred into smaller groups could easily augment an arithmetic lesson.

Figure 4.5: Everett Anderson's Year

When an artist chooses woodcut, a strong image usually results, as shown here. The bold, blocky silhouette of the main character is softened only a little by the crayon color laid down around the figure. For the book jacket itself, the san serif type face of the title is printed in an orangy red, while the figure is in a deep brown, and the color beneath him is printed in a greyed blue, resulting in three-color art. You could look at this in the context of illustrations Grifalconi did for the *Village of Round and Square Houses,* in which she used an impressive array of hues in the pastel medium.

EVERETT ANDERSON'S YEAR

by LUCILLE CLIFTON • *Illustrations by* ANN GRIFALCONI

About the poet and artist

Livingston's (1990) comments help us understand why Valerie Worth is an important poet. Frasconi's own book, Against the Grain *(1974) is helpful in understanding his work.*

Ann Grifalconi prints her woodcuts using a limited array of three colors, brown, orange, and a greyed blue, to illustrate *Everett Anderson's Year*, one of a series of stories by Lucille Clifton about this young black character and his family. With just two or three sentences on each double-page spread, and only one spread per month, Clifton tells us, and Grifalconi shows us, a range of Everett's emotions, from delight in the rain of April, to apprehension about the return to school in September.

Antonio Frasconi is perhaps the preeminent name among American practitioners of the art of woodcut. In the illustrations accompanying Valerie Worth's poems in *At Christmastime*, he provides the kind of richly complex shapes and subtle colorations for which he has become justly well known. Some of the colors are vivid, as on the second opening for the poem, "Light String," and on the sixth opening for the two poems featured there. In other cases, the printing is impressively subtle: see, for example, the double spread on the last opening, to illustrate "Spring." In the less than full-page, small vignettes, as on the third and eighth openings, we see the compact tightness possible in woodcut. As always, Worth's poetry is succinctness personified.

Robert Sabuda used an array of subtle colors in printing his linoleum cut illustrations for *The Log of Christopher Columbus*, selected by Steve Lowe. Rather than choosing primary hues, Sabuda gives us a rich variety of blues, greens and purples, to show the sea and the sky, in good weather (as in the selection for September 6, 1492) and in turbulent weather (as in the selection for September 26). The marks cut by the gouge provide interesting repeated textures, as in the sails in the illustration for September 25; in the birds' feathers, in the illustration for September 19; and in the sailors' clothing, as in the illustration for October 11. The text is presented in bordered rectangles, set on top of the illustrations, which are double spreads bled to the page edge. The closeness of the tonalities makes for an integrated page.

Blair Lent provides more complex illustrations, slightly less angular than those of Nonny Hogrogian but also in limited color, for an old Japanese tale, *The Wave* by Margaret Hodges. These illustrations are done in cardboard print, which looks much like block print. In this technique, pieces of cardboard—often of varying textures—are cut to the shapes the artist desires, and then glued to a larger piece of cardboard which forms a background. Paint is applied with a brayer, and because of the difference in heights between the background and the applied pieces, a print can be pulled. In this book, the author, a noted storyteller and children's librarian, adapted a story first brought to America in the late nineteenth century. Lent's illustrations in brown, grey, and black reflect both the initial tranquility of life in a house above a valley and the later uproar as the convoluted shape of the tidal wave gathers force and strikes the village below.

More recently, Lent has used the same technique in *Bayberry Bluff,* featuring stylized, almost doll-like characters which are less important than the architectural detail, from tents to finished village, which the artist obviously enjoys creating. The fresh blues and greens contrast well with the stark, real white of the page, where backgrounds are purposely kept minimal so the color contrasts can sing out. The concluding note tells how the simple story is based on the actual account of how Oak Bluffs on Martha's Vineyard developed in the early part of the nineteenth century. There's no strong story conflict here, or vivid characters to identify with. Rather, it's the simple delight of the decorative art work, enhanced with the many textures Blair Lent achieves using this medium.

Other variations

In *Stella and Roy*, Ashley Wolff contrasts the bike Stella enjoys for its speed with little Roy's more leisurely coasting here and there. The artist uses a linocut technique to show this contemporary story of two friends enjoying an afternoon in the park. The crisp black patterning of the block print is brightened with watercolors painted on after the prints were made. There's a pleasant rhythmic quality in the illustrations, and also in the repeated text line, "And Roy rolled right on by."

Another artist who augments the black printing of the block with color applied with brushes, rather than printed from a color block, is Christopher Manson. His woodcuts for *Over the River and through the Wood*, a well-known Thanksgiving poem by Lydia Maria Child, show a rural landscape in strongly patterned illustrations enhanced with large undesigned areas. Manson uses the gouges made by his cutting tools to create the texture of the trees (on the seventh opening), of the blacksmith's forge (on the sixth opening), and the lattice-work of a gazebo (on the tenth opening). For all of his double-page spreads, he lightly strokes more pastel watercolors to augment the blackness of his woodcuts.

Manson used the same technique with success in *The Tree in the Wood*, an adaptation of a classic old accumulative song, thought to be French in origin. The jacket cover, with its repeated branch, leaf, and berry design, is reminiscent of the work of William Morris (1843-1896), leader of the Arts and Crafts Movement in England. Inside, the endpapers, with their strong design of repeated tree trunks and crowns, is similarly related to design principles of the Arts and Crafts Movement, where natural forms were used but were systematized and regularized into flat patterns. The heavily-bordered text and picture pages, in an array of pleasantly subdued natural colors, continues the flavor throughout the book.

In *Where the Great Bear Watches*, artist Lisa Flather painted some areas of the paper with acrylic paints, and then printed linoleum cuts—also done in acrylics—over the top of the painting. This accounts for the interesting contrast between the softer-edged painted areas, and the crisper, more typical cut edges in the linoleum printed areas. This serious story, written by James Sage, is narrated by a young Inuit boy who sings a song to all the creatures who live in this desolate, white North.

Arts and Crafts Movement

In the arts and crafts movement, design elements grew from the movement's philosophy of the desired relation between people, art, and work. Anscombe and Gere (1978) describe the context in which these ideas were nurtured and the distinctive art which grew from it.

Evans G. Valens combines linoleum cuts with lift (or transfer) prints to illustrate his dramatic book *Wildfire*. Valens first transferred the grain of the wood and the design of small plant and leaf forms to paper. He applied paint to the surface of the objects, placed a piece of paper over them, and rubbed the paper to lift the design (similar to the way children do a pencil rubbing of a penny). The small animals were cut in linoleum blocks and printed in the usual manner. Many pages are printed in black and white, but some also include red and green. The full-page spreads convey the extent of the forest and the magnitude of the damage done by the fire very effectively.

A more elaborated version of printing with "found" objects is also related to constructing collage. This variation is called collagraphs. As explained in *Only One* by Marc Harshman, this is a technique in which paper and other materials are glued down on cardboard. The assembled plate is then inked and printed on an etching press. The artist, Barbara Garrison, used materials such as sandpaper, masking tape, string, and feathers to assemble the plates for this book. After the prints were made and dried, the artist applied watercolor washes for additional color. The book is a concept book showing relationships. For example, "There may be 12 eggs, but there is only one dozen." It ends with a very affirmative statement about the wonder that there is only one of each of us.

Block printing is beyond the capabilities of most young children, primarily because of the danger involved in using sharp gouges to prepare the blocks. With careful instruction and close supervision, however, middle school students can create their own linoleum cuts. The action of cutting the block and the ability to make many copies of one design appeal to children.

Activity: See Hurwitz & Day, 1991, for suggestions about working with students to make block prints.

Etching

Etching is an ancient process, probably begun around A.D. 1450, in which drawings are reproduced from a metal plate, into which fine lines have been bitten by acid. A clean copper plate is covered with a thin coat of acid-resisting ground (often composed of wax or resin, more recently of spirits in a solvent). The artist uses a steel needle, exposing the metal surface wherever the lines are to appear. Then the plate is immersed in an acid bath, which attacks the exposed metal. After this, the ground is removed with a solvent. The artist next rubs ink into the lines and cleans the surface where ink isn't wanted. The plate, covered with damp paper, is run through a press, forcing the paper into the ink-filled lines, which transfers the design (Haggar, 1962).

This is a time consuming medium which requires extra care because of the dangerous materials involved, and few artists of picture books use it. An example of one who does is Arthur Geisert, in both serious books, as in *The Ark*, and in delightfully silly ones, like *Oink Oink*. The oversized (11^1/2" x 9") horizontal format used for *The Ark* provides a panoramic space for Geisert's individual etchings, presented on facing pages with text beneath. Using a cream-colored background, the artist prints his minutely detailed etchings, full of hatching and crosshatching which show how much variety is possible without using color. One can't help but be impressed with the amount of work such detailed illustrations on this scale require.

In a much lighter vein, *Oink Oink* shows primarily through pictures the adventures of Mama Pig's eight restless piglets. These are determined piglets: they persist to the extent of swimming to a river island in order to enjoy the purloined corn. In this case, as with the previous book, *Oink* (the only word used in both books), the artist relies mostly on the black-etched line but does print parts of the picture in a porcine pink.

Elizabeth Coatsworth talks in spare language of several animals, all waiting *Under the Green Willow* for crumbs, in a book originally published in 1971, and reissued more recently. The book is handsomely produced: the cover is done in green paper, imprinted with a blind stamp of a symbolic tree, bound in a white linen sleeve binding, with the words printed in gold. Inside, the endpapers are a complex, abstract layering in collage fashion of strips of green and yellow papers, some of which are textured. Janina Domanska's etchings are done in shades of moss green, lime green, and bright yellow, in a highly patterned, geometric style that remains two dimensional on purpose. The turtle's shell, for instance, isn't at all realistic: rather it becomes a repeated pattern which Domanska plays with, because it contrasts so effectively with the pattern on the duck's wing and the fishes' scales.

Etching is a graphic technique, i.e., the artist makes plates from which the final art is printed. That contrasts with making the art directly, as in painting. Another graphic technique is evident in *What Kouka Knows* by Truus, a Belgian artist. She engraved her images into thin zinc plates and then printed the pictures from the plates. The result is a set of illustrations featuring simplified, abstracted animal shapes, printed on a stark white, featureless background. The contrast highlights the unusual colors and interesting surface textures this artist achieved using this graphic technique.

Scratchboard

Another technique which involves scratching a picture into a surface makes use of scratchboard—a two-layer, smooth-surfaced board, most often in black or white. The artist scratches away the top surface, using dots, or thin lines which results in a very precise, sharp illustration. Often shading is accomplished by using hatching (parallel lines), crosshatching, or stippling to create roundness of form and depth.

An early example of this technique is Barbara Cooney's illustrations for *Chanticleer and the Fox*, a Caldecott Medal winner. This adaptation of Geoffrey Chaucer's *Canterbury Tales* presents a variety of authentic flowers, grasses, birds, and architecture. Here Cooney augments the crisp black and white with solid highly saturated blue, green, gold, and orange.

The black and white vigor of scratchboard is readily apparent in the illustrations Leonard Everett Fisher did for the information book, *All Times, All Peoples: A World History of Slavery*, written by Milton Meltzer. This book for older readers presents in nine chapters the facts about slavery from the time of the Egyptians, some four thousand years ago to the much more recent tragic history of black slaves brought to this country from Africa. On nearly every page, there are both small margin vignettes, and full-page illustrations of slaves and the jobs they performed. Fisher's use of crosshatching adds drama to the sharply contrasting dark and light, here printed on a heavy cream-colored paper.

For an information book, *Giants in the Land* by Diana Appelbaum, Michael McCurdy did strong black-and-white scratchboard drawings. The tall vertical rectangle ($7^3/4''$ x $11^3/4''$) provides an effective context for his drawings of the giant pine trees, more than 250 feet tall and four feet wide, which once filled New England forests. Scratchboard is an apt medium for conveying the textures of animals (i.e., the coats of oxen used to

Activity

For an interesting comparison of a similar scene done in two contrasting media, look at the margin drawing, "Aztecs Sacrificing Slave," p.19 of All Times, *with the full-page, black-and-white painting of Aztecs sacrificing a victim on the ninth opening of Fisher's* Pyramid of the Sun, Pyramid of the Moon, *a book described more fully in chapter 2.*

Figure 4.6: The Ballad of Belle Dorcas

There's a constantly moving quality in this art, the result of the many small lines. The fact that the artist chose to provide no empty places to rest a viewer's eyes contributes to a vague sense of anxiety, reflecting the tension in this text about the conjur woman and the young lovers. More recently, Pinkney has used the same scratchboard medium for a more tranquil, first person account narrated by young Menlik in *Day of Delight,* which describes a Jewish sabbath in Ethiopia.

transport the trees, as on the ninth opening) and the variety of textures in tree bark, branches, leaves, and other growing things (i.e., on the second opening). Throughout, the stark contrast between intense black and white makes the patterns stand out more clearly.

In a longer book for older readers/listeners, Brian Pinkney has provided brooding, dark illustrations that are touched but not brightened appreciably with color washes over the scratchboard. His pictures for *The Ballad of Belle Dorcas* by William H. Hooks, accompany this tale set in the Carolinas in the early 1800s. Pinkney has used a full spectrum of colors, but they are less important than the swirling white lines which pervade, in the clothes of the people depicted, as well as in elements of the setting like trees, the smokehouse, and the interior of Granny Lizard's home. Everywhere we look we see the white scratched lines giving an agitation to a story which is filled with conflict, and even foreboding. The lines give a palpable dimensionality to Joshua's face and body (the second opening), to the bodies of the bloodhounds which pursue Joshua (ninth opening) and a sense of deep space, as in the picture where Cook watches the houseboy run back from the smokehouse (12th opening).

More recently, Brian Pinkney has augmented his scratchboard drawings for *Seven Candles for Kwanzaa* with overpaintings in oil pastel. This information book by Andrea Davis Pinkney traces the development of this modern American holiday to its ancient African roots, explaining (and giving phonetic pronunciations for) the many unfamiliar words for objects and foods which have symbolic significance in the celebration. Such things as mkeka (a straw placemat representing tradition) and muhindi (corn) are important as are the principles like umoja, which means family unity. The many crosshatched white lines add textural richness to the realistic scratchboard drawings of a modern family celebrating the holiday. These are bordered, sometimes on the sides, at other times on the bottom, in African motifs.

To help children think about how the media used affects the final look of a book, you might compare this book, done in scratchboard, with another on the same topic. *Celebrating Kwanzaa* uses full-color photographs by Lawrence Migdale, in many different settings, and showing many different people, to accompany the text by Diane Hoyt-Goldsmith. The overall feeling of the two books is quite different, because the art in each is so different. The variety of typefaces in the *Celebrating Kwanzaa* book is effective in differentiating visually the continuous body of the text from the informational sidebars on several of the pages. Different sizes and styles of type make the captions easy to see, as well.

Collage and other paper techniques

The term *collage*, from the French *papier collé* (meaning "glued papers"), refers to the process of attaching fragments of printed matter, colored papers of various weights and textures, photographs, fabrics, and other materials to a solid background to make a composite picture. The desired arrangement can be sketched in pencil beforehand, or the entire creation may be spontaneous. The technique of collage was first used in 1912 by the painter Pablo Picasso, who was attempting to break from more traditional approaches to the painting style in vogue at the time. Since then, it has become an accepted medium for artists.

Collage *by Herta Wescher is an exhaustive text. On every third page are full-color, full-page reproductions of collages, from early works by Georges Braque and Juan Gris to works by contemporary artists.*

Marantz (1992) described Frederick at greater length, suggesting particular parts of it adults could have children observe, and suggesting followup art activities. Her book shows how to use the 43 titles she includes to develop children's visual perception.

About the artist

Lionni (1984) has talked both about the influences on his work and also about how illustrations in books help children develop and expand their own store of mental images.

Many children's illustrators use collage. For example, Leo Lionni, whose books have four times been named Caldecott Honor winners, created many popular books for children (Smith, 1991). In *Frederick*, his gentle story about a mouse, Lionni uses grey torn-paper shapes with cut-paper ears and tails to depict Frederick and his friends. The large and blocky designs, spread across facing pages, are simple but effective, printed on a heavy quality matte paper. It's always important to try to obtain a copy of the first edition of works, as illustrated with this particular title. *Frederick* as originally presented in a separate picture book, is quite unlike the presentation in *Frederick's Fables*, where several pieces of the original art are omitted, and some of those included are severely cropped. The presentation on a glossy paper in this newer edition does enhance the colors.

Another well-known collage illustrator was Ezra Jack Keats, whose *The Snowy Day* won a Caldecott Medal. Bold shapes and interesting surface textures characterize this innovative book,

Figure 4.7: Frederick

Like many of Lionni's works, this is a fable and like most of his art, this is a collage. The contrast between the ragged shapes with torn edges and those with smooth cut edges, is effective. Other of Lionni's titles like *Cornelius* and *An Extraordinary Egg*, continue with similar texts and art, though this latter title makes more use of paint than is usual in Lionni's books.

Figure 4.8: The Snowy Day
The abstract simplicity of this art was more unusual to viewers in 1962 when it was first published than it seems to us today. Look at this Caldecott winner in the context of illustration by Bernarda Bryson, for *The Sun is a Golden Earring* by Natalia Belting and Maurice Sendak's art for *Mr. Rabbit and the Lovely Present* by Charlotte Zolotow, both of which were named Honor books that year. Had you been on the committee, would you have made the same, or a different choice? Why?

which pioneered in the portrayal of black children in natural settings (Hopkins, 1983). Keats also used collage in the minimal but pleasant story of *Jennie's Hat*. Endpapers with an intricate design introduce Jennie, whose dress is of the same material. Birds decorate her plain hat with a variety of printed papers, painted shapes, leaf-vein forms, and Victorian cutouts of flowers, hearts, and photographs, turning it into a "garment of brightness" (Lanes, 1984).

Eric Carle uses transparent tissue papers, lightly streaked with paint, to form collages for his counting book *1, 2, 3 to the Zoo*. It features brightly colored creatures transported by minimal train cars. The lions are suitably fearsome, the crocodiles flash their teeth, and the monkeys' curved tails intertwine in Carle's sharp-edged collages. Carle again uses tissue papers streaked with paint to illustrate a story about *The Lamb and the Butterfly*, written by Arnold Sundgaard. The bodies of the main characters are rendered in vibrant shades of transparent color that overlap. The lamb's body includes some interesting stipple effect, probably dabbed on with a sponge and further enriched with a purposely "scrawly" crayon overlay. Carle combines his familiar full-color collage with paper engineering in *The Honeybee and the Robber*. On each page, there is something that moves. In the center of the book is the most spectacular display—a butterfly with opened wings that springs up when the pages are spread.

About the artist
Eric Carle: Picture Writer, *distributed by Searchlight Films for Philomel Books, received the Andrew Carnegie Medal for Excellence in Children's Video, given by the American Library Association.*

Though the story itself is fiction, Carle provides two pages of factual information about honeybees inside the back cover.

Patricia Mullins used tissue paper collage for illustrations in *Crocodile Beat* by Gail Jorgensen, who is—like the illustrator—an Australian. A simple description of animals, their activities, and the sounds they make, this is full of repeated words that children will delight in saying along with the adult presenting the story. The ducks go: "Quack Quack Quackity," for example. On every double-page spread, Mullins provides vibrant illustrations full of enriching transparencies. On the fifth opening, we see how the transparency of the heron's wings affects the several different shades of green over which the white is applied. Another strength of Mullins' art is the textures she develops. On the first opening, the skin of the crocodile is particularly interesting. On the third opening, notice the way she has purposely applied the tissue paper irregularly, so it creates the wrinkled skin of the elephants. These are joyous pictures: despite the lurking menace of the crocodile, readers know, because of the cheerful colors, that all will end well.

Elisa Kleven's richly detailed collage mosaics of paper and paint provide an enthusiastic, patterned accompaniment to Arthur Dorros's story celebrating urban ethnicity, in *Abuela*. The wonderfully sunny pictures of young Rosalba and her abuela (Spanish for grandmother) juxtapose more patterns than one can easily take in, so repeated viewings are necessary before one has savored all the delights in this book. We are close up, and far away from the two aerial adventurers, looking straight on, up, and down at the pair. Because of the motif of flying, this evokes images of the Russian-born Marc Chagall (1887-1985), an artist whose work this might be compared with.

These are but a few of the artists working in collage today, for as Evans points out in an article on trends in book illustration, the children's book world is "experiencing a renaissance of cut paper and collage mixed with other media and sometimes combined with found objects."[3]

Young children enjoy the tactile experience of arranging bits of fabric, ribbon, paper, cardboard, etc., on paper to create their own collages. For teachers who have not tried doing collage with children, *The Collage Book* by Hannah Tofts is very helpful. The instructions are written simply enough so intermediate grade children can read the book themselves, but the pictures are large enough so a teacher of younger children could use the ideas with

About the artist

One useful source about this artist is Marc Chagall *by Ernest Raboff, from the "Art for Children" series, which features full-color illustrations on nearly every page; the series now runs to over a dozen artists.*

a group, reading or paraphrasing the text. Junior high school students may enjoy creating montages, combinations containing only photographs.

A slightly different use of paper places the emphasis not on contrasting types of paper, but rather on how papers used can be manipulated in layers and photographed to indicate depth. For instance, in *Ragged Shadows*, a collection of poetry selected by Lee Bennett Hopkins, artist Giles Laroche creates depth by folding and bending the paper, so when it is photographed the originally flat paper casts shadows. The result gives an appearance of dimensionality. As pieces are positioned, but not glued flat on top of other pieces, it is possible to achieve an effective layering.

Shadows are equally important in enhancing the art which Grace Bochak did for *Paper Boats*, a single poem by the Nobel Prize-winner, Rabindranath Tagore of India. Though there are different kinds of paper used here, the emphasis is on how the paper can be layered, one piece on top of another, to create depth.

Figure 4.9: Paper Boats
The backgrounds are decorative in this art, and provide some minimal additional information, for instance, about the types of animals living in this setting. But because of the placement, and his size, the boy main character in this poem remains the major focus. Throughout the book the individual pieces of art have been photographed very carefully, so the paper used to make the collage casts shadows which are captured in the photographs.

Because the paper isn't tightly attached everywhere, the photographer was able to capture the shadows cast by pieces which are above other pieces. The abstract simplicity of the shapes, and the largely plain backgrounds, make for a very tranquil mood.

Author/illustrator David Wisniewski used an X-Acto knife with incredible precision, as he cut the art for *Elfwyn's Saga*, a tale he retold from tenth century Iceland in the Viking age, and in *Rain Player*, derived from the Mayan culture (ca. A.D. 300 to 900). A note in the first book relates that it took 1,000 blades to cut the art. Vibrantly colored papers are cut into intricate designs, and many layers are juxtaposed one over the other, so that the layers underneath show through. It is interesting to note that the photography is so critical in presenting this sort of art that the photographer, Lee Salsbery, is acknowledged in both books. Both of these have much longer, more involved text than is commonplace in picture books, probably making them of more interest to intermediate than to primary grade children.

A different use of paper is evident in *Saint Valentine* by Robert Sabuda, a retelling of the life of the ancient Roman Christian priest, whose name has become linked with one of our prominent holidays. In panels of varying sizes, placed on both left and right pages, Sabuda uses thousands of tiny rectangles of colored paper to create mosaics which swirl and move with curving lines to show details. Some of the panels are tall, thin rectangles, showing people only in silhouette, as in the illustration on the right half of the third opening. In others, we get intricately detailed representations of the faces of characters, and Sabuda uses varying shades of the same color to show clothing. The choice of paper mosaic as a medium was appropriate for this story, since in Roman times actual ceramic and glass mosaics were such a prominent part of the decoration of public buildings.

Another artist doing innovative paper work is Denise Fleming, as in her book, *Lunch*. She creates illustrations using paper pulp in various colors. This mixture is squeezed from bottles onto a background of wire mesh screen, into shapes controlled by hand-cut stencils. Each shape requires a separate stencil and the different colors are built up into layers. The pulp painting, when complete, is put into a drying press for three days. What results is in essence a piece of handmade paper, with the colored shapes an integral part of, not applied to, the paper itself. The story in *Lunch* is very simple: the little mouse eats various vegetables of differing colors, until he is too full to move. Fleming's boldly

Plate 6: Lunch

Artists can indeed transcend the limitations of a medium making for example, watercolor look like oil paint. But the most honest use of a material is to work within its characteristics. Here, Fleming uses her unusual medium (described in the text), to create art which explores shapes in a unique way. One of the limitations of this medium is that it can't easily be used to make lines. The boldness of her unequivocal shapes makes line unnecessary, however. Look at Fleming's continuing use of this medium, *In the Small, Small Pond*. In this she is achieving line (rather than applying it) by overlapping colors and not quite matching up the underneath color: what results is a thin sliver of the bottom color which acts as a line. *(See full illustration in color plates follwing p.174.)*

simplified shapes are resolutely abstract, though they remain recognizable. They splash loudly, but tastefully, across the double-page spreads; the close-up views allow us to enjoy the variety of shades Fleming is able to get in any one given color. The art in this gains subtlety in two details. Notice that the table top is always tilted, rather than being straight across, a more interesting division of the background space. Also, on each page a different color of the spectrum is used for the background color.

Fleming used the same medium for *In the Small, Small Pond,* an equally simple story of the movements the pond inhabitants make, told in rhyme. On several openings the white she uses crisps up the highly saturated colors; on several other openings children can be encouraged to notice the variety of shades. On the sixth opening, for instance, point out the many different shades of blue in Fleming's palette.

Fabric

Fabric is becoming a common material in illustrations for children's books. One artist who uses fabric effectively is Edda Reinl, who works in batik, a Javanese hot-wax resist technique that involves painting designs with wax and dying the fabric in several stages. Her book *The Three Little Pigs* is a swirl of color. The opening endpapers feature dancing pigs that are appealing without being cloying; the concluding endpapers feature the decorative designs of the pigs' houses. On the pages in between, Reinl uses batik impressively: each picture is exuberant and filled with details that add to the total effect rather than calling attention to themselves. The artist's palette ranges from the warm yellow/orange/red range used most often in depicting the pigs to the chilly blue/green/purple combination used in showing the fearsome wolf as he stalks his quarry, huffs at their house, and finally explodes startlingly. Even though the pictures for the most part simply illustrate and do not expand or extend the text in significant ways, the colors are so joyous and the partitioning of space is so effective that the book is a delight.

Reinl also did the illustrations for her own story, *The Little Snake*, a gentle tale which mixes elements of reality and fantasy. It begins quite realistically, describing characters and events that are believable, and that is interesting because of the contrast between the realism of the text itself and the brightly colored, patterned, abstract batik designs. In the middle of the story, when

For more information
To learn how to do this technique, read Krevitsky (1964). Though most of the illustrations are in black and white, the book shows carefully the steps involved in this complex, and ancient craft. The author sets this in the historic and cultural context from which it developed.

the snake finds a friend, "a rare and lovely flower," the words go in a different direction, into fantasy. Here, the contrast between the words and pictures is less apparent. Even the dark pages, i.e., the one set in the "quietest part of the night," sing with highly saturated color, in patterns which spring across the pages.

Another example of batik, this time done with dyes on silk cloth, is provided by the Japanese artist, Yoshi, in the alphabet book *A to Zen*, written by Ruth Wells. In a tall vertical rectangle (8^1/$_2$" x 11^1/$_4$"), Yoshi painted full-color, quite detailed illustrations for each facing page, set above the paragraph of text, including the word for each letter printed in both Roman letters as well as in characters. The book is bound from "back" to "front" in our Western way of thinking.

Patricia MacCarthy did bold and bright batik illustrations for *The Horrendous Hullabaloo* by Margaret Mahy, the New Zealand author and winner of the Carnegie Medal. This tells the improbable tale of Peregrine the pirate, whose aunt and parrot party while he is away. The highly saturated colors, a vivid patchwork splashed exuberantly across double-page spreads, are intensified because the vigorous line is done in white, not the more usual black or other dark tone.

Though batik is often done in high intensity colors with much contrast, there isn't anything inherent in the medium that makes this necessary. *Little Eagle Lots of Owls*, by Jim Edmiston, features art by Jane Ross which is instead characterized by very close tonalities. The subtle illustrations feature many different tints and shades of color, and she outlines her shapes in grey, rather than using black as the last color, which is more typical. A small, narrow, vertical rectangle on the left text page faces a larger horizontal illustration on the right page. These are bordered with varying, semi-abstract patterns, and within the illustrations themselves the shapes are often broken up into smaller areas of subtly contrasting tonalities.

Other artists, instead of dying cloth, use different kinds of fabric to construct pictures, sometimes in the process not simply applying them to a base fabric, but in addition, giving them a three-dimensional quality. An example is *Come to My Party*, in which Salley Mavor combines a number of different kinds of cloth textures into pictures which have been photographed close-up so the surface qualities of the materials show very plainly. The simple, and rather unlikely story by Judith Benet Richardson about a tiger's birthday party, provides a framework within which the artist has displayed her bordered pictures: even the single rows of stitching in the border are clearly three dimensional. Several of the animal shapes have been padded from beneath to give them visual weight. The work is enhanced by the photography, which had to be very carefully done to capture the often minimal shadows cast by the slightly raised portions of the pictures.

Jeannie Baker used a similar technique to illustrate *Polar* by Elaine Moss, a story about a teddy bear white "as snow on a dark dark night," written for young readers/listeners. Working almost entirely without any backgrounds except the pale cream of the paper, Baker cuts fabrics of many different textures, reproduced in close-up so we can see the tactile qualities. She includes such other real objects as a tiny safety pin and band-aid, to create illustrations that invite the viewer to reach out and touch.

Stone lithography

Lithography, a term derived from the Greek word *lithos* (meaning "stone" and "-graphy" mean writing), is a technique devised by the Bavarian dramatist Senefelder in 1798. The artist draws with a greasy crayon on the smooth surface of a heavy limestone slab. The stone is then treated with a mixture of gum arabic and nitric acid, which eats away areas not protected by the crayon. When the stone is inked, the ink sticks only to areas containing grease deposits from the original drawing. The artist places paper on the inked stone and forces both through a press, transferring ink from the stone to the paper. The process is both strenuous and messy, and therefore few book artists use it. Though artists can now use lighter-weight materials such as zinc and aluminum, many printmakers still favor the more traditional slabs of limestone.

Among the best-known lithographers are Ingri and Edgar Parin d'Aulaire, who used this medium in many large books—including their *Book of Greek Myths, Norse Gods and Giants*, and *d'Aulaires' Trolls*—which alternate monochrome with full-color lithographs. Their *Abraham Lincoln*, which won the Caldecott Award in the year of its original publication, has recently (1993) been rereleased in a large (8³/4" x 12") format paperback, which satisfactorily shows off the artists' technique. When first published, the book was lauded by Becker for "the humor of these designs...," while Buell commented that though the book will be considered for its illustrations, she felt it was most distin-

For more information

You may want to browse in the book by Mann (1970), to learn more about lithography. This extensive work gives more history of the development of lithography than you will need, but the extensive section of plates shows the amazing variety possible when using this medium.

guished for the "high standard it sets in the field of biography for children under 10." Horning has talked about the problems inherent in subsequent editions of an award-winning title: often they look "very different" than the edition which won the award.[4] Analyzing the d'Aulaires' *Abraham Lincoln*, Horning points out that subsequent editions of this award winner were significantly less effective than the edition which won the award.

Another author/illustrator who used lithography is Robert McCloskey, winner of a Caldecott Medal for *Make Way for Ducklings*. Reproduced in soft brown, his illustrations show the casual, sketchy, and grainy quality of lithographs.

Lynd Ward created realistic lithographic character studies in two books by his wife, May McNeer. In *The Canadian Story*, he depicts the rugged strength of the Indian, French, English, and Eskimo people who shaped the Canadian frontiers. In a companion book, *The Mexican Story*, Ward's illustrations are similar lithographs but their colors are harsher and less interesting.

Felix Hoffman also uses lithography to portray people in two traditional tales by the German folk literature collectors, the Brothers Grimm, but his work is very different from others. In retelling *The Sleeping Beauty*; the figures advance the story but never become the highly individualized people represented in lithographs by Ward. Hoffman also illustrated *The Seven Ravens*, about a brave little girl who sets out alone to free her brothers from imprisonment as birds.

Photography

An increasing number of children's books are being published with photographs as illustrations. Like other photographers, those who illustrate books for children often prefer to work in black and white, because they believe that color can be a distraction from the dramatic quality of an image.

Tana Hoban is one well-known photographer whose work helps children see the drama in everyday objects. In *Push-Pull Empty-Full*, her photos of children, objects, animals, and birds illustrate a book of antonyms for young readers. Clear black-and-white photographs of contrasting concepts (up/down, front/back) face each other across double-page spreads. The photographs catch every wrinkle, blemish, light, and shadow and thus bring out details people often miss when looking at well-known objects. In *Shapes and Things*, Hoban uses photograms, shadow-

About the artist
Make Way for Ducklings *is one of several of his books which McCloskey discussed in an interview with Heins (1988).*

For more information
Ward (1978) has described this complex graphic technique at greater length in a book which includes many artists writing about their mediums.

like photographs made by placing objects between light-sensitive paper and a light source. The technique yields a high-contrast outline with no interior details.

Hoban also uses color photography. *Is It Rough? Is It Smooth? Is It Shiny?* presents full-page, full-color photographs of, for the most part, single objects evoking a sensory response. A child's hand holding pennies is shot so close up that the many fine creases in the palm form an interesting contrast to the metallic, lettered coins. The photo of a girl in a foil costume contrasts that surface with the softer texture of the girl's hair, and the grainy texture of the pillar against which she leans (eighth opening). *A Children's Zoo*, by Hoban, is even more elegantly produced. Black high-gloss pages contrast vibrantly with stark white lowercase letters, which spell out two adjectives and a verb. These words are in the upper right-hand corner of the page; in the middle, in the same typeface but in all capital letters, the animal's name is given. On the facing page is a single photograph of the animal, bordered in white and set on black.

Photographs by George Ancona have an impressive, direct honesty. In *Faces*, a book by Barbara Brenner, the minimal text calls attention to the wonder of a face and what it can do. Ancona's black-and-white photographs—including both close-ups and longer shots—are the most interesting part of the book. With a class you could look at these in the context of Ancona's use of color photography, in the illustrations for Remy Charlip's *Handtalk*. A variety of close-up photographs of different adults signing the alphabet are in some places clear, and in other places blurred, to show the motion of the hand. These are purposely shot against completely plain backgrounds, to emphasize the content.

Shirley Glubok, an artist who earned respect for her impressive series of books on the art of various cultures, often used black-and-white photography not to interpret but to record with clarity. In *The Art of Photography*, Glubok turns her attention to the art of "writing with light," to make a permanent image. The first photograph included is from 1837 and the last from 1961, though the majority of those featured are from the earlier years considered. Glubok's usual stylish production prevails in this volume from cover to cover. The binding contrasts pale beige with warm brown, in a vertically divided, off-center arrangement featuring a particularly distinctive sans serif lettering in black. The endpapers show Eadweard Muybridge's horse-and-rider studies, which represented a major breakthrough in photographic technique. This innovative photographer is described in a double-page spread, as are more than 16 other important photographers, such as Alfred Steiglitz and Edward Steichen. There is never more than one photograph on each generous (nearly ten inches square) page; as a result, all the photos are large enough to show details clearly.

In addition to Glubok's contemporary photographs of historic art objects, book designers sometimes use actual historic photographs, as in *Brown Angels* by Walter Dean Myers. The author's poetry about children accompanies photographs from a wide variety of sources: what unites them is the formal poses, and the equally formal clothing most of the children were wearing when the photographs were taken. Printing this book on an elegant cream matte paper enhances the variety of sepia tones in which these photographs were originally reproduced.

Small Worlds Close Up, by Lisa Grillone and Joseph Gennaro, is an effort to make viewers more aware of their environment. The book is illustrated with pictures taken using a scanning electron microscope (in which an electron gun bombards an object with a thin stream of millions of electrons). These micrographs, as they are called, are arranged in three categories: animal, vegetable, and mineral. A brief explanatory paragraph introduces each section, followed by closeup views of common objects (such as needles, hair, and cotton) and less common objects (such as dolphin skin, an opal, and a xylem tube). The dramatic black-and-white micrographs are captivating, causing the viewer to marvel anew at objects in the everyday world.

Sometimes photography is used with other media to add interest. In *My Sister Lotta and Me* by Helena Dahlback, we see an unusual combination of sepia photographs, and full color. Artist Charlotte Ramel did vivid over-paintings on top of the photographs of an antique doll house in this story of two little girls and their adventures there. The slightly formal, quite serious nature of the photos contrasts interestingly with the somewhat casual, rather slap-dash paintings of the children.

A more fanciful use of photography is apparent in Brooke Goffstein's *Our Prairie Home. A Picture Album* with full-color photos of minute wooden figures the artist carved herself. Those familiar with this author's earlier, minimalist works, will recognize her spare text as typical. What is unusual for this artist who usually does her own pictures, is the use of photographs to set up a miniature, self-contained, and highly static world. Little girls will empathize with the joy the artist must have had in moving around the tiny figures, furnishings, and architectural details, arranging and rearranging her scenes. There are a lot of referents here that young children won't understand, i.e., sending in jokes to a radio station. They will wonder about objects, i.e., what is that round white thing sitting beside the sink (second opening)? Nonetheless, young children entranced with tiny things will enjoy looking at this assemblage, lovingly photographed.

An even more unusual use of photography is apparent in Flint Born's art for *An Alphabet in Five Acts* by Karen Born Anderson. Helpfully, an artist's note tells us that: "The art for this book consists of hand-colored photocollage. The cut-out elements of each collage were arranged on two or more planes of suspended glass. The structure, lit to cast shadows creating a three-dimensional effect, was then photographed." Having read that, viewers know they are looking at photographs of photographs, something they might not have known without the note.

For more information

Information concerning other books that contain photographs is included in Paulin (1982), in a compendium that is descriptive rather than evaluative.

Computer-generated graphics

Many teachers and librarians are concerned about the amount of time children spend playing computer games, but the reality is that computers have become pervasive in our lives today. One of the possibilities in computers is the generation of graphics. And so it is inevitable, be that either good or bad, that artists would see the possibility of generating entire books of graphics on the computer. J. Otto Seibold had done just that, in *Mr. Lunch Takes a Plane Ride*, which was named one of *Publishers Weekly*'s Best Picture Books of the year. This tells of how the main character, a dog, is invited to a television talk show to display his bird-chasing skills. En route to this media opportunity, Mr. Lunch mixes up the baggage of several passengers, and what begins as disaster when these same passengers perform on the television show, ends with a positive, if slightly unbelievable, conclusion. The graphics themselves have the sort of hard-edged, mechanistic quality one might expect, and an intensely-patterned, frenetic quality because of the number of objects shown on each page. The prevailing brown/orange tones which are so consistent throughout the book are most often contained within an unvarying black line. The graphics were done on an Apple Macintosh computer, using Adobe Illustrator software. Is this the wave of the future? Or will individual artists prefer to put their own individual stamp on a book with all the individual eccentricities of design that human creators devise? It is too early to answer such a provocative question.

Sculptured media

Barbara Reid has taken a commonplace medium in early education classrooms, plastine, and turned it into a reputable art form, in *Have You Seen Birds?* by Joanne Oppenheim. Sculpting impressive small details, she creates pictures of complexity which, when photographed carefully, clearly reveal their dimensional nature. Notice, for instance, the variety of feather shapes, colors, and patterns on the heron on the 11th opening. Each page is full of precisely-crafted shapes of natural forms with clearly defined edges and distinct colors. The decorative nature of this art encourages viewers to enjoy Reid's rhythmic repetition.

In her own *Two By Two*, Reid continues this visual vocabulary, but adds texture, by incising lines into, for instance, Noah's beard, the bear's fur on the dust jacket, and the grassy hills (pp. 28-29). Her interior view of the ark (p. 23) is testimony to her patience in creating intricate designs.

What media was used?

The previous section described individual media used by artists, in a way which may have suggested that it is always possible to determine the materials the artist used. That is really an oversim-

Figure 4.10: Have You Seen Birds?
You might use this as a starting point for a unit on how artists depict birds. Compare these detailed, but stylized depictions with those by Bert Kitchen, as in his *Animal Alphabet,* which are shown without backgrounds, enhancing his skilled renderings. Another useful book, *Wings Along the Waterway* features full-color bird art on nearly every page, by Mary Barrett Brown.

plification, for in fact, detecting what material, or what combination of materials the artist used, isn't an easy task for two reasons. One, sometimes one material can be made to look like quite a different material, once the art work is completed. Highly saturated watercolor can, for instance, be put on with such definite edges that it ends up looking much more like tempera paint. Two, more and more artists are today experimenting with combinations of mediums, and that also makes the detective task more difficult.

Unfortunately, it isn't yet commonplace for the publisher to provide this information for readers/viewers. It is very helpful when a publisher indicates at least the media used, and even better when a few lines are provided about the way the material was used. For example, we read in *The First Night* by B. G. Hennessy:

> In preparing the art for the book, butternut wood was chosen for its texture. The sketch for each painting was drawn on the wood and the lines cut in with a carving tool, while the outer edge was shaped with a jigsaw. Two layers of gesso were applied—one white, one black—after which acrylic paints were used. Sandpaper and a carving tool were used to create a weathered edge. The art was then photographed and the color transparencies used for reproduction in the book.

This may indeed be more information than the general public wants about the media and art processes involved, but it is extremely helpful to teachers and librarians in understanding how the art was created. As Behrmann (1988) points out in an article about her detective work concerning media in Caldecott books, having this information available educates our eye in seeing the art more completely.

Involving children in studying media

The chapter commented on the tissue paper collage by Eric Carle. You might gather several of his books, and then compare them with the art in Mem Fox's *Shoes from Grandpa*, illustrated by Patricia Mullins. In this cheerful intergenerational story, Mullins uses many transparent shapes as Carle does, but she also includes heavier materials, and some nonpaper items like knitted fabric and feathers. These are arranged against white backgrounds that give crispness to the wide variety of colors used.

Levin (1980) has called Hopper the "major twentieth-century American 'realist' and one of the giants of American painting." Her book is useful for familiarizing adults with Hopper's work, though because of the small size of the illustrations, the book isn't useful with children directly.

Activity

McCall and Grossman (1987) suggest other art activities for children, including setting up a still life under a floodlight, so that light and shadows become apparent.

Plate 7: Greyling

David Ray's art for this book reflects the relentless swirling motion of the sea waves: in the clothes of the people, in the twisting shapes of their bodies, in the roundness of the rocks and the boat, this repeated movement is apparent. Find a copy of this, and of the earlier edition with art by William Stobbs so you can notice similarities and differrences. *(See full illustration in color plates following p.174.)*

It would be interesting to help children look at Chris Van Allsburg's work in the context of that by the American painter, Edward Hopper (1882-1967), an artist whose work often exemplifies the sharp contrasts of light and dark which are apparent in Van Allsburg's work. In addition to a similar approach to tonality variation, there is also a similar emptiness of Hopper's and Van Allsburg's art. In each, though there are people and activity shown, the pervading sense is one of an unusual emptiness.

A story told by Jane Yolen, *Greyling*, is useful because it has been illustrated twice, by artists with very different styles. Both editions may be available in libraries. The illustrations by William Stobbs show the effect of tooth in watercolor paper. There are many places in each illustration where the white shows through, accentuating the brilliance of the colors. Stobbs also mixes many shades of color in his illustrations. For example, the colors of the sea and rocks in the scene where the villagers watch the grey seal dive into the sea make this particular illustration as impressive as any formal watercolor painting.

In contrast to these illustrations are those by David Ray, who did full- and double-page spreads, painted to the page edge. These are full of circular movement. The pages include no white space showing at all, so the contrast with the previous edition is very noticeable.

Picture books in other media

Several manufacturers produce film or video versions of favorite stories. There are differences between the film and book formats. The advantages of using a book include:

1. The child can shift position to examine a picture more closely or from some distance to perceive the total effect.

2. The child can adjust the pace of reading, moving slowly to savor a particular enjoyable section or moving more quickly in an exciting part of the story.

3. The child can go back to a previous page to check details, to compare illustrations, or to enjoy a description in relation to what she or he is currently reading.

The child, in essence, remains in control of the experience (Shaw, 1985). In contrast, film viewing has certain disadvantages:

1. The filmmaker controls the point of view, what is seen, and the distance from which a scene is viewed.

2. The pace is preestablished and cannot be varied.

3. It is not possible to go back, unless the entire film is rewound and started over.

Despite these drawbacks, film and video versions of picture books also offer several advantages:

1. Sound effects, skilled narrators, and music can enhance the printed word.

2. Children can experience the film as a group, and valuable discussion can follow.

3. Many visual effects--superimposition of images, close-ups, perspective views, and animation of static images--provide visual experiences the average book cannot achieve.

Teachers should be aware that several different types of filmed literature for children are available. Nancy Larrick identified four basic kinds of films about children's books:

- **Live Action** (*Rapunzel, Rapunzel*, Tom Davenport Films, RR 1, Box 527, Delaplane, VA 22025);
- **Puppets** (*Dick Whittington and His Cat*, Sterling Educational Films, 241 E. 34th Street, New York, NY 10016);
- **Animation** (*Anansi the Spider*, Landmark Films, Inc., 3450 Slade Run Drive, Falls Church, VA 22042); and
- **Iconography** (*Andy and the Lion*, Weston Woods Studios, Weston Woods Street, Weston, CT 06880).

For more information
Larrick includes a complete list of different kinds of audiovisual adaptations of children's books. This popular resource book is available in an updated version—with annotated children's titles—from Bantam (1982), but the film material has been dropped.

When teachers choose a media version of a book, they need to consider fidelity to the original. Fidelity does not mean complete correspondence with the original version, which is impossible, but rather a sensitive adaptation of it to a new mode. Blair Lent, an artist who made puppets for a film based on one of his books, comments, "I do not think that the filmed version of a story should correspond exactly with that of the book. Film is a different medium, and it is most effective when telling a story in its own way."[5] He believes that what is added in the film must be sympathetic to the book content and should not overshadow the original concept.

Even very young children can be encouraged to think about and respond to differences between print and film/video versions of stories. Stone (1988) provides a succinct, yet telling description of how her 5-year-old son responded to seeing a film version

For more information: Stewig (1988) reported on responses of fifth grade children to filmed and printed versions of the same tale.

of "Snow White" after having heard a print version read aloud. Stone followed up by telling him her own version, which he then directed her to change in particular ways. Throughout this experience, she reports that he was "working through" the different presentations, creating his own version. Stone believes the child was responding to the "explicit and implicit content" of the story, as well as to the differing means through which this was presented.[6]

Teachers could help intermediate-grade youngsters compare Lent's ideas about filmmaking with those of Tom Davenport (1981), who describes how he made the live-action "Rapunzel" (mentioned above). Davenport's fascinating account might encourage teachers to attempt live productions of fairy tales in the classroom, because his rules of production could be applied to informal drama. One of his basic precepts is that "how an actor looks and moves is more important than his voice or facility with dialogue." In addition, Davenport talks of the need to understand the story thoroughly and seriously, to follow the original story as carefully as possible, and to look for the intrinsic dramatic elements in the story.

Most film versions retain the original artwork and avoid distorting the story. Unfortunately, some companies pirate stories and add artwork they feel is more appealing. Shoddy artwork is more likely to occur in filmstrip versions; these need to be evaluated carefully to make sure their quality is good enough to make them worth sharing with children. In this area, as in other areas of children's literature, there are valuable resource books that provide comprehensive information to help teachers make selections. May (1981) annotated nearly three hundred films and filmstrips, presented alphabetically, indexed by subject and theme.

Today, even more than film, videotape has become a pervasive visual medium. Children are influenced by the adaptations of literature they see on commercial television. In addition, several manufacturers are offering video adaptations of literature. Some of these efforts rise to the quality teachers have come to expect from such suppliers as Weston Woods; other efforts have met with less success in making an effective transfer from book to media.

In addition to film and video, many manufacturers of computer programs are now doing book adaptations to that medium. What is the quality of such transformations? It is distressing that often reviews and articles don't address the issue of fidelity to the original. For example, in a typical article, Wepner (1990) describes many new computer programs which incorporate in various ways, adaptations of children's books. The problem is that she nowhere in the article addresses two important questions: 1) What kind of changes or deletions have been made in the text; and 2) Is the original art used? For teachers concerned about faithfulness to the artist's and author's original ideas, it is difficult to find out necessary information.

Bibliography of children's books

Amoss, Berthe. *Old Hasdrubal and the Pirates*. New York: Parents' Magazine Press, 1971, now o.p.

Ancona, George (Ill.) *Faces* by Barbara Brenner. New York: E. P. Dutton, 1970.

Ancona, George (Ill.). *Handtalk. An ABC of Finger Spelling and Sign Language*. New York: Parents Magazine Press, 1974.

Ardizzone, Edward. *Little Tim and the Brave Sea Captain*. New York: Henry Z. Walck, 1955.

Baker, Jeannie (Ill.). *Polar* by Elaine Moss. New York: Greenwillow, 1990.

Bender, Robert. *The Three Billy Goats Gruff*. New York: Henry Holt, 1993.

Bochak, Grace (Ill.). *Paper Boats* by Radindranath Tagore. Honesdale, PA: Caroline House, 1992.

Born, Flint (Ill.). *An Alphabet in Five Acts* by Karen Born Anderson. New York: Dial Books, 1993.

Brown, Mary Barrett. *Wings Along the Waterway*. New York: Orchard Books, 1992.

Bryan, Ashley. *The Cat's Purr*. New York: Atheneum, 1985.

————(Ill.). *Climbing Jacob's Ladder. Heroes of the Bible in African-American Spirituals*, selected by John Langstaff. New York: Margaret K. McElderry Books, 1991.

————. *Sing to the Sun*. New York: HarperCollins, 1992.

Bryson, Bernarda (Ill.). *The Sun is a Golden Earring* by Natalia Belting. New York: Holt, Rinehart and Winston, 1963)

Byard, Carole (Ill.). *Africa Dream* by Eloise Greenfield. New York: Harper Trophy, 1992.

————. *The Black Snowman*. New York: Scholastic, 1989.

Carle, Eric. *1, 2, 3, To the Zoo*. Cleveland: World Publishing, 1968, now o.p.

————. *The Honeybee and the Robber*. New York: Philomel Books, 1981, now o.p.

————(Ill.). *The Lamb and the Butterfly* by Arnold Sundgaard. New York: Orchard Books, 1988.

Cole, Alison. *Eyewitness Art. Color*. New York: Dorling Kindersley, 1993.

Cooney, Barbara (Ill.). *Chanticleer and the Fox*, adapted from Geoffrey Chaucer. New York: Thomas Y. Crowell Co., 1958.

Cooper, Floyd. (Ill.) *Be Good to Eddie Lee* by Virginia Fleming. New York: Philomel Books, 1993.

d'Aulaire, Ingri, and Edgar Parin d'Aulaire. *Abraham Lincoln*. Garden City, NY: Doubleday, 1939.

———. *Book of Greek Myths*. Garden City, NY: Doubleday, 1962.

———. *d'Aulaires' Trolls*. Garden City, NY: Doubleday, 1972, now o.p.

———. *Norse Gods and Giants*. Garden City, NY: Doubleday, 1967.

Domanska, Janina (Ill.). *Under the Greenwillow*. New York: Greenwillow Books, 1984.

Falwell, Cathryn. *Feast for 10*. New York: Clarion Books, 1993.

Fisher, Leonard Evertt (Ill.). *All Times, All Peoples: A World History of Slavery* by Milton Meltzer. New York: Harper and Row, 1980.

Flather, Lisa (Ill.). *Where the Great Bear Watches* by James Sage. New York: Viking, 1993.

Fleming, Denise. *In the Small, Small Pond*. New York: Henry Holt and Co., 1993.

———. *Lunch*. New York: Henry Holt and Co., 1992.

Frampton, David (Ill.). *Whaling Days* by Carol Carrick. New York: Clarion Books, 1993.

Frasconi, Antonio (Ill.). *At Christmastime* by Valerie Worth. New York: HarperCollins, 1992.

Gammell, Stephen (Ill.). *Song and Dance Man* by Karen Ackerman. New York: Alfred A. Knopf, 1988.

Garrison, Barbara (Ill.). *Only One* by Marc Harshman. New York: Cobblehill Books/Dutton, 1993.

Geisert, Arthur. *The Ark*. Boston: Houghton Mifflin, 1988.

———. *Oink Oink*. Boston: Houghton Mifflin, 1993.

Glubok, Shirley. *The Art of Photography*. New York: Macmillan, 1977, now o.p.

Goffstein, Brooke. *Our Prairie Home. A Picture Album*. New York: Harper & Row, 1988.

Grifalconi, Ann (Ill.). *Everett Anderson's Year* by Lucille Clifton. New York: Henry Holt and Co., 1974, 1992.

———. *The Village of Round and Square Houses*. Boston: Little, Brown, 1986.

Grillone, Lisa, and Joseph Gennaro. *Small Worlds Close Up*. New York: Crown, 1978, now o.p.

Henwood, Simon. *A Piece of Luck*. New York: Farrar, Straus and Giroux, 1989.

Himler, Ronald (Ill.). *Dakota Dugout* by Ann Turner. New York: Macmillan, 1985.

Hoban, Tana. *A Children's Zoo*. New York: Greenwillow, 1985.

———. *Is It Rough? Is It Smooth? Is It Shiny?* New York: Greenwillow, 1984.

———. *Push-Pull Empty-Full*. New York: Macmillan, 1972.

———. *Shapes and Things*. New York: Macmillan, 1970.

Hoffman, Felix. The Seven Ravens. New York: Harcourt Brace, 1962, now o.p.

————. *The Sleeping Beauty*. New York: Harcourt Brace, 1959, now o.p.

Hogrogian, Nonny (Ill.). *Hand in Hand We'll Go* by Robert Burns. New York: Thomas Y. Crowell, 1965.

Johnson, Steve and Lou Fancher (Ills.). *The First Night* by B. G. Hennessy. New York: Viking, 1993.

Keats, Ezra Jack. *Jennie's Hat*. New York: Harper & Row, 1966.

————. *The Snowy Day*. New York: The Viking Press, 1962.

Kitchen, Bert. *Animal Alphabet*. New York: Dial Books, 1984.

Kleven, Elisa (Ill.). *Abuela* by Arthur Dorros. New York: Dutton Children's Books, 1991.

Laroche, Giles (Ill.). *Ragged Shadows*, selected by Lee Bennett Hopkins. Boston: Little, Brown and Co., 1993.

Lent, Blair. *Bayberry Bluff*. Boston: Houghton Mifflin, 1987.

————(Ill.). *The Wave* by Margaret Hodges. Boston: Houghton Mifflin, 1964.

Lionni, Leo. *Cornelius*. New York: Pantheon Books, 1983.

————. *An Extraordinary Egg*. New York: Alfred A. Knopf, 1994.

————. *Frederick*. New York: Pantheon Books, 1967.

————. *Frederick's Fables*. New York: Pantheon, 1985.

Locker, Thomas. *The Mare on the Hill*. New York: Dial Books, 1985.

Lucht, Irmgard. *In This Night ....* New York: Hyperion Books for Children, 1993.

MacCarthy, Patricia (Ill.). *The Horrendous Hullabaloo* by Margaret Mahy. New York: Viking, 1992.

Mackain, Bonnie (Ill.). *One Hundred Hungry Ants* by Elinor J. Pinczes. Boston: Houghton Mifflin Co., 1993.

Mak, Kam (Ill.). *The Moon of the Monarch Butterflies* by Jean Craighead George. New York: HarperCollins, 1993.

Manson, Christopher (Ill.). *King Wenceslaus* by John Mason Neale. New York: North-South Books, 1994.

———— (Ill.). *Over the River and Through the Wood* by Lydia Maria Child. New York: North-South Books, 1993.

Mavor, Salley (Ill.). *Come to My Party* by Judith Benét Richardson. New York: Macmillan Publishing Co., 1993.

McCloskey, Robert. *Make Way for Ducklings*. New York: The Viking Press, 1941.

McNeer, May. *The Canadian Story*. New York: Ariel Books, 1958, now o.p.

Migdale, Lawrence (Ill.). *Celebrating Kwanzaa*. New York: Holiday House, 1993.

Mullins, Patricia (Ill.). *Crocodile Beat* by Gail Jorgensen. New York: Bradbury Press, 1988.

————(Ill.). *Shoes From Grandpa* by Mem Fox. New York: Orchard Books, 1990.

Myers, Walter Dean. *Brown Angels*. New York: HarperCollins, 1993.

Pinkney, Brian (Ill.). *The Ballad of Belle Dorcas* by William H. Hooks. New York: Alfred A. Knopf, 1990.

Pinkney, Brian (Ill.). *Day of Delight* by Maxine R. Schur. New York: Dial Books for Young Readers, 1994.

———(Ill.). *Seven Candles for Kwanzaa* by Andrea Davis Pinkney. New York: Dial Books for Young Readers, 1993.

Ramel, Charlotte (Ill.). *My Sister Lotta and Me* by Helena Dahlbach. New York: Henry Holt and Co., 1993.

Ray, David (Ill.). *Greyling* by Jane Yolen. New York: Philomel Books, 1991.

Reid, Barbara (Ill.). *Have You Seen Birds?* by Joanne Oppenheim. New York: Scholastic Hardcover, 1987.

———. *Two By Two*. New York: Scholastic Hardcover, 1993.

Reinl, Edda. *The Little Snake*. Boston: Neugebauer Press U.S.A., 1982.

———. *The Three Little Pigs*. Natick, MA: Picture Book Studio, 1983, o.p.

Ross, Jane (Ill.). *Little Eagle Lots of Owls* by Jim Edmiston. Boston: Houghton Mifflin, 1993.

Sabuda, Robert. (Ill.) *The Log of Christopher Columbus*, selected by Steve Lowe. New York: Philomel Books, 1992.

———. *Saint Valentine*. New York: Atheneum, 1992.

Sendak, Maurice (Ill.). *Mr. Rabbit and the Lovely Present* by Charlotte Zolotow. New York: Harper & Row, 1962.

Shimin, Symeon (Ill.). *Listen, Rabbit!* by Aileen Fisher. New York: Thomas Y. Crowell, 1964.

Siebold, J. Otto (Ill.). *Mr. Lunch Takes a Plane Ride* by Vivian Walsh. New York: Viking, 1993.

Stobbs, William (Ill.). *Greyling* by Jane Yolen. Cleveland: World Publishing, 1968.

Valens, Evans G. *Wildfire*. Cleveland: World Publishing, 1963, now o.p.

Van Allsburg, Chris. *The Garden of Abdul Gasazi*. Boston: Houghton Mifflin, 1979.

———. *Jumanji*. Boston: Houghton Mifflin, 1981.

Ward, Lynd. *The Canadian Story*. New York: Ariel Books, 1958.

———. *The Mexican Story*. New York: Ariel Books, 1953, now o.p.

Wiesner, David (Ill.). *Night of Gargoyles* by Eve Bunting. New York: Clarion Books, 1994.

Wisniewski, David. *Elfwyn's Saga*. New York: Lothrop, Lee & Shepard Books, 1990.

———. *Rain Player*. New York: Clarion Books, 1991.

Wolff, Ashley. *Stella and Roy*. New York: Dutton Children's Books, 1993.

Yoshi (Ill.). *A to Zen* by Ruth Wells. Saxonville, MA: Picture Book Studio, 1992.

Professional references

Anscombe, I. and C. Gere. (1978). *Arts and Crafts in Britain and America*. London: Academy Editions.

Becker, M. L. (1939, April 30). Review. *Books*, p. 10.

Behrmann, C. (1988). "The Media Used in Caldecott Picture Books: Notes Toward a Definitive List." *Journal of Youth Services in Libraries*, 1(2), 198-212.

Brown, M. (1986). *Lotus Seeds. Children, Pictures and Books*. New York: Charles Scribner's Sons.

Buell, E. L. (1939, June 18). Review. *The New York Times*, p. 10.

Davenport, T. (1981). "Some Personal Notes on Adapting Folk-Fairy Tales to Film." *Children's Literature*, 9, 107-115.

Evans, D. (1992, September). "Black-and-White Magic." *Booklinks*, pp. 49-53.

————. (1992, November/December). "An Extraordinary Vision: Picture Books of the Nineties." *The Horn Book Magazine*, pp. 759-764.

Fieser, S. (1992). "Solving the Picture-Book Puzzle." *The Artist's Magazine*, 9(2), 78-83.

Frasconi, A. (1974). *Against the Grain*. New York: Macmillan.

Frezzolini, S. (1992). "Glossary of Terms in Art and Design of Children's Books." *CBC Features*, 45(2), unp.

Haggar, R. G. (1962). *A Dictionary of Art Terms*. New York: Hawthorn Books, Inc.

Heins, E. L. (1988). "From Mallards to Maine: A Conversation with Robert McCloskey." *Journal of Youth Services in Libraries*, 1(2), 187-193.

Heller, S. (1988, September-October). "Extending the Territory." *Print*, 76-84 and ff.

Hopkins, L. B. (1983). "Remembering Ezra Jack Keats." *School Library Media Quarterly*, 12, 7-9.

Horning, K. T. (1988). "Are You Sure That Book Won the Caldecott Medal? Variant Printings and Editions of Three Caldecott Medal books." *Journal of Youth Services in Libraries*, 1(2), 173-176.

Hurwitz, A., and M. Day. (1991). *Children and Their Art*. San Diego: Harcourt Brace Jovanovich.

Krevitsky, Nik. (1964). *Batik. Art and Craft*. New York: Reinhold Publishing Co.

Lanes, S. G. (1984, September/October). "Ezra Jack Keats: In Memoriam." *The Horn Book*, 551-558.

Larrick, Nancy. (1971). *A Parent's Guide to Children's Reading*. Garden City, NY: Doubleday (pp. 155-156).

Lent, B. (1971). "How the Sun and the Moon Got into a Film." *The Horn Book*, 47, 589-596.

Levin, G. (1980). *Edward Hopper: The Art and the Artist*. New York: Norton, and the Whitney Museum of American Art.

Lionni, L. (1984, November/December). "Before Images." *The Horn Book Magazine*, 727-734.

Livingston, M. C. (1990). *Climb into the Bell Tower. Essays on Poetry*. New York: Harper & Row, Publishers.

Mann, F.H. (1970) *Artist's Lithographs*. New York: G.P. Putnam's Sons.

Marantz, S. S. (1992). *Picture Books for Looking and Learning*. Phoenix, AZ: Oryx Press.

May, J. P. (1981). *Films and Filmstrips for Language Arts*. Urbana, IL: National Council of Teachers of English.

McCall, C.H., and C.A. Silberg Grossman. (1987). "Unraveling the Mysteries of *Jumanji* and *The Garden of Abdul Gasazi*." *The Dragon Lode*, 6(1), 4-6.

Paulin, M. A. (1982). *Creative Uses of Children's Literature*. Hamden, CT: Library Professional Publications.

Raboff, Ernest. (1988) *Marc Chagall*. New York: J. B. Lippincott.

Rothenstein, Michail. (1962) *Linocuts and Woodcuts*. New York: Watson-Guptill.

Sendak, M. (1988). *Caldecott & Co. Notes on Books and Pictures*. New York: Farrar, Straus and Giroux.

Shaw, F. C. (1985). "The Limitations of Motion Picture Adaptations to Contribute to Reading Development in Pre-Schoolers." *The Advocate*, 5, 36-46.

Smith, A. (1991, April 5). "The Lively Art of Leo Lionni." *Publishers Weekly*, pp. 118-119.

Stewig, J. W. (1988). "Children's Preferences in Film." *Journal of Visual and Verbal Language*, 8(1), 74-78.

Stone, K. (1988). "Three Transformations of Snow White." In J. M. McGlathery (ed.), *The Brothers Grimm and Folktale* (pp. 52-65). Urbana: University of Illinois Press.

Tofts, Hannah. (1990). *The Collage Book*. New York: Simon and Schuster Books for Young Readers.

Triado, Juan-Ramon. (1990). *The Key to Painting*. Minneapolis: Lerner Publications Company.

Ward, L. (1978). "Doing a Book in Lithography." In L. Kingman (ed.), *The Illustrator's Notebook* (109-114). Boston: The Horn Book, Inc.

Wepner, S. B. (1990). "Wholistic Computer Applications in Literature-based Classrooms." *The Reading Teacher*, 44(1), 12-19.

Wescher, Herta. (1968) *Collage*. New York: Abrams.

Book Design Elements

5

Beyond the quality of the illustrations themselves, several considerations influence the final look of a picture book. Some of these components are rather subtle. In choosing books to use with children, a teacher or librarian should assess the effectiveness of the book designer's decisions concerning: 1) shape, 2) size, 3) binding, 4) endpapers, 5) paper, 6) typefaces, and 7) page layout. In some books construction details provide movement of one sort or another. Here, we shall isolate each of these elements and examine them separately for instructional purposes. However, when we look at a book, we shouldn't notice any given element as calling attention to itself. In fact, as Goldenberg points out, book design is "most successful when (it is) not immediately apparent ...."[1] The chapter closes with a section suggesting ways to involve children in studying book design elements.

Shape

A book designer carefully chooses a book's shape to enhance the text and pictures. Although constraints are imposed by the practicalities of printing and the problem of shelving unusually shaped books, the designer has a range of options.

The most common shape for books is the rectangle. Some books that are rectangular are taller than they are wide. For example, the tall shape of *Up Goes the Skyscraper!*, by Gail Gibbons, effectively ties in with the subject, but the solid colors and pervasive thin, black line of the illustrations are utilitarian, merely providing the necessary factual details about the construction of buildings. A tall, thin shape was also used by the book designer for *Jack and the Beanstalk*, retold by Walter de la Mare. The artist, Joseph Low, stretched the illustrations (especially the one of the beanstalk) to the full height of the page. Using black crayon with bold splashes of color, Low created pleasantly casual illustrations to accompany the detailed story. A different approach to the same story is a square-shaped version with illustrations by Matt Faulkner, who uses soft, pastel-hued crayon.

Or, you might look with children at the solution devised by Gail Haley in *Jack and the Bean Tree*. In this horizontal rectangle format, which extends a full 20 inches wide on the double-page spread openings, she stretches the pictures across the gutter, leaving space on either the left or right margin for the block of text. However, on the spread showing the giant pursuing Jack down the tree, the picture is printed "sideways," i.e., one must turn the book upright to orient the picture properly. After enjoying the drama of this wordless spread, we return the book to normal viewing position, as Haley concludes using the horizontal rectangle possibilities of the format.

About the artist

The art for Aesop's Fables *by Zwerger was included in the 1989 Bologna International Book Fair, a juried competition of over 847 entries from 45 countries, narrowed to a show of 80 artists* (Annual '89).

Sometimes the book designer provides a tall rectangle shape, but the art doesn't particularly make use of that shape. For example, Lisbeth Zwerger's art for *Hans Christian Andersen Fairy Tales* is showcased in a $13^{1}/2$"-tall shape. The art for the book by this often-honored artist is done in her usual, pleasantly understated watercolor which focuses on the characters and minimizes background details. But for the most part the art isn't done in tall rectangle shapes; far more often it is in rectangles where the vertical and horizontal dimensions are very close. As a result, the art doesn't reiterate the book shape. The pages themselves are an elegant showcase for the blocks of text, providing margins more generous than in most books.

The book designer, on the other hand, may choose a rectangular shape that is longer in the horizontal dimension. In *Carol Barker's Birds and Beasts*, Barker uses darkly intense colors with swirling patterns to develop a menagerie of wild beasts. The illustrations spread across facing pages, giving an impression of extended horizontal space. The chameleon, with rotating eyes and spotted skin, extends the full width of the open book, nearly 21 inches. Several other animals are almost as long. The horizontal dimension is also exploited effectively in *A Boy Went Out to Gather Pears*, by Felix Hoffman. The text is an old verse about a boy who, instead of picking pears, waits for them to fall; his master sends out a dog, a stick, fire, and four other messengers to stir the boy to action. The artist fills the 17-inch-wide horizontal spreads with angular illustrations in limited but cheerful shades of orange, yellow, blue, green, brown, and black.

In *The Sea and I*, Harutaka Nakawatari gives viewers realistic paintings, bled to the page edge, showing the variety of moods of the sea, depending on time of day and type of weather. The paintings open to a full 23 inches in the horizontal dimension. The small boy narrator worries about the father, and is relieved when all is well at day's end. There is one particularly effective vertical spread, showing the height of the lighthouse headland, which viewers must turn the book in order to see.

Lois Ehlert used a $6^1/2$"-tall rectangle which opens to a full 22 inches in width, and she stretches her shapes to take full advantage of that dimension, in *Fish Eyes*, a counting book. Crisply-edged shapes, in neon-vivid colors create these imaginative fish, and we look through the die-cut circles which form their eyes at the colors on the following page. The lower-case serif lettering of the text, i.e., "10 ten darting fish" is printed in a brilliant, true white, which vibrates against the dark blue background.

At the other end of the realism/abstraction continuum are the paintings Gary Blythe did for *The Whales' Song* by Dyan Sheldon. This nine-inch-tall book opens to a full $22^1/2$" double-page spread, with paintings which extend across the gutter. The subtle gradations of paint color are enhanced by the texture of the rough canvas on which the illustrations were painted. The lyric story is of the conflict between Lilly's grandmother's and her great uncle's views of the whales: in the end Lilly comes to her own conclusions.

In his Caldecott Honor book, *Freight Train*, Donald Crews also used a horizontal rectangle to maximum effectiveness, as the double-page spreads stretch to a full 19 inches across. This provides ample room for the boldly simplified shapes presented in highly saturated colors Crews uses to show the variety of places, and the ways of traveling, that the train exemplifies. The bold san serif lettering, printed on different pages in a variety of colors, is a dramatic addition to the page.

Seymour Chwast made clever use of a rectangular shape in *Tall City, Wide Country. A Book to Read Forward and Backward*. The shape is $6^1/4$"x$11^1/2$" and is either vertical or horizontal in orientation, depending on which of the two segments one is reading. Opening the "wide country" side, we find Chwast's flat, decorative, humorous illustrations spread across the double-page

Serif

A serif is a short line used to finish off a main stroke of a letter.

Sans Serif

A letter or typeface with no serifs, or extending lines.

spreads, to achieve a horizontal dimension that stretches to a full 22 inches. He uses a green, rather than black outline to show us people, objects, and events in the countryside. The center, transition page is vertigo-producing, as the airplane travels between the country and the city. Readers then turn the book to the vertical position and see that the things in a city fit comfortably in that dimension, stretching tall to a full 22 inches. Stilt walkers, apartment buildings, and elevators are also outlined in the green line Chwast used earlier in the book. We can read through to the end. Or, we start at the "back," i.e., the vertically oriented "tall city" side, and read backwards toward the country at the front of the book.

A clever use of both the horizontal and vertical dimension of a book's shape is apparent in Mordicai Gerstein's illustrations for *The Cataract of Lodore* by Robert Southey. Southey, a nineteenth-century writer who was England's Poet Laureate, has done a description of an adventure in a veritable deluge of rhyming words which children will enjoy hearing. The book opens conventionally, with horizontal single and double-page spreads, but at the seventh opening, where the three children and their father begin to tumble down the waterfall, the reader/viewer must turn the book sideways. Once in vertical position, the water falls to a full 20 inches from top to bottom for the next six openings, until the family lands safely at the bottom. The book is then returned to the conventional horizontal position for the remainder of this rhymed adventure, which children will enjoy vicariously.

Another alternative for a book designer is to choose a square shape. *The Fish* is a square book (about six inches on a side) containing a not very believable story about a fish who rescues a little girl. Prolific artist Dick Bruna rendered the fish, swans, ducklings, and little girl in flat, intense colors boldly outlined with a uniform black line. The illustrations' blocky shapes are well suited to the book's square format.

More elegant illustrations appear in the realistic story *Toad*, by Anne and Harlow Rockwell. This almost square book (about eight inches by eight inches) tells of the dangers and pleasures of a year in the life of a toad. Illustrations that are both rectangular and square are mostly placed rather formally on the pages, with a border of color surrounding them.

Board books, printed on heavy cardboard with just a few pages, are designed for infants and toddlers and are often done in a square shape. *Ding Dong! And Other Sounds* by Christine Salac

Activity

Toad *could be used in conjunction with a more recently published work by the Rockwells, such as* In Our House *so children can notice changes in the artists' style.*

Dubov, in a six-inch-square format, features full-color photographs by Elizabeth Hathon of preschool youngsters using simple instruments to make sounds. The solid-color backgrounds and single word for each sound on a page make it easy for very young children to understand the ideas presented.

Barbara Reid, who has developed plasticene as a serious art medium, in *Zoe's Rainy Day* presents a wordless story of her adventures in several locations, in a five-inch-square format. Three other books in the series explore outings in other seasons of the year. Reid juxtaposes intricate shapes, offering a great deal to look at on any opening.

For slightly older children, Ann Morris and Maureen Roffey used a five-inch-square format to present *Night Counting*, in which simple watercolor and ink line art shows a variety of children counting objects up to ten. The endpapers, featuring simplified and stylized sheep jumping fences, make an effective introduction to the book.

Sometimes, particularly in the category often labeled "toy books," publishers experiment with less conventional book shapes. One example is the Dial "Playshapes" series, in which the publishers produced Arnold Shapiro's *Triangles* and *Circles*, both about nine inches in dimension. *Triangles* opens along the spine, to reveal objects like a pine tree and a tent. The half-circle shape opens to full in *Circles*, depicting such objects as a pizza and a clock. Both are printed on heavy cardboard stock in full, bright colors with cartoon-like illustrations designed for the preschool or early childhood crowd.

Page shape

In addition to the outside shape of the book, at times the artist varies the shapes of the internal pages. Perhaps the best known use of half pages is in the books of John Goodall, who some time ago began experimenting with a half page inserted between two full pages. On any given opening, the half page obscures part of the right hand page, and when flipped to the left, reveals a different scene. In essence, the use of the half page moves the action along, by showing two half pages of difference between the double-page spread. For example, in *Shrewbettina's Birthday*, an early (1970) book, Goodall depicts an appealing animal heroine on a shopping excursion. He continued using the half-page format throughout his career, and later books, like *Paddy to the Res-*

cue, show that careful bookmaking is essential in this format. The half-pages must align objects exactly for the device to be effective. In addition, the color match is critical.

A variation of this device was used by Brian Wildsmith in a much larger format, in contrast to Goodall's small-scale work. *Shrewbettina*, for example, is only 7"x 5". In contrast, Wildsmith, working in a vertical rectangle which is $9^3/4$"x$12^1/4$", depicts *Daisy*, the discontented cow, unhappy in her field. Working in his usual con brio visual style, Wildsmith juxtaposes colors and patterns to create this imaginary world. The half pages between a double-page spread help vary the action. For example, on the seventh opening, we see Daisy on the photographer's stand when the half page covers the right side; when it is flipped to cover the left side, it reveals Daisy in a bubble bath, posing for an advertising spread. Because of the size of the book, the half page gives Wildsmith much more space in which to work than it did for Goodall.

Another example of an artist using a half page is Clive Scruton in *Mary's Pets*, a simple story for beginning readers about a little girl's search for her temporarily missing animals. The text, phrased in question format, makes it easy for children to guess which animal will be revealed next as the vertical half-page is flipped from right to left. The very simple watercolor wash and pen line illustrations in cartoon style vary the viewing distance greatly. The artist shows Mary at middle distance when she is looking for what turns out to be her dog, Sam. In contrast, on the page where Flip Flop, the duckling, appears, we are so close to Mary that her head takes most of the page. The bright colors and simple shapes are appropriate to the age group the brief text suggest.

Lark Carrier in *There was a Hill...*, split soft grey pages vertically, and used a simple san serif lettering. This gives the first part of the sentence when the half page is on the right, for example, "There was a hill...." When the page is flipped left, it reveals the rest of the sentence, "...that was a bear," and viewers see that what at first appeared to be one thing is indeed something else. The book is really only accessible to individual viewers, as the pastel illustrations are so incredibly subtle that they couldn't be seen at a distance in a group. These pictures need to be studied close up as there is almost no light and dark contrast: as a result individual shapes are difficult to see. For example, when the tree stump is revealed to be a wolf, children will have to look carefully to discern this.

In contrast to a half page split vertically, Laura Rader split her whole pages horizontally, in *Mother Hubbard's Cupboard*. The humorous cartoon-like ink line and watercolor drawings open the rhyme and then advance the action. When the top half of the split page is flipped, some indication of what is happening is revealed, a foreshadowing of what becomes apparent when the bottom half is flipped. For example, on the "Hickory, dickory, dock" page, when the top half is moved, we see the mouse running down, his eyes wide in amazement. It isn't until the bottom half is moved that we discover the cause: there is a large, menacing cat hiding at the bottom of the clock! On most of the openings the color match is satisfactory, but on the "Jack and Jill" page, there is too substantial a difference in the green of the grass when the half pages are flipped.

Sometimes pages are trimmed so that each succeeding page is wider than the previous one, which makes a part of each visible when the first page is opened. For example, the first two pages of Eric Carle's *The Grouchy Ladybug* are conventional size (identical with the size of the book). When we turn to the third opening, however, we see that the right page of this double spread is only two inches wide. This makes it possible to see the edge of the fourth opening (2$\frac{1}{2}$" wide), the fifth opening (3" wide) the sixth opening (3$\frac{1}{2}$" wide) and so on. The edge of each following page is exposed, and printed at the top of these exposed edges are clock faces showing the passage of time central to the plot. By the time viewers are at the 15th opening, the page has "grown" back to the full size of the beginning. An even more interesting production detail was the die cutting done on the 17th opening: the right-hand page, showing the whale's tail, is cut into the shape of a tail.

Lois Ehlert used this device of increasingly wider pages in her *Planting a Rainbow*. The first eight openings, which describe in simple language the process of gardening, are full size. The words are set in large serif lettering topping the abstract shapes this artist favors. Beginning on the ninth opening, where the right page is only five inches wide, we see the array of succeeding pages, gradually growing wider, each solid vertical stripe providing a pleasant contrast to the energetically patterned flowers for that color. In the end, the pages are back to the beginning size, providing a generous space in which Ehlert presents, horizontally

Plate 8: Planting a Rainbow
A streamlined and simplified attention to shapes characterizes this work, which is a visual descendant of the work done several decades earlier by Ann and Paul Rand. Their *Sparkle and Spin* is now available again, and you might look at it in the context of Ehlert's art. Her latest book is *Crocodile Beat*, a collection of animal poem-songs. (*See full illustration in color plates following page 174.*)

across both pages, the dazzling bouquet which results from the summer's labor.

Another way to affect the look of a page is by cutting away part of it, so that something on the following spread is revealed. This is called die-cutting. At times the opening is a consistent size and shape throughout the book. For example, in *Old Mac-Donald Had a Farm*, Carol Jones provided detail-packed water-color wash and ink line drawings. On the first opening, the left page shows the farmer, while the text on the right page accompanies a circle/hole, through which we look at part of the illustration on the succeeding opening. When we move to the next page, the entire painting is revealed, while the die-cut page (which has been flipped left) now shows the farmer on the previous opening. This process of looking at first the right, then at the left page through the hole provides a pleasant, predictable experience. The traditional folk song is presented in naturalistic, humorous pictures done in earth tones. The illustrator used the same technique, incorporating much crosshatching to indicate textures, in her *Hickory Dickory Dock*.

About the artist

Ehlert has talked about the process of creating her books, in an article by Goddard (1992).

In contrast to such a regular use of die-cut openings, two vibrantly colored books are printed on a paper of such thickness that it is almost cardboard, with openings of different sizes and shapes on every page. Lois Ehlert's *Color Farm* begins with a rooster, and when the page is turned we see that part of the head is the *square* opening cut into the page. On the next opening, we read the word *square*, and see that the animal revealed is a duck. We turn that page to see the octagon opening reveals a chicken on the following page, and so the pattern continues. The artist's solid, highly saturated colors bear no relationship to naturalistic colors of the birds and animals depicted. In addition, the highly simplified shapes used to depict the rather abstract heads of the animals present a challenge for literally minded viewers. She uses the same approach in her *Color Zoo*.

Another sort of page variation, though not of shape, per se, is the use of clear transparent pages with printing on them, inserted between conventional pages. This, then, allows for two different views of the same scene when the transparent page is shifted. For example, in an information book on *Ancient Greece* by Rowena Loverance and Tim Wood, we see both the outside and the inside of several locations. The pages entitled "Public Life" show the outside of the Athenian Agora (printed on the acetate). When this transparent sheet is flipped to the left, the interior view of the buildings is revealed. These cut-away views help child readers understand more fully the construction details. This is part of a four book series entitled "See Through History," which also examines Aztec, Egyptian, and Roman culture.

Size

Within certain limits, publishers will experiment with book size to create specific effects. However, very small or very large books are difficult to print, mail, and shelve. A designer considers the topic, the potential audience, and the total visual presentation desired when selecting a size.

Undoubtedly the best-known creator of small books is Beatrix Potter. Generations of young listeners have become familiar with the legion of small, personified animals that this artist began presenting in book format early in this century. *The Tale of Peter Rabbit* is probably the best known, though in the 23 other books still available from her publisher, Potter created kittens, pigs, squirrels, and mice, among others that charm young children. Potter's books follow a very consistent internal format: on each opening a small, close-up unbordered illustration in soft pastel colors faces a few lines of text. Potter wrote in the language she felt appropriate, and assumed children would follow even though vocabulary is often difficult. Such words as implored, permission, and intending, among others, don't reflect the kind of vocabulary control which today sometimes renders books lifeless.

Though children won't necessarily notice, it is interesting for adults to compare editions of her work published some time ago, with the new editions continuing the original small size (5⅝"x4¼"). In 1987, the publisher, Warne, reissued the entire series of books, with new color reproductions shot from the original art. Advances in photography and printing technology make these new books interesting in two ways: 1) the color gradations are much more noticeable than previously and 2) the clarity of line, and thus of the forms defined by line, is much sharper than before.

Although Potter's stories are usually accompanied by her own illustrations, *The Tale of Tuppenny* is available with pictures by another artist, Marie Angel. Angel's pictures are softer than Potter's but are quite appropriate to the story. This book's miniature size, similar to those illustrated by Potter herself, reinforces the charm of the story. To see just how important size is, compare

About the artist
The biography by Taylor, Whalley, Hobbs, and Battrich (1987) provides a helpful introduction to Potter's life and work.

Potter's illustrations for her stories with those by Stephanie Britt, Lulu Delacre, or David McPhail. Each artist has illustrated the tale of Peter Rabbit, yet each has chosen a much larger size. Despite some interesting visual qualities in each of these alternate editions, none has the cozy charm of Potter's originals. Allen Atkinson's edition tries a compromise: on a large (7³/4"x10") page size, he produced several illustrations which are in many cases almost as small as Potter's. Despite the attempt, these remain at best a compromise.

Maurice Sendak's illustrations for his "Nutshell Library" predate by a year his Caldecott-winning and trend-setting phenomenon, *Where the Wild Things Are*. Though less well known, this set of four books is equally interesting, especially in its original small format of only 2⁵/8"x 3³/4". The set includes an alphabet book (*Alligators All Around*), a counting book (*One Was Johnny*), a book of months (*Chicken Soup with Rice*), and a cautionary tale (*Pierre*). Presented in a full-color slipcase, the books themselves are illustrated in shades of yellow, blue, green, and grey, with the type of finely drawn pen crosshatching typical of Sendak's early work. The pictures in *Alligators* are bordered with a thin black line, while in the other three books they are unbordered, featuring animals—clothed and unclothed, as well as the kind of squatty children which were an early Sendak trademark. The books were reissued with brighter internal colors and given four-color covers, in a paperback edition in 1991. At that time, the size was increased to 4¹/4" x 5³/4" and the distinctively diminuitive quality was lost.

A similar presentation was devised for Leonard Baskin's *Miniature Natural History,* four books (3³/4" square) with their own full-color dust jackets inside a patterned slipcase. These show a single creature on each page, done for the most part without backgrounds, in richly dark colors.

Graham Percy also used a tiny format for his *The Tortoise and the Hare and Other Favorite Fables*, four books in a cardboard sleeve. Full-page, soft crayon drawings face a page of text. In each case the endpapers introduce the characters in silhouette, and other silhouettes are placed at the foot of each block of text.

Large size can also make a book more effective. Tomi Ungerer, author and illustrator of over 50 books, chose a large, rectangular shape (9"x12") for the humorous story of *Zeralda's Ogre*. The innocent farmer's daughter uses her culinary skill to

For more information

Other examples of books available in small trim sizes are described by Donahue (1992), in an article which examines the motivations and successes of publishers' efforts to experiment with both small and large trim sizes.

Figure 5.1: The Tale of Peter Rabbit
These two reproductions show the point in the story where Peter is seeking to elude Mr. McGregor, in whose garden he has been feasting. He might have escaped "…if he had not unfortunately run into a gooseberry net got caught by the large buttons on his jacket." Notice the differences in the position of Peter's body, where he is in relation to the birds and to the ground, and his orientation on the page (here facing left, in the McPhail facing right). (Page size: 4" x 5¹/₂")

Figure 5.2: The Tale of Peter Rabbit
David McPhail's work brings viewers closer to the main character during his misadventure, and provides larger art, easier to share with a group. The four-color art throughout the book is accompanied by more complete backgrounds than is Potter's art. To learn more about McPhail's art, look with your class at his illustrations for *Annie & Co.*, with a human main character who has many animals. (Page size: 8" x 8")

win over the grumpy ogre and solve the villagers' problem. Ungerer takes full advantage of the generous space the large size affords.

Another large book, the same size as *Zeralda's Ogre*, is William Steig's pleasant *Roland the Minstrel Pig*. This illustrator was honored by being nominated for the Hans Christian Andersen Award, given to an internationally known illustrator for an entire body of work. In this particular book, Roland, who has a beautiful voice, aspires to be rich and famous but falls in with bad company—a voracious fox. Until the king fortuitously passes by and rescues him, he is in danger of being roasted and eaten. The illustration for the crisis point in the story gains in intensity by being spread across two pages. A wide variety of pastel shades are employed in the detailed illustrations. In an article about his own work, Steig describes himself, "basically I'm a doodler," but he goes on to say that his best work is "spontaneous and unconscious," qualities which are apparent in *Roland* and other of his work.[3]

An even larger vertical format ($10^{1}/2$"x $14^{1}/2$") is used for *Orlando The Marmalade Cat. A Camping Adventure*, reissued in 1990 with illustrations originated from lithographs prepared by the author Kathleen Hale in 1959. The first book in what eventually became an 18-book series, the story was originally published in 1938. There is an elegance of mixed color and a grainy quality to these illustrations that merits careful study. The artist uses some double-page spreads, and at other places one and two illustrations on a single page, to present this bucolic story of personified cats, setting out in their red convertible for a trip to the country. The artwork in this could be compared with what Hale did for *Orlando's Evening Out*, originally issued during World War II in a much smaller, horizontal rectangle format ($9^{1}/2$"x $7^{1}/2$") and with color on only every other opening. The publisher is in the process of reissuing all the books, with Hale herself supervising the color correcting of the new editions.

To see how important scale is in illustration, you could compare the reissued editions of *The Story of Babar. The Little Elephant*, and *The Travels of Babar*, both by Jean de Brunhoff. Through the years since the original publication in the 1930s, the popular stories about the orphan elephant who adapts to city ways have been issued in a variety of formats, a fact which Feaver (1977) laments. In 1985 they were reissued in an elegantly oversized $10^1/2$"x 14" format which showcases the artist's primitive-style drawings, done in flat colors. In this size they create a remarkably more powerful impact than they do in the smaller (8"x $10^7/8$") size in which editions done by Random House in 1961 were published. Another, not unimportant, consideration is that in this reissue, the text was presented again in the original (or connected) cursive script. That fell out of use in intervening editions, and having the books available in script makes a pleasant contrast to more conventionally typeset books.

Looking further at these two variant editions, we notice other differences. For example, in the 1985 *Story of …*, the background color of the cover is distinctly orange, instead of red as in the 1961 edition. The interior colors are approximately the same, though the background brown of the endpapers in the 1961 edition has been replaced with a green, picking up a predominant color from the inside illustrations. In looking at the pair of *Travels of …*, we notice that the blue on the cover, and indeed throughout the 1985 edition, is far more vivid than the blue in the 1961 edition. A very vibrant red is used in the 1985 edition for the background of the end papers, which is quite an improvement on the flat brown used in the 1961 edition. In both *Travels of …* and *Story of …*, the back cover featured a photograph of four animals, bearing absolutely no relationship to the interior art. In the 1985 edition, this irrelevant photograph has been replaced by a solid color. In all ways, the 1985 edition is a much more satisfactory showcase for presenting the stories than was the earlier edition.

Throughout this section on size, the focus has been on the book itself. But there are other ways in which book artists are concerned with size. In *What Do You Like?*, a note about Michael Grejniec's illustrations points out that watercolor art, done on a highly textured Colombe paper, is reproduced in the book at 250% larger than the original paintings. That was done to accentuate the details and the rough edges of the paintings. As a result, the texture becomes a very palpable part of the illustrations, and it is easy to see the way in which watercolor bleeds into the paper, giving a distinctive "raggedy" edge. More recently he has used the same enlargement technique effectively in *Look*, a clever story about a small boy sick in bed who discovers the façade of the building he can see out his window isn't nearly as boring as

About the book

For readers interested in knowing about the creation of Travels of … *and* Story of … *and their author/illustrator, the book by Weber (1989) is very helpful.*

he first imagined. As a separate story unfolds in each of the windows, there's a plethora of detail for children to discover.

At other times, an artist will work on a much larger space, making it easier to show details, with the art then being reduced in size when photographed for the final book. A note in *Whisper from the Woods* points out that A. Scott Banfill's personified forest settings were originally painted in acrylics in a 17"x 23" size, finally reduced to 8"x 10³/₄". The variety of natural textures he evokes would have been more difficult to create had they been done in the smaller size originally. It would, incidentally, be interesting to compare the humanized trees in this book with those often found in the work of the widely popular Arthur Rackham, done much earlier in this century. For example, you could compare these trees with the ones Rackham did for Washington Irving's *The Legend of Sleepy Hollow*, in a facsimile of a 1928 edition.

Binding

The binding is carefully chosen by the designer to give a book an attractive and durable exterior. In planning a cover, the designer gives careful consideration to the visual impression that will be created. To ensure that the cover is representative of the book, a designer will sometimes use a design motif or picture that appears elsewhere in the book, or will tie in the color.

Higher-quality picture books are often hardbound with a cloth cover. A very handsome black linen cover with a gold-stamped ship's wheel, a design element that is repeated on the title page, introduces *Steamboat in a Cornfield* by John Hartford. Black was an appropriate color choice for this cover, given the thin black line that borders the sepia-toned photographs in the book. These photographs were taken during the first decade of this century, when the steamboat Queen City traveled from Pittsburgh to New Orleans. A brown linen cover would have been the more obvious but less effective choice.

Sometimes the cover is a combination of cloth and paper. The designer of *Half a Moon and One Whole Star*, by Crescent Dragonwagon, chose dark blue paper with a linen spine edging of even darker blue. Visually, this cover leads directly into the book, in which Caldecott Honor winner Jerry Pinckney's richly interesting watercolors show a similar midnight blue. A cloth-and-paper binding in two shades of orange, one bright and one burnt,

For more information

Stamped color designs are created under pressure using a brass die. If no ink is used, the sunken image is referred to as a blind stamp. An example of a blind-stamped design is found on the vivid purple cover of A Color of His Own, *by Leo Lionni.*

introduces *A Regular Rolling Noah* by George Ella Lyon. Throughout the book, artist Stephen Gammel's full-page watercolors in a variety of browns, golds, and other oranges echo the introductory colors.

Sometimes a contrast in tonality on a cover is quite effective. *Babushka's Doll* by Patricia Polacco has a cheerful, true red paper cover, with a bright white linen spine binding. The contrast between the two is repeated throughout the book: on many pages Polacco uses the white of the page space to intensify her colors, and on many pages the red appears in the illustrations. The brightness of the cover is an apt introduction to the brightness of the book itself.

In *Chicken Sunday*, Polacco continues to provide arresting contrasts in dust jacket, binding, and endpapers. An appealing interracial and intergenerational story, this won a Golden Kite Award in 1992 for illustration, given to an outstanding book of

Figure 5.3: Chicken Sunday

In this, as in other of her books, Polacco explores the ways groups of people from unlike backgrounds work out their differences harmoniously. The cheerful, clear colors which pervade this book are accented by the largely plain white backgrounds. The palette Polacco uses is somewhat more subdued in *Pink and Say*, and the enhancing use of white is less pervasive, but the theme is similar.

fiction by the Society of Children's Book Writers. The dust jacket shows only Miss Eula, Winston, Stewart and Patricia, set against a start white background which contrasts effectively with the soft brown and pink tones of the illustration itself. Opening to the endpapers, we discover a rich, solid, deep purple, not encumbered with design. Removing the dust jacket, viewers come across the high sheen texture of a paper binding, in pleasantly casual flower design, white with gold center, splashed against an intense dark blue and olive green. The green of the cover, and the purple of the endpapers are repeated at several places throughout the book, most effectively on the page full of the motion of the upraised arms (13th opening), as "Our hearts sang along with the choir that Sunday."

Because of increasing production costs, books are often bound in a paper-over-boards format. A particularly well-done example of this less expensive binding is *Wallaby Creek*, by Joyce Powzyk. The high-gloss finish of the cover sets off its deep blue border, lighter aqua type, and naturally colored animal painting.

The same type of cover is used effectively for *Noah's Ark* by Lucy Cousins. The high-gloss cover accentuates the saturated colors Cousins uses in her simplified, primitive-style illustration showing Noah, two giraffes, and the ark. These are arranged in a depth-less space, and Cousins concentrates on the patterning, rather than on any realistic representation of the objects shown. The cover leads to endpapers showing other animals done in this folk-like style. Throughout the book the simplified retelling is pleasantly decorated with Cousins' flat shapes.

Sometimes the same as, sometimes different than the binding, the book jacket has been described as "a small poster wrapped around a book."[4] The art editor will at times simply reproduce the cover, though on a different surface. At other times, for example, when a plain linen binding is used, the jacket may be a full-color illustration (or two), taken from within the book.

Endpapers

Opening a book, readers discover another important visual element, the endpapers. Endpapers are the first and last spreads of a book. One side of each spread is glued to the inside of the cover; the other side is not pasted down. Endpapers are usually of heavier paper than are the printed pages. These may have a design that comes from a motif or an illustration used elsewhere in the book, or they may simply be a solid color.

A very simple endpaper design that is nonetheless effective is found in *Ruff Leaves Home*, by Anne Carter. A blue silhouette of a fox faces left on the front endpapers and right on the back endpapers, nicely framing the story in between. The blue is repeated as the background color on the title page and in the book's realistic paintings by John Butler.

Coby Hol, in the endpapers for *Tippy Bear's Christmas*, uses just two shapes and four colors to create a pleasant repetitive design which effectively leads into the simplified sharp-edged collage illustrations in the book.

Scenic endpapers which establish the setting of a gentle animal fantasy are different in the front and back of the book, in *Farmer Duck* by Martin Waddell. Artist Helen Oxenbury shows a panoramic view of the farm, on an overcast wintry day with clouds threatening, for the front endpapers. This undergirds the plight of the overworked duck, forced to do all the work for the lazy farmer. On the back endpapers, we see the same view but lightened and brightened, with the fields in verdant growth—an optimistic scene which reflects the duck's changed status. In between, Oxenbury uses her fluid watercolor technique to show the long-suffering duck in all kinds of weather: bringing the cow into the barn from the rain drenched fields, and sheep from the hill in a snowstorm. The animals solve their own problem as they evict the pot-bellied farmer. The endpapers show the changed mood of the story without the text ever mentioning the mood, per se.

More elaborate scenic endpapers are found in *Katie Morag and the Two Grandmothers*, by Mairi Hedderwick. The front endpapers show the story setting, the Isle of Struay in Western Scotland, by day, with the buildings labeled. Pleasant watercolors are enhanced by a liberal use of white. The back endpapers show the same scene at night, without the labels, in the glow of moonlight. Hedderwick's illustrations within the book are also done in watercolors that are pleasantly kinetic, using much white for contrast and a thin brown line to define shapes. The same endpapers are used again in *Katie Morag and the Tiresome Ted*, also characterized by Hedderwick's light, bright palette.

It was logical for Hedderwick to use the endpapers to depict the environment, since she is telling stories in which the setting is an integral part of the action. Schwarcz and Schwarcz (1991) comment that in some stories the place is a dramatic part of what happens, almost becoming another character. Though Hedderwick doesn't develop this idea through the words, it is well developed throughout the illustrations. We see the dramatically darkening skies, the roiling waves smashing against the breakwater, the crashing of lightning at night, and the incoming tide tossing objects onto the shore. At the end, though it is again not specifically discussed in the words, we notice the gradually calming sky becoming brighter and lighter, to reflect the cheering mood of the conclusion.

In her *P.D. Peebles' Summer or Winter Book*, Hedderwick uses a similar light, airy palette with lots of white space to brighten the watercolors, showing a baby with a mind of his own. The endpapers are simpler, just an informal sketch of P.D., getting himself into trouble in both seasons. Inside, the illustrator presents one season on a double-spread opening, but on the right side there is a nearly page-size flap to be lifted which shows the same activity in the other season.

The handsome, dark endpapers in *East O' the Sun and West O' the Moon* by Irish illustrator P. J. Lynch, set the mood for this epic story of rags and riches, magic and mystery. This artist won, in 1987, the Mother Goose Award in England, as the most promising newcomer to children's book illustration. That is apparent in these richly-detailed, realistic, full-page paintings which show the Prince and the lassie who outsmart the old hag and her ugly

Figure 5.4: P.D. Peeble's Summer or Winter Book
What a helter-skelter home P.D. and his family inhabit: things are always cluttered and (minor) catastrophes happen amidst the comfortable disarray. Hedderwick's watercolors rush out to and spill beyond the page edge, in a style well-suited to the story.

daughter. The endpapers, in many shades of brown and green, with black ink line, show a map of the world, with personified portraits of the four winds in each of the corners.

Another example of a map endpaper is in *My Father's Dragon*, by Ruth Stiles Gannett, not a picture book, but rather chapter book, with black and white interior illustrations by Ruth Chrisman Gannett. The book won a Newbery Honor designation when first published in 1948, and was recently reissued in a near-facsimile of the first edition. Teachers reading this aloud to classes might want to prepare a color overhead of the endpapers, showing Wild and Tangerina Islands, so children can follow the location of the action.

In *Mike Mulligan and His Steam Shovel*, author/illustrator Virginia Lee Burton makes the endpapers into a teaching tool. Since children may not know the parts of a steam shovel, the end-

Activity
Children could speculate about what kind of a story these endpapers might introduce.

Figure 5.5: My Father's Dragon

Maps were, until relatively recently, decorative in addition to being informative. These endpapers follow that tradition, in presenting a map which helps readers of this longer illustrated book (not a picture book, per se) follow the adventures of the young narrator and the elusive dragon. Throughout the book, the black and white illustrations include many different shades of grey presented in a soft, grainy quality which resembles a lithograph. The humans are stylized in a way reminiscent of the art of Lois Lenski.

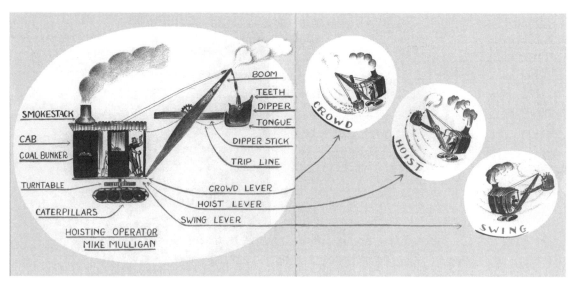

Figure 5.6: Mike Mulligan and His Steam Shovel
In a well-loved book which is fondly remembered from childhood by generations of adults, with the anthropomorphized main character who can talk, and feel. The fictional tale of how Mary Anne dug the basement seems unrelated to the gritty realities of life today, and yet preschool children still respond to the story. The information provided on the endpapers helps viewers better understand a machine now long out of use.

About the book

For a description of Mike Mulligan *as a whole, including some of the visual perplexities it presents, see Nodelman (1984).*

About the book

In a comment on a children's book within a children's book, Beverly Cleary lets the main character in Ramona the Pest *give her reaction to* Mike Mulligan *during her first day in kindergarten. Ramona's delight in the story is shared by many real children.*

papers provide a diagram. These show, in bright colors, a side view of the steam shovel, with each part labeled; small drawings to one side show the steam shovel at work. Though nearly 50 years old, the story remains a favorite.

No one uses teaching endpapers more effectively than does Deborah Nourse Lattimore. An example is *Why There Is No Arguing in Heaven.* Done just in shades of blue, the elaborately designed endpapers show the Mayan glyphs for numbers, for common words, like house, and for various Gods this group worshipped. Inside, this ancient Mayan story of the creation of the world is accompanied by full-color illustrations, which also incorporate visual motifs drawn from the culture.

Another illustrator, Peter Spier, often designs endpapers that set the tone for or expand upon the story within a book. For example, for his extended wordless retelling in *Noah's Ark*, Spier presents from one to three illustrations on each page. The opening endpaper alludes to the events that led up to Noah's task, and the closing endpaper shows what Noah did after he left the ark.

Sometimes the endpapers serve another utilitarian purpose. In the case of *Sam Panda and the Thunder Dragon* by Chris Conover, both front and back endpapers are printed with a board-

Figure 5.7: Noah's Ark
The variety in size of the illustrations in this book, from as few as two on an opening to as many as seven on an opening, contributes to the interest. Some of the illustrations (like the one showing the ark in the deluge) are virtually detail-less; others (like the spread showing the animals entering the ark) are crowded to excess with details. Spier used the same visual approach, though in a book with words, in *Father, May I Come?*, a more recent, yet still historic book depicting trouble off the Dutch coast. Look at this, compare it with his Caldecott winner, *Noah's Ark*, and try to decide which children will find more interesting.

game design. Children can use a button or coin to play, helping the bear attain the apple. Done in a subtle array of pastel colors which introduce the tonality that pervades the book, this is something kids will return to again and again.

Whether or not they are illustrated, endpapers are frequently of a color that is the same as or in contrast to the cover. The color of the endpapers can also reflect the book's mood. A dark grey stock is used for the endpapers in *The Something*, by Natalie Babbitt. Ugly Milo and his uglier mother live in a cavelike home. Milo is afraid of an unknown thing, which he believes will invade his bedroom. Babbitt creates an ominous effect on the endpapers with fine, black lines. She doesn't outline the shapes of the interlocking trees but rather uses the fine lines to create the background in a reverse effect. After listening to this story, children may enjoy discussing their own fears and comparing them to Milo's.

In *The Sign in Mendel's Window*, the plain lavender endpapers pick up shades and tints of purple that appear in, but do not dominate, author/illustrator Margot Zemach's watercolors. Similarly, in *Henry's Fourth of July*, the light blue endpapers reflect various shades of that color used by Margot Zemach throughout the book, to illustrate this story by Holly Keller.

Paper

Since children are very sensorially oriented, they should have the luxury of fine paper in their books. The smell and feel of good quality paper can be a delight to them, just as it often is to adults.

Papers basically have one of two finishes: matte or shiny. A matte finish is a dull surface. Matte finish paper is often heavy, with an interesting texture that does not reflect but rather absorbs light. The kind of pleasurable delight to be derived from fine, matte finish paper is apparent in the thick, cream-colored stock used for *Grandmother's Pictures*, reminiscences of Sam Cornish, a major black poet. The heavy paper has a velvety surface and is completely opaque; no hint of an illustration on the reverse side of a page ever shows through. *Under the Green Willow*, by Elizabeth Coatsworth, a U.S. nominee for the Hans Christian Andersen Award, was first published in 1971 and was recently reissued. Janina Domanska's geometric drawings, alive with repeated patterns in shades of just green and yellow, show up well on the heavy, white, textured matte paper. Also printed effectively on heavy, white matte paper, but very different stylistically from Domanska's drawings are Brock Cole's realistic watercolors for *The Winter Wren*.

Ann Jonas's *Round Trip* is an intriguing story idea and an interesting printing example, as well. *(See illustration on page 87.)* The story reads from front to back, and we follow the unnamed narrator through fields, mountains, valleys, and shores. When we reach the end of the book, we turn it around and reread the story from back to front. What had been the bottom of the pictures now becomes the top. In the process, graphics that had shown one scene on the first trip through show a different scene. The pictures mesh in such a way that, for example, what had been bridges (ninth opening) become telephone poles when the book is turned upside down.

Another notable aspect of the book is the printing. The paper is a heavy, quality matte paper. But, instead of using conventional black ink, which would have printed glossy on the matte paper, the book designer chose to use an ink which prints flat black. The contrast between the white of the paper and the black of the ink becomes more intense because both of them are matte finishes. A careful attention to detail like this makes the book more effective than using a regular glossy ink would have.

In contrast to matte finish papers are those with a shiny, light-reflecting surface, technically called coated papers because they

For more information

Maurice Sendak makes this point in an interview in which he talked about his work and bookmaking in general (Haviland, 1980).

For more information

Round Trip *is one of the books which Burke (1990) recommends in an introductory text with a helpful section on evaluating illustration.*

About the book

Jonas has talked about the creation of Round Trip *in an interview with Marantz and Marantz (1987).*

are created in a complex process in which a coating of clay and adhesive is applied. The smooth, glazed surface creates a very different effect than does a matte finish surface.

The Golem, a picture book for older children, was named a Caldecott honor book in 1976. Author/illustrator Beverly Brodsky McDermott used massive, rather abstract shapes to illustrate this retelling of a Jewish legend. The paper's high sheen and the light that it reflects deepen and intensify the dark colors McDermott uses. Heavy black line, which liberally outlines many of the objects, is kept from being oppressive by the paper. In another example, Lydia Dabcovich tells of the hibernation of *Sleepy Bear* in less than 50 words. Her bold but limited-color illustrations are enhanced by the coated paper on which they are printed. Lillian Hoban's casual pictures for Miriam Cohen's book *Starring First Grade* are similarly enriched by glazed paper.

In *Demi's Secret Garden*, the coated paper is especially effective in enhancing the art. Double-page, and larger spreads (accomplished by folding some longer sheets), provide an ample format for such garden creatures as the cicada, housefly, bee, and spider, among others. The art is presented on pale, solid-colored backgrounds, which contrasts effectively with the detailed, but imaginative patterns on the creatures; the metallic gold (not simply yellow or orange color) used in the pictures is enhanced by the paper. Poems from American, British, and Asian poets are mostly quite brief.

Typefaces

Although few readers ever pause to consciously consider the typefaces selected by a book's designer, the type chosen does affect the final look of a book. Typefaces are basically of two kinds: text faces and display faces.

Text faces are those used to set the body of the book's copy and are usually much simpler than display faces. Text faces feature easy-to-read shapes that do not tire the reader's eye. These are examples of text faces:

Old Mother Hubbard
Went to the cupboard,
To give her poor dog a bone,
(Garamond)

For more information

An extended but interesting technical consideration of binding and paper is provided by Groban and Lowe (1982), who base it on their experiences working in publishing. In a text characterized by its insights into many matters about picture books, Nodelman (1988) provides as perceptive a section on paper quality as is available anywhere. His ideas about the distancing which occurs when a book designer chooses a glossy paper help us see the role of paper choice as critical.

Old Mother Hubbard
Went to the cupboard,
To give her poor dog a bone,
(New Century Schoolbook)

Old Mother Hubbard
Went to the cupboard,
To give her poor dog a bone,
(HelveticaNarrow)

Old Mother Hubbard
Went to the cupboard,
To give her poor dog a bone,
(Universe)

Old Mother Hubbard
Went to the cupboard,
To give her poor dog a bone,
(Times Roman)

Close observation of the text types will reveal subtle differences. Take one letter and compare its form in the five samples. How are the a forms, the *w* forms, or the *g* forms the same or different?

Display faces often have unusual shapes that will attract and hold readers' attention. Display faces are used on the title page and for chapter and section headings in longer books. Since fewer words are set in display faces than in text faces, readability is not the prime consideration. When selecting a display face, the book designer searches for a type that will reflect the tone or enhance the message of the book.

Children in Literature
(Bellvue)

Children in Literature
(Tekton)

Children in Literature
(Falstaff)

Children in Literature
(Helvetica Black)

CHILDREN IN LITERATURE
(STENCIL)

CHILDREN IN LITERATURE
(BEE/KNEE/)

Compare the letter forms of the display types above, noting ways they are alike or different. Can you make any inferences about the reasons why a book designer might choose one or another of these typefaces?

All typefaces are categorized either serif or sans serif (without serif). Serif letters have short extensions off the extremities of the basic letter forms, as in the first, third and fifth examples of display faces above. Sans serif letters, however, are unadorned; the lines forming each letter just end, with no flourish, as in the second, fourth and last examples.

Serif: Children in Literature

Sans serif: Children in Literature

Recently, aware of interest in such matters, more publishers have been including information about technical aspects of book production. Often included on the copyright page, readers now can frequently learn the name of the typeface used, and sometimes even the size of type.

Some children's books utilize reproductions of hand-lettering rather than being set in type. Hand-lettering adds to the cost of a book's production, but is sometimes considered worth it for the diversity it brings. One example is found in the works of Wanda Gag, who hand-lettered her enduringly popular *Millions of Cats (See illustration on the next page.)*, as well as her other picture books. In *Panda*, artist Susan Bonners uses soft-edged watercolor, dark and very wet looking, to portray the life cycle of a young cub. The text is hand-lettered in a precise fashion that gives it the look of print.

As mentioned earlier in this chapter, Jean de Brunhoff wrote the text to *The Story of Babar* in script (cursive or connected writing),

Serif

A serif is "the short finishing stroke set across or projecting from the end of a letter stem," according to Geoffrey Glaister in *An Encyclopedia of the Book*. This book includes many terms, arranged alphabetically, related to paper making, printing, bindings, and publishing.

For more information

Gag is one of many authors and illustrators whose brief biographies are included in Carpenter and Prichard, 1984.

Figure 5.8: Millions of Cats
One of the oldest pieces included in this book, like the *The Tale of Peter Rabbit* by Beatrix Potter, this is truly a classic work for children. Also like the Potter, this book is considerably smaller in scale than the lavish, four-color, and over-sized books we're used to today. But use this with your young viewers who will delight in the just-right conclusion to the story, after they've enjoyed saying the repeated refrain with you.

They took the kitten into the house, where the very old woman gave it a warm bath and brushed its fur until it was soft and shiny.

which is used in children's books even less often than hand-lettering, though children enjoy the challenge of reading the script.

Paul Cox, in *The Riddle of the Floating Island*, also uses cursive hand lettering, and like de Brunhoff, presents this in an oversized format ($10^{1}/4$"x $14^{1}/4$"). One of three books in a series originally published in France, "The Adventures of Archibald the Koala on Rastepappe Island," tells simple adventure stories about a group of koalas and a group of badgers living in the tropics. In *The Case of the Botched Book*, the author experiments even more extensively with hand-lettered text, using both cursive and manuscript. Within the manuscript samples included in the book which forms a story within a story, several different styles including variation of letter form and size are used. In another interesting parallel, the art in the three books is done in a naive style reminiscent of de Brunhoff's art.

If a book designer decides that a book should be set in a conventional typeface, he or she then must specify the type size and placement. Typefaces come in different sizes, called points. There are 72 points in an inch. Points are used to measure both the size of typefaces and the space between lines of type. Some picture books for beginning readers feature type that is thirty-six points high, but books for mature readers may use type that is one-third that size or smaller.

One, two three, four… (12 pt.)

One, two three, four… (18 pt.)

One, two three, … (24pt)

Sometimes a book designer varies the type size to make a particular visual point. In Gene Baer's *THUMP, THUMP, Rat-a-Tat-Tat*, for example, the type size grows from the beginning of the book to the middle, and then becomes smaller again. This reflects the marching band coming nearer to the audience (the book reader) and moving away. As the sound made by a band would seem to grow louder, so the type size increases to suggest that. Lois Ehlert's illustrations show the same increase in size of objects. On the first page, the marchers nearest the viewer are only $1^1/2$" high, while on the double-page spread in the middle of the book where they are nearest us, they are so large that only their heads and torsos fit on the $8^3/4$"-high page.

In Glen Rounds' book, *Three Little Pigs and the Big Bad Wolf*, type size is varied to emphasize the drama of the words. For example, with the line: "He HUFFED and he PUFFED and he BLEW the little pig's house in," the important words are done all in capital letters, which emphasizes them. In addition, in the following line, "And then he ate the little pig!" the sentence is set in 42-point type, which is dramatically bigger than the 18-point type used for the preceding sentence.

You might look with children at the uses of type in Maira Kalman's *Max Makes a Million*. The dust jacket, cover, and title page feature a purposely crude hand lettering, while the interior pages are marked by type going this way and that, set in straight lines, curving lines, zigzag lines. At times the blocks of type are set flush left, while at other times they follow a shape in the illustration. On the second opening, for example, the words are shaped so that the outside letters form the shape of the Eiffel tower, a landmark in Paris where the story is set. Most children won't make that association, and it isn't mentioned in the text; but it shows the sort of visually sophisticated playing with type placement the artist does in the book. In addition, the size varies: where the word screeches is set, the word begins with a very small letter, and each succeeding letter increases in size. Kalman

Activity

There are many picture book editions of "The House that Jack Built," which the one with pictures by Emily Bolam identifies as having first been published over two hundred years ago, with roots in the oral tradition far earlier still. Her purposely blocky illustrations with repeated patterns but little fine detail, are done in highly saturated colors which vibrate against each other. You could help children compare these with the collages by Jenny Stow done in multimedia with transparencies achieved by rubbing and sponging, in a version set in the Caribbean.

continues this playful experimentation with where and how type is placed in *Max in Hollywood, Baby*, in which dog-poet Max and his new wife Crepes Suzette heed the call to go West to make a film. The many references to the people and places of this environment will probably be funnier to adults than to children.

The amount of white space between the lines of type is controlled by the *leading*. Originally, pieces of lead of different heights were used to determine the space between lines of hand-set type. Today, this spacing is controlled by computer, but it is still called leading. The amount of white space between lines (together with the width of the margins) determines whether the page will have an open, airy look or a tight, compressed appearance.

To help children understand many of these concepts, presented in an easily accessible, and attractive picture book format, use Cathryn Falwell's *The Letter Jesters* with a class. The imaginative playing with type faces which she does will intrigue children; the book itself requires no previous knowledge. Particularly useful as a way to initiate a unit of study on type and its place in book design with intermediate age children.

Page layout

Where the type is placed on the page is another important design consideration. In some children's books, the type occurs in the same place on every page; in some, it is placed in the same relative position on alternate pages. For example, in *All the Way Home*, by Lore Segal, a pleasant, cream-colored paper sets off James Marshall's humorous three-color illustrations of a parade of caterwauling animals which follow a girl and her mother home. The illustrations are formally placed on the right-hand pages, surrounded by a colored border, and the type always appears on the left-hand pages, adding to the book's predictable progression. This story is a literary cumulative tale meaning that characters or action are added in sequence and it was written by an identifiable author. It is interesting because of its similarity to folk cumulative tales like "The House That Jack Built," which have the same general additive form but are from the oral tradition and have no one identifiable author.

In *The Wreck of the Zephyr*, author/illustrator Chris Van Allsburg uses a similar, very consistent format. The pictures are always on the right page of the opening, facing a block of type of the left page, always bordered with two fine rules (or lines), placed very closely together, the outside one larger than the inside one.

In some books, the type is placed in a variety of locations. In *Parade*, by Tom Shactman, the type appears above and below as well as to the left and right of the full-color photographs. In addition, the type is placed on both left-hand and right-hand pages, presenting more variety than is evident in other books.

Picture book designers must also decide where to place the illustrations. Several types of page placement are possible. In some cases, the designer simply puts one picture on each page. The entire picture is contained on the page, creating a particular effect. Wanda Gag, who illustrated most of her own work, uses this placement technique. *Gone is Gone* is a petite book meant for sharing with a single listener, in which Gag tells the whimsical story of an old man who wants to swap jobs with his wife.

The illustrations for *The Princess and the Froggie*, three short tales for very young children, by Harve and Kaethe Zemach, are examples of self-contained pictures. Margot Zemach, a U.S. nominee for the Hans Christian Andersen Medal, provided pleasant pastel sketches, located below or above brief lines of type and surrounded by generous white margins. Each picture, which generally has a minimal background and no border, can stand alone.

Sometimes the illustrator places the picture within a formal frame, a device that Dooley (1980) identifies as one of the oldest conventions in book art. Dooley examines frames, visual points-of-view, and captioning as options available to artists. She opens with a consideration of various framing devices, including formal ones such as curtains or stage architecture, parts of the picture itself, and decorative frames. In framing a picture, an artist calls special attention to its boundaries, creating in the process a more formal effect than when a picture is bled to the page edge.

Derek Collard creates a somber effect in his detailed linoleum cuts for the highly original *The Squirrel Wife*, by Philippa Pearce. Collard's brown leaf-and-flower border is printed on light brown paper. On some pages, the border sets off a full page of type; on others, it frames complex illustrations reminiscent of the Norwegian expressionist painter Edward Munch.

Geometric and curvilinear plantlike forms are combined in the imaginative frame for the illustrations in *Whinnie the Lovesick Dragon*, by Mercer Mayer. Artist Diane Dawson Hearn

About the artist

A lot of real-life characters described in Self-Portrait: Margot Zemach *turn out to look very similar to the fictional characters in the artist's illustrations for her books. These are homey, somewhat dumpy, but charming characters.*

About the artist

There is more historic detail in Eggum's (1984) book about Munch than most teachers and librarians will need. Nonetheless, the large, full-color reproductions show clearly the design qualities which distinguish this artist's work.

has breached the frame in a variety of ways. For example, one character rests his elbows on it; another lifts a leg to crawl over it; on one page a boy holding a flag actually becomes part of the frame.

Jan Brett is an artist who consistently employs pictorial borders to provide additional information which augments the details included in her realistic illustrations. In *Annie and the Wild Animals*, for instance, she depicts the story of the young child, despondent over the apparent loss of her pet cat, Taffy, who tries to attract another pet to replace the cat. *(See illustration on page 77.)* Sometimes the double-page spreads aren't divided in the middle while on other openings two separate pictures are each framed separately. The borders on the sides tend to be narrow, and primarily decorative. Throughout, borders on top and bottom of pages are wider (about an inch in depth) and show miniature scenes related but not central to the main action of the story. Even in these smaller border vignettes, Brett's penchant for realistic detail is apparent.

A different kind of framing is present in *The Story of Chicken Licken*, by Jan Ormerod, a book in which the entire story is recreated by child actors in costume, watched by an audience presented in silhouette. Above, the performers on stage are in full-color costumes, their words in cartoon-strip balloons. Below, the silhouettes making up the audience vary on each page, so a continuing "story" develops there, too. Children may need to look at these illustrations more than once to perceive the dual stories. This presentation is an effective way of framing the pictures, even though there is no all-around border.

Sometimes borders don't completely surround a picture, but rather underline and cap a set of illustrations. In *The Honey Hunters* by Francesca Martin, a retelling of a tale from the Ngoni people of Africa, this artist paints watercolor borders that frame three sides of the first opening. The right side is unbordered, directing the eye to the following spread. All the succeeding spreads have borders running only along the top and bottom. On the final spread, the eye follows along to the border which is now on the right edge, stopping the action visually that the text has also concluded.

For more information

For a more extended analysis of silhouette in children's book illustration, see Cleaver (1990).

Activity

You might look with children at the use Ormerod makes of silhouette in The Story of Chicken Licken, *and then examine how it is used in Mitsumasa Anno's* In Shadowland. *Full-color pages face pages of silhouette (both bordered in bands of different color and width); in some cases the sharp patterns of the silhouettes are punctuated with small painted details.*

Double spreads

The book designer may spread an illustration across facing pages, creating a double-page spread, which has two advantages. First a double-page spread enhances the dimensions established by the book's shape. For example, a double-page spread in a book with a horizontal rectangular shape makes that rectangle wider, changing its proportions dramatically. In *Two Hundred Rabbits*, by Lonzo Anderson, Adrienne Adams used soft, sometimes transparent watercolor to create serene, pastoral landscapes and richly detailed court scenes for the story in which a young boy tries to think up a way to entertain the king. (The rabbit narrator finally helps solve the boy's problem.) In several places, the illustrations extend all the way across the 19-inch double-page spread, with the type arranged below.

The second advantage offered by the double-page spread is that it allows the artist to use both vertical and horizontal pictures in one book. For example, in *George's Garden*, by Gerda Marie Scheidl, illustrator Bernadette Watts fully utilizes the potential of the book's shape, which is a vertical rectangle. On some pages, upright pictures stretch the full height (almost 12 inches). This height is particularly effective, for example, for the picture showing the high wall separating the two gardens. In other cases, pictures extend horizontally across two pages, for a width of more than 16 inches. This layout allows Watts plenty of space in the picture showing the variety of birds, animals, and flowers in George's garden.

There is an intrinsic bookmaking problem with double-page spreads, however. The place where two facing pages come together is called the gutter and careful bookmaking is necessary to ensure that the two halves of an illustration match up exactly across this division. The designer must take into account the portion that will disappear into the binding when the pages are sewn together. Children have a clear eye for detail and will notice any missing parts or misalignment in pictures that extend across the gutter. In fact, Lacy points out that there is one spread in *Make Way for Ducklings* by Robert McCloskey in which the gutter wasn't adequately considered: as a consequence, there are "just seven babies to waddle along behind Mrs. Mallard."[5] It is a single flaw in an otherwise rightly classic book. The illustrator and book designer must weigh the gains of using double-page spreads against the added problem presented by this arrangement.

An even more significant problem is apparent in Anne Wilsdorf's *Princess*, a modernized takeoff on Hans Christian Andersen's "The Princess and the Pea." Prince Leopold sets off to find his wife in a pleasantly splashy array of watercolor and pen line drawings, of varying sizes and placements on the page. Problems become apparent on opening four, where the fire coming from the horn of the "ferocious antiseptyx" is partially lost in the gutter. But the disadvantage of this page layout is critical on the sixth opening, where the princess being threatened by the bombachyderm charges directly into the gutter so that her arm and hand seem to be coming out of her head, which has lost most of its profile. Certainly a slight mismatch of a mountain top is less critical than losing a foot, as this princess does. In all, one might expect more capable planning from such an experienced illustrator as Wilsdorf.

Careful bookmaking can minimize the problems inherent in double-page spreads. For example, in *The Moon's Choice* by John Warren Stewig, artist Jan Palmer does watercolor illustrations of the Italian countryside which include many thin brown lines defining the shapes of the mountains, trees, and lakes. These require an exact match, which was achieved in the copy of the book used for this description. Similarly, on the scenic endpapers, there is a large brick bridge, the two halves of which must match exactly, for the illustration to be convincing. This tale, which dates back to a print version of 1885, centers on three sisters; the youngest is the most beautiful, in a motif reminiscent of "Cinderella."

Leo and Diane Dillon, in art for *The Tale of the Mandarin Ducks* by Katherine Paterson, devised another way of dealing with the problem of the gutter. In this retelling of a popular Japanese folktale, human greed contrasts with the wild creature's desire for freedom. These are indeed double-page spreads, rather than independent pictures on two facing pages. That is, the action and characters shown on the left page are depicted in the same location and at the same time as those on the right page. However, rather than running the single picture across the double spread, the Dillons simply stop the picture, allowing a white margin at the gutter to divide the picture into two parts. As in the style of the art, in this acceptance of the gutter, the Dillons were using solutions developed by the earlier ukiyo-e woodcut.

Instead of containing the illustration totally within the page area, book designers sometimes use another type of placement, called a *bleed*, in which the illustration extends all the way to the edge of the page and then seems to fall off of it. Placing illustrations in this manner can be very effective. Sometimes the bleeds are so unobtrusive that they are almost unnoticeable. *Bang Bang You're Dead*, by Louise Fitzhugh and Sandra Scoppettone, is illustrated in black line with much cross-hatching to create realistically shaded boys with exaggeratedly homely faces. The pictures sometimes extend off the page, but what bleeds off is not of any real significance to the pictures. Parts of a room, rocks, and tree branches extend off the edge, but the figures of the characters are usually contained on the page.

Other artists make more noticeable use of bleeding. In *While the Horses Galloped to London*, by Mable Watts, illustrator Mercer Mayer had the illustrations bleed off the page, which creates a sense of people being jammed into a carriage. The fussiness of the ink line and the close-up view taken by the illustrator increase the effect of crowdedness in these pictures.

Even more innovative use of bleeds was made by Caldecott Award winner Ezra Jack Keats in his bold, colorful, thickly-painted illustrations for *The King's Fountain*, written by Lloyd Alexander. All the pictures bleed off the page, and often only parts of the characters are contained on the page. Several illustrations show just the characters' torsos and heads. For example, the fifth opening shows three merchants in a warm beige-and-brown close-up painting; the tops of their heads are cut off by the page edge. The same is true on the next opening, a picture of the metalsmith, the top of whose head and lower body are cut off. Keats's technique is reminiscent of that used by such French painters as Edgar Degas and Henri de Toulouse-Lautrec, who often included only part of a figure or object within the frame of a painting. Doing so allowed these artists to focus on the momentary, or transitory nature of people and actions they depicted. There's another way in which some of these paintings are similar to those of Toulouse-Lautrec. On the seventh opening, notice that the figures in the back standing in the door are fully painted, while those near the front of the picture plane are done in silhouette. Toulouse-Lautrec sometimes painted closer figures in a flat color, without detail, showing them cast in shadows contrasting with the theatrical lighting he often used.

You could help children study Lautrec's work, using the volume titled with his name, in the "Art Start" series by Ernest

For more information

In a bleed the illustration is actually printed slightly larger than the final page size. When the paper is trimmed to the page size, so is the illustration. This effect is described with clarity by Henry C. Pitz in Illustrating Children's Books.

Raboff. This fine series features large, full-color reproductions of each artist's work. An accompanying text tells enough background detail so children can learn to look at what is on the page, but doesn't overwhelm them with facts and dates. Full color, nearly page-size illustrations help children *Meet Edgar Degas* in a book by Anne Newlands. The few paragraphs of text describing each picture are written as if by Degas himself.

Some books show a variety of page placements. In *One Monster After Another*, Mercer Mayer at times contains his aggressive, crowded illustrations within a black-line edge, surrounded by a white border. In other places, the picture is bounded on the bottom by a black line but spills off the top and sides. In still other places, no border at all contains the picture, which simply takes the space of the objects in it.

Lorna Balian used a very consistent bleed-off approach to the double-page spreads in her *Humbug Rabbit*. The trees on either

Figure 5.9: Humbug Rabbit
The many small details, i.e., tree leaves and roots, depicted in the book itself in delicate pastel colors, link this work visually with some of the art of Barbara Cooney. For example, in her illustrations for *The Year of the Perfect Christmas Tree* by Gloria Houston, we see similar design qualities. Or, look at this art in the context of Cooney's pictures for *Only Opal. The Diary of a Young Girl* to see the visual similarities.

The Rabbit children have discovered the Easter eggs!

Color Plates

This section contains all color plates discussed in chapters 1–6. The page numbers in the captions here indicate the location of the descriptive caption and textual material about the illustration, artist or genre. A black and white portion of each illustration has been included with the text to serve as a quick reference to the color plates.

Plate 1: Crafty Chameleon. By Mwenye Hadithi, illustrations by Adrienne Kennaway. (p. 10)

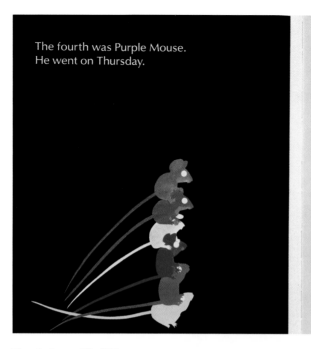
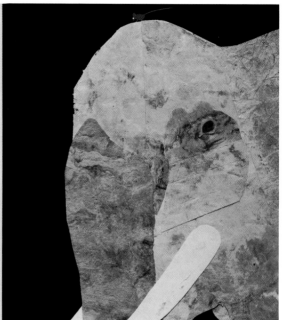

Plate 2: Seven Blind Mice. By Ed Young. (p. 46)

Plate 3: The Nightingale. Translated by Eva le Gallienne, illustrations by Nancy Ekholm Burkert. (p. 53)

Plate 4: Zoo. By Anthony Browne. (p. 66)

Plate 5: Abuela. By Arthur Dorros, illustrations by Elisa Kleven. (p. 85)

Plate 6: Lunch. By Denise Fleming. (p. 122)

Plate 7: Greyling. By Jane Yolen, illustrations by David Ray. (p. 132)

Plate 8: Planting a Rainbow. By Lois Ehlert. (p. 147)

Plate 9: Black & White. By David Macaulay. (p. 175)

Plate 10: Stevie. By John L. Steptoe. (p. 202)

Plate 11: Mufaro's Beautiful Daughters. By John L. Steptoe. (p. 202)

But it is mute.
It never speaks.
It listens.
It comes sliding right up
behind the storyteller.
Then when the last fire is out
it goes back to the forest.

Plate 12: Shadow. Translated and illustrated by Marcia Brown. (p. 216)

side of the spreads serve as a frame. But what makes this interesting is the double story Balian tells, by dividing her spreads in half horizontally. Above, she shows us the tale of Granny, troubled because she can't find the eggs her hen Gracie lays; she wants to use them for her grandchildren's Easter egg hunt. Below, in a cutaway view showing Father and Mother Rabbit's burrow, we see the parallel story of the five rabbit children, convinced their father is the Easter Bunny, despite his insistent, reiterated denials. It is Barnaby, "that devilish cat," who makes everything, albeit inadvertently, turn out all right. The device of the cutaway view on the lower half of the pictures is a clever way to make it possible for the viewer to enjoy both stories simultaneously.

It would be useful with children to compare Balian's book with Arlene Mosel's retelling of a Japanese tale, *The Funny Little Woman*, which predates Balian's use of the horizontal page split by two years. In this story, an old woman falls through her kitchen floor into underground caverns, and there continues to hunt for her run-away dumpling, in a motif similar to the Gingerbread Boy. Blair Lent pictured the main character's adventures below ground in watercolors; the goings-on above ground at the same time are depicted in smaller, black-line drawings.

Perhaps the most perplexing page layout for librarians and teachers to understand and use with children is that found in David Macaulay's *Black and White*, which won the Caldecott Award and was named an American Library Association Notable Book. A complex interlocking of four related stories, this splits each double-page opening into quarters. A reader-viewer can select, for example, the upper right quarter, and follow just that story on each page until the conclusion, then returning to the front of the book to select another story to follow. Or, readers can try to read and follow the four separate strands on each opening in succession. Each of the four stories is quite different, not only in illustration but even in type face used. "Seeing Things" is done in very loosely applied watercolor, without an appreciable use of line. "Problem Parents" is done in a much tighter style, including a determinedly constraining pen line, with a limited array of brown tones, black, and white. "A Waiting Game" is done using a broader range of colors and also includes line but a less determined one than in "Parents." Finally, "Udder Chaos" uses a more abstract style of shapes defined without line.

Plate 9: Black and White

Illustrators have often explored ways to break up space on a page. Ann Jonas (in *Round Trip*) and Lorna Balian (in *Humbug Rabbit*) are examples included elsewhere in this book. But that space breakup has usually served a single, connected story. Here, Macaulay does something quite different. Because these appear to be four different stories, presented in apparently different visual styles, we as viewers must look for connections. In what ways do these four pieces of art seem related to you? (*See full illustration in color plates following page 174.*)

About the book

Paley (1992) has described what he sees in Black and White.

About the artist

A broader consideration of Macaulay's body of work is provided by Cobb (1992).

It's a book which needs careful examination, several times. For instance, on the tenth opening, what had been four compartmentalized stories is suddenly breached when the word-flakes from "Seeing Things" (top left) begin to float down into "Problem Parents" (bottom left). The established organization dissolves completely on the 13th opening, when everything turns black and white only. On the last double spread, the expected arrangement is reestablished. To what end? We probably won't agree on the reasons for this and other perplexities in the book. And, if we believe Macaulay's own description of the book, it isn't important that we do. What he has made us do is study this with more care than we need to give to other, more easily accessible books. For he is concerned that children understand "it is essential to see, not merely to look" and that thinking doesn't necessarily need to take place "in a straight line to make sense."[6]

We might think that page layout is too esoteric a topic for children, but Crago and Crago (1983) have commented on this. In a longitudinal, naturalistic study of their child Anna's immersion in picture books, they record her development in relation to entire books, to visual elements like color, and to design features like layout. Details in their anecdotal journals of her development suggest to them her "incipient awareness of page layout" as early as three years. If children this young do respond in ways which suggest they are aware of layout, surely some conscious attention to it in school settings can enhance their ability to respond.

Construction details

Though most adults might think of books as having flat pages to be turned, book designers and paper engineers have in fact experimented with a variety of ways to transcend the inherent two-dimensional quality of book pages. One of the ways is through a variety of paper engineering techniques.

Popup books

Using a heavier grade of paper (or indeed, thin cardboard), paper engineers fold, crease, glue together, and attach with a variety of tabs, pieces which, when the page is opened in some way, move out of the flat position in which they are folded to create dimensionality. These may be quite simple constructions, as found in "Marc Brown's Play Pops" series in his *Can You Jump*

Like a Frog? Each double-page spread opens to show, for example, the gull's wings moving, the duck's foot lifting, and other animal movements. In a small format (5¼"x 6¾"), these usually contain only one or two moving parts.

At the other end of the scale are such books as *Looking Into the Middle Ages* by Huck Scarry, in which when one of the double spreads is opened, an entire medieval castle rises up in three dimensional accuracy. In another opening, a cathedral is depicted in four different depths, and one can literally start at the front of the page, turn the book to view one side, turn again to look at the rear of the building (also printed in full-color detail), and continue the final turn to look at the fourth side of the cathedral. This is so cleverly constructed that we get both inside and outside views of the building. This is one of several picture books recommended by Greenlaw (1988) as appropriate for use in middle school.

Two non-story books make exemplary use of popup construction. *A is for Animals* by David Pelham is a trip through the alphabet with popup animals behind each of 26 different flaps to be lifted. Each large, vertical rectangle, double-page spread contains four smaller flaps. What pops up varies in complexity: behind the *G* (for giraffe) flap, only the animal's head and neck move, while behind the *A* (for animals) flap, nine animals move into position in a clump of grass. In a much larger format, Jan Pienkowski's *ABC Dinosaurs* uses several real dinosaurs (phonetic pronunciations included) with imaginative, highly colored popups of the beasts, incorporating the letter of their name as part of the design. After the page is opened and the dinosaurs have popped up, there are additional flaps to be lifted, and tabs to be pulled, showing other things. This was included as part of the American Bookseller Pick of the Lists.

In Kees Moerbeek's *New at the Zoo 2*, the popups are either (fairly) realistic, or imaginary, depending on how the pages are turned. Each page is split in half horizontally as well as fitted with popup components. When both halves of the pages are turned in regular, consecutive order, they reveal actual animals, like an owl (first opening). However, if either the top or the bottom of the page is flipped, imaginary animals are created. If the top of the owl page is flipped but not the bottom, we see a "rabl" (combining owl and rabbit). If the bottom of the owl page is flipped but not the top, we get "owbit."

For more information

Other recent examples of popup book construction were reviewed by Cooper (1991).

Activity

For teachers interested in having children try making their own popups, Irvine (1992) is a useful reference.

Lift the flap, or pull the tab

In other books children lift a flap to reveal what has been printed beneath. *January Brings the Snow*, based on a poem by the British poet, Sara Coleridge, features art by Elizabeth Falconer. The left-page, bordered illustration shows the human children doing something seasonal, while on each right facing page there is a tab to be lifted, showing the mouse family also doing something seasonal. Lifting the sled shows the mice making a snowman, opening the side of the barn shows the mice dying Easter eggs, while opening the hollow in the tree shows the mice donning their Halloween costumes.

Marie Angel, in her *Woodland Christmas*, combined the lift the flap feature with an accordion fold construction. The pages are not conventionally bound but rather are so constructed that as they unfold in fan arrangement, they make one long accordion panel, which is indeed printed on both sides of the heavy cardboard used. Each of the small, numbered panels lifts to reveal some other, intricately detailed small vignette of animal life during December. For another example of an accordion fold, look at Rick Brown's cartoon illustrations for *Old MacDonald Had a Farm* with flat colors contained with a pervasive black line. The large size makes the book appropriate for group sharing: when unfolded, the panel extends to a full 80 inches.

At other times, readers pull a tab which activates some sort of movement. *Dinner With Fox* combines popup and pull tab construction. Korky Paul's pictures show Fox looking into his cupboard door for something to eat when one opens the double-page spread. The popup is effectively done in three dimensions. On another page, when one pulls the tab, Fox slams shut his oven door. The book also includes lift the flap construction, as when readers open the door, Red Fox, come visiting, is revealed. The paper engineering is quite detailed: when we open Pink Pig's mailbox, we can lift out the separate piece of paper which is Fox's note of invitation.

This idea of a container, holding another piece of paper to be lifted out and read, was actually originated earlier than Paul's book, by Janet and Allan Ahlberg, in *The Jolly Postman or Other People's Letters*. This charming fantasy strings together different storybook characters, each of whom receives a letter or post card from another character in their story. For example, the three bears receive a letter of apology from Goldilocks. The letter is done in childlike drawings and script, replete with misspellings, and after the text introduces the idea of the letter, the reader lifts it out of its "envelope" to read it. The clever text is enhanced by the varying formats, i.e., the witch in Hansel and Gretel receives a flyer advertising the products from Hobgoblin Supplies Ltd., and the giant gets a postcard from Jack, off on holiday spending the proceeds of his thefts, among other equally imaginative ideas.

Revolving wheels

In another kind of construction detail, a wheel is inserted between two pages which are then glued together. A small cut-out piece of page or a movable tab makes it possible to turn the internal wheel, revealing in holes cut into the paper whatever was printed in different places on the inside wheel. Linda Weller's pictures for *A Turn and Learn Book. Colors* is an example. On each page we begin with one large illustration of Panda painting the color named on the page. When the tab turns the wheel, we see five smaller illustrations of objects of that color.

Sliding panels

Some artists make use of sliding panels, as Stephen Savage did in his *Making Tracks*. Before the tabs are pulled to move the panels, the pages, constructed of thin cardboard with several die-cut holes evident, don't reveal visually the content described in the text. When the tab is pulled, it moves another thin piece of cardboard inserted between the pages, to reveal the animal and to show its tracks in color.

Toy books

Often today books go even further toward crossing the line from being conventional books into becoming toys which can be played with. *Mouse in the House* by Lizi Boyd is an effective example. This comes with a $7^3/4$"-square cardboard book which unfolds along a central spine to reveal, not individual pages of the kind we're used to, but rather four connected rooms (with openings between); two of these when tied together with a ribbon make this unit into a completely three-dimensional "house." Included in the package is a three dimensional felt mouse and an assortment of felt squares which can be cut to make clothes for the mouse. Directions for how to do this are provided in a small booklet which also gives suggestions for furnishings made of found objects. The two dimensional art is outlined in simple black lines yielding symbolic art appropriate for the intended preschool audience.

Involving children in studying book design elements

Details of physical format are important to book designers, to teachers and librarians who share books with children, and, eventually, to the children themselves. When adults share books with children, they can call attention to such details as an interesting paper color, a striking typeface, or an unusual page layout. There is no need to talk at length about these details; casual comments made incidentally over a period of time will make children aware that a book is more than just the story.

We can also heighten children's awareness of physical format by asking incidental questions such as the following when sharing a book with children:

1. Did you notice the paper in this book? Feel it with your fingertips, and think of a word or words which tell how the paper feels.

2. Where have you seen a color like the one in this endpaper? What does this color suggest to you about the kind of story that may be in this book?

3. Did you notice the letters used for the title of this book? Based on the typeface, what ideas do you have about the kind of person the main character is?

4. Where are the illustrations placed on the pages in this book? Can you think of a book in which the illustrations were placed in another way? Why is there a difference in where the illustrations are placed?

Comparing variant editions

An interesting experience for children would be to examine books available in two different sizes, so they can think about how this affects their reaction to the book. For example, Eric Carle's *The Very Hungry Caterpillar* is available in a conventional size ($11^3/4$"x $8^1/2$"), but it was also issued in a diminutive (5"x $3^3/4$") size. The sweeping effect of the art work is very different in the larger format than in the smaller one.

Though most of the art is the same, there are some subtle differences which children could be helped to notice. For example, on the second opening, the face of the sun has been redone (both the eyes and the mouth are different), and on the last opening, the designs in the butterfly's wings are different. Throughout the book there are some subtle color differences in the two print runs, which children could observe.

In the same way, Carle's *The Mixed-Up Chameleon* is available in a larger size ($8^1/4$"x $11^1/4$") vertical rectangle, with a subsequent publication of a miniature ($3^3/4$"x 5") edition. In addition to the color run differences, it is interesting to note that on the first two openings of the miniature edition, the type is set in different line lengths than in the larger book.

Studying book details

Earlier in this chapter, Graham Percy's illustrated version of four fables was recommended. You might examine with the children *The Tortoise and the Hare and Other Favorite Fables* and then over several days look at the same fables as included in *Anno's Aesop*. Children could, with your help, compile two charts, identifying ways the books are the same and how they are different. This might focus on:

1. *The nature of the art itself* (Anno uses watercolor to create mostly flat shapes, while Percy uses crayon to create more three dimensional shapes).

2. *The page placement* (Anno incorporates text into the space including the art, and also places it below the pictures, while Percy always faces the art with a block of text on the left page).

3. *Construction details* (Anno includes many tales in one large book, while Percy binds the four tales in separate, tiny books).

After children do this sort of comparing of different editions, they can be encouraged to tell or write which they prefer. Which of the two mentioned would most children like better? That is always difficult for adults to tell, so the way to make sure is to ask children themselves. Groups might find one or the other of these two preferable, or they might be drawn to:

1. The scratchy pen drawings overlaid on watercolor wash by Paul Galdone in his *Three Aesop Fox Fables*. The tall rectangular shape provides ample vertical space for the unbordered, informal art.

2. The realistically-detailed black etchings printed on sepia backgrounds with Arthur Geisert did for *Aesop and Company* by Barbara Bader. The introductory material on Aesop will be useful to teachers, though children may enjoy these drawings, done in a variety of different shapes and sizes.

3. John Hejduk's boldly abstracted shapes which revel in repeated flat patterning, to create a bright, flat world of unrealistic design. The morals are always set apart from the rest of the text and accompanied with a fragment of design repeated from the facing picture page.

4. The elegantly realistic, elaborately bordered formal illustrations by Heidi Holder, done in soft pastels with a pervasive sepia influence. The decorated capital letters used for the first word of each fable repeat design elements from the pictures.

5. Claire Littlejohn's three dimensional art in a book which features both pull tabs and popup features, all softly stroked with crayon color.

6. Minutely detailed, realistic animals shown by Robert Rayevsky for an edition of the fables retold in verse by Tom Paxton. These double spreads push to the page edge; brown tones predominate, brightened by cheerful reds.

Studying book production

Children are intrigued with the processes involved in producing a picture book. The most ideal way to learn about this is through a field trip to a production facility, but that often isn't possible. As an alternative, there are books which describe this process; using one of these will help children become more aware of the complexity of modern picture book production.

From *Picture to Picture Book*, by Ali Mitgutsch, is from the publisher's "Start to Finish" series, designed for young children. It begins when the artist, shown in the full-color, full-page illustrations facing the text pages, has an idea. The process is followed through days of sketching and painting the ideas, conferring with the editor, photographing the art, producing four color plates, printing, binding, and selling the book in a bookstore. Finally the book is enjoyed by a father and his son. It is all an easily understood, charming look at an unfamiliar process. There are some problems involved. For example: there's no mention made of any editing of the manuscript, and the printing process is oversimplified to the point children may think individual sheets of paper are printed, rather than large sheets which are then trimmed to become individual ones. Nonetheless, as an introduction this is admirable.

For slightly older children, *How a Book is Made* by Aliki, an IRA Children's Choice award winner, stresses that many people are involved in this process, a feature missing in the Mitgutsch book. This includes description of the work of such people as the designer, the production director, the color separator, and others. It even distinguishes between the publisher and the editor. As an author-illustrated book, this shows the process of creating a dummy and the finished artwork. It deals with technicalities of storing text in a computer, and using a typesetting machine with a typestyle disc. The page on color separation is much more complete than in the Mitgutsch book as appropriate for older readers. There's even a diagram showing the inside of a four-color offset printing press. Some of the information is more technical than may interest readers: how side sewing is different than other ways to sew the signatures isn't easy to understand. Nonetheless, Aliki's thoroughness and accuracy is a plus in this presentation. The book even details the fact that there are problems to be solved: i.e., one of the small cartoon drawings shows the editor asking the author: "Do you think this word is clear?" Another: the production schedule is "delayed because of the holidays." When the staff is checking the proofs, the production director notes: "The red doesn't match the art. Let's add some yellow." In all, a very satisfactory introduction, for upper intermediate or middle school readers, to a process that most of them won't know first hand. Aliki's brightly-colored cartoon illustrations pack each page with a lot of information.

A Book Takes Root by Michael Kehoe is also for upper-intermediate grades or middle school. It starts out by personalizing the topic, as we follow an author, Betsy Thomas, and her desire to write. Full-color photographs on every page follow the process, from author to editor, on to the artwork and the book

Signature
A printed sheet folded in four or a multiple of four, to page size, for binding together to create a book.

designer. Explaining technical processes, like keylining, is carefully done in easy-to-understand terminology, and at times with the process shown in several smaller photographs, rather than the larger ones earlier in the book when the processes involved didn't require more photos. The use of margin headings, and ample white space on the page, help direct the reader to the final stage of children enjoying the book.

In addition to books, there are audiovisual presentations of this content. "The Making of a Storybook," featuring storyteller Mary Calhoun is available from Chip Taylor Communications (15 Spollett Dr., Derry, NH 03038). In addition to materials for children, authors and illustrators write widely about these ideas for teachers and librarians, in articles which will help you better understand this. For example, Halsey (1992) has written about how using a storyboard helps her plan the flow of her books.

Recommended children's books

Adams, Adrienne (Ill.). *Two Hundred Rabbits* by Lonzo Anderson. New York: Viking, 1968.

Aliki. *How a Book is Made*. New York: Thomas Y. Crowell, 1986.

Angel, Marie (Ill.). *The Tale of Tuppenny* by Beatrix Potter. New York: Frederick Warne, 1971.

———. *Woodland Christmas*. New York: Dial Books for Young Readers, 1991.

Anno, Mitsumasa. *Anno's Aesop*. New York: Orchard Books, 1989.

———. *In Shadowland*. New York: Orchard Books, 1988.

Atkinson, Allen (Ill.). *The Tale of Peter Rabbit and Other Stories* by Beatrix Potter. New York: Alfred A. Knopf, 1982.

Babbitt, Natalie. *The Something*. New York: Farrar, Straus and Giroux, 1970.

Balian, Lorna. *Humbug Rabbit*. Nashville: Abingdon, 1974.

Banfill, A. Scott (Ill.). *Whisper from the Woods* by Victoria Wirth. New York: Green Tiger Press, 1991.

Barker, Carol. *Carol Barker's Birds and Beasts*. New York: Franklin Watts, 1971.

Blythe, Gary (Ill.). *The Whale's Song* by Dyan Sheldon. New York: Dial Books for Young Readers, 1991.

Bolam, Emily (Ill.). *The House That Jack Built*. New York: Dutton Children's Books, 1992.

Bonners, Susan. *Panda*. New York: Delacorte, 1978.

Boyd, Lizi. *Mouse in a House*. Boston: Little, Brown and Co., 1993.

Brett, Jan. *Annie and the Wild Animals*. Boston: Houghton Mifflin, 1985.

Britt, Stephanie (Ill.). *The Adventures of Peter Rabbit* by Beatrix Potter. Chicago: Children's Press, 1985.

Brown, Marc. *Can You Jump Like a Frog?* New York: E. P. Dutton, 1989.

Brown, Rick. *Old MacDonald Had a Farm*. New York: Viking, 1993.

Burton, Virginia Lee. *Mike Mulligan and His Steam Shovel*. Boston: Houghton Mifflin, 1939.

Butler, John (Ill.). *Ruff Leaves Home* by Anne Carter. New York: Crown, 1986.

Carle, Eric. *The Grouchy Ladybug*. New York: Thomas Y. Crowell, 1977.

———. *The Very Hungry Caterpillar*. New York: Philomel, 1983; miniature edition, same publisher, 1986.

———. *The Mixed-Up Chameleon*. New York: Harper Trophy, 1988; miniature edition, same publisher, 1991.

Carrier, Lark. *There was a Hill...* Natick, MA: Picture Book Studio, 1985.

Chwast, Seymour. *Tall City, Wide Country. A Book to Read Forward and Backward*. New York: The Viking Press, 1983.

Cleary, Beverly. *Ramona the Pest*. New York: Morrow, 1968.

Coatsworth, Elizabeth. *Under the Green Willow*. New York: Greenwillow, 1984.

Cole, Brock. *The Winter Wren*. New York: Farrar, Straus, and Giroux, 1984.

Collard, Derek (Ill.). *The Squirrel Wife* by Philippa Pearce. New York: Thomas Y. Crowell, 1971.

Conover, Chris. *Sam Panda and the Thunder Dragon*. New York: Farrar Straus and Giroux, 1992.

Cooney, Barbara. *Only Opal. The Diary of a Young Girl*. New York: Philomel Books, 1994.

——— (Ill.). *The Year of the Perfect Christmas Tree* by Gloria Houston. New York: Dial, 1988.

Cousins, Lucy. *Noah's Ark*. Cambridge, MA: Candlewick Press, 1993.

Cox, Paul. *The Case of the Botched Book*. New York: Green Tiger Press, 1992.

———. *The Riddle of the Floating Island*. New York: Green Tiger Press, 1992.

Crews, Donald. *Freight Train*. New York: Greenwillow Books, 1978.

Dabcovich, Lydia. *Sleepy Bear*. New York: E. P. Dutton, 1982.

de Brunhoff, Jean. *The Story of Babar*. New York: Random House, 1984.

———. *The Travels of Babar*. New York: Random House, 1985.

Delacre, Lulu (Ill.). *The Tale of Peter Rabbit and Other Stories* by Beatrix Potter. New York: A Little Simon Book, 1985.

Demi. *Demi's Secret Garden*. New York: Henry Holt and Company, 1993.

Dillon, Leo and Diane (Ills.). *The Tale of the Mandarin Ducks* by Katherine Paterson. New York: Lodestar Books, 1990.

Ehlert, Lois. *Color Farm*. New York: J. B. Lippincott, 1989.

———. *Color Zoo*. New York: J. B. Lippincott, 1990.

———. *Crocodile Beat*. New York: HarperCollins, 1994.

———. *Fish Eyes. A Book You Can Count On*. San Diego: Harcourt Brace Jovanovich, 1990.

———. *Planting a Rainbow*. San Diego: Harcourt Brace Jovanovich, 1988.

————(Ill.). *THUMP, THUMP, Rat-a-Tat Tat* by Gene Baer. New York: Harper Collins, 1989.

Falconer, Elizabeth (Ill.). *January Brings the Snow* by Sara Coleridge. New York: Orchard Books, 1989.

Falwell, Cathryn. *The Letter Jesters*. New York: Ticknor and Fields, 1994.

Fitzhugh, Louise, and Sandra Scoppettone. *Bang Bang You're Dead*. New York: Harper and Row, 1969.

Gag, Wanda. *Gone is Gone*. New York: Coward, McCann, 1935.

————. *Millions of Cats*. New York: Coward, McCann, 1928.

Galdone, Paul. *Three Aesop Fox Fables*. New York: The Seabury Press, 1971.

Galli, Letizia (Ill.). *Inside Noah's Ark* by Laura Fischetto. New York: Viking Kestrel, 1989.

Gammel, Stephen (Ill.). *A Regular Rolling Noah* by George Ella Lyon. New York: Bradbury Press, 1986.

Gannett, Ruth Stiles. *My Father's Dragon*. New York: Random House: 1986.

Geisert, Arthur (Ill.). *Aesop and Company.* by Barbara Bader. Boston: Houghton Mifflin Co., 1991.

Gibbons, Gail. *Up Goes the Skyscraper!* New York: Four Winds, 1986.

Gerstein, Mordicai (Ill.) *The Cataract of Lodore* by Robert Southey. New York: Dial Books for Young Readers, 1991.

Goodall, John. *Paddy to the Rescue*. New York: Atheneum, 1985.

————. *Shrewbettina's Birthday*. New York: Harcourt Brace, 1970.

Grejniec, Michael. *Look*. New York: North-South Books, 1993.

————. *What Do You Like?* New York: North-South Books, 1992.

Hale, Kathleen. *Orlando The Marmalade Cat. A Camping Holiday*. London: Frederick Warne, 1990.

————. *Orlando's Evening Out*. London: Frederick Warne, 1991.

Haley, Gail E. *Jack and the Bean Tree*. New York: Crown Publishers, Inc., 1986.

Hartford, John. *Steamboat in a Cornfield*. New York: Crown, 1986.

Hathon, Elizabeth (Ill.). *Ding Dong! And Other Sounds* by Christine Salac Dubov. New York: Tambourine Books, 1991.

Hearn, Diane Dawson (Ill.). *Winnie the Lovesick Dragon* by Mercer Mayer. New York: Macmillan, 1986.

Hedderwick, Mairi. *Katie Morag and the Tiresome Ted*. Boston: Little, Brown, 1986.

————. *Katie Morag and the Two Grandmothers*. Boston: Little, Brown, 1985.

————. *P.D. Peebles' Summer or Winter Book*. Boston: Little, Brown and Co., 1989.

Hejduk, John (Ill.). *Aesop's Fables*. New York: Rizzoli, 1991.

Hoban, Lillian (Ill.). *Starring First Grade* by Miriam Cohen. New York: Greenwillow, 1985.

Hol, Coby. *Tippy Bear's Christmas*. New York: North-South Books, 1992.

Holder, Heidi (Ill.). *Aesop's Fables*. New York: The Viking Press, 1981.

Jonas, Ann. *Round Trip*. New York: Greenwillow Books, 1983.

Jones, Carol. *Hickory Dickory Dock and Other Nursery Rhymes.* Boston: Houghton Mifflin Company, 1990.

―――. *Old MacDonald Had a Farm.* Boston: Houghton Mifflin Company, 1988.

Kalman, Maira. *Max in Hollywood, Baby.* New York: Penguin Books, 1992.

―――. *Max Makes a Million.* New York: Viking Penguin, 1990.

Keats, Ezra Jack (Ill.). *The King's Fountain* by Lloyd Alexander. New York: E. P. Dutton, 1971.

Kehoe, Michael. *A Book Takes Root. The Making of a Picture Book.* Minneapolis: Carolrhoda Books, Inc., 1993.

Lattimore, Deborah Nourse. *Why There Is No Arguing in Heaven. A Mayan Myth.* New York: Harper and Row, 1989.

Lent, Blair (Ill.). *The Funny Little Woman* by Arlene Mosel. New York: E. P. Dutton, 1972.

Lionni, Leo. *A Color of His Own.* New York: Pantheon, 1975.

Littlejohn, Claire. *Aesop's Fables.* New York: Dial Books for Young Readers, 1988.

Loverance, Rowena, and Tim Wood. *Ancient Greece.* New York: Viking, 1993.

Low, Joseph (Ill.). *Jack and the Beanstalk* by Walter de La Mare. New York: Alfred A. Knopf, 1959.

Lynch, P. J. *East O' the Sun and West O' the Moon,* translated by Sir George Webb Dasent. Cambridge, MA: Candlewick Press, 1992.

Macaulay, David. *Black and White.* Boston: Houghton Mifflin, 1990.

Marshall, James (Ill.). *All the Way Home* by Lore Segal. New York: Farrar, Straus, and Giroux, 1973.

Mayer, Mercer (Ill.). *While the Horses Galloped to London* by Mable Watts. New York: Parent's Magazine Press, 1973, now o.p.

Martin, Francesca. *The Honey Hunters.* Cambridge, MA: Candlewick Press, 1992.

McPhail, David. *Annie & Co.* New York: Holt, 1991.

―――. (Ill.) *The Tale of Peter Rabbit* by Beatrix Potter. New York: Scholastic Inc., 1986.

Mitgutsch, Ali. *From Picture to Picture Book.* Minneapolis: Carolrhoda Books, 1988.

Moerbeek, Kees. *New at the Zoo 2.* New York: Random House, 1993.

Morris, Ann and Maureen Roffey. *Night Counting.* New York: Harper and Row, 1986.

Nakawatari, Harutaka. *The Sea and I.* New York, Farrar, Straus & Giroux, 1992.

Newlands, Anne. *Meet Edgar Degas.* New York: J. B. Lippincott, 1988.

Ormerod, Jan. *The Story of Chicken Licken.* New York: Lothrop, Lee and Shepard, 1985.

Oxenbury, Helen (Ill.). *Farmer Duck* by Martin Waddel. Cambridge, MA: Candlewick Press, 1991.

Palmer, Jan (Ill.). *The Moon's Choice* by John Warren Stewig. New York: Simon and Schuster Books for Young Readers, 1993.

Paul, Korky (Ill.). *Dinner With Fox* by Stephen Wyllie. New York: Dial Books for Young Readers, 1990.

Pelham, David. *A Is for Animals.* New York: Simon & Schuster Books for Young Readers, 1991.

Percy, Graham (Ill). *The Tortoise and the Hare and Other Favorite Tales.* New York: Henry Holt and Co., 1993.

Pienkowski, Jan. *ABC Dinosaurs.* New York: Lodestar Books, 1993.

Pinckney, Jerry (Ill.). *Half a Moon and One Whole Star* by Crescent Dragonwagon. New York: Macmillan, 1986.

Polacco, Patricia. *Babushka's Doll.* New York: Simon and Schuster, 1990.

———. *Pink and Say.* New York: Philomel Books, 1994.

———. *Chicken Sunday.* New York: Philomel Books, 1992.

Powzyk, Joyce. *Wallaby Creek.* New York: Lothrop, Lee and Shepard, 1985.

Potter, Beatrix. *The Tale of Peter Rabbit.* London: Frederick Warne, 1987.

Raboff, Ernest. Henri de Toulouse-Lautrec. *Art for Children.* New York: J. B. Lippincott, 1988.

Rackham, Arthur (Ill.) *The Legend of Sleepy Hollow* by Washington Irving. New York: Morrow, 1990.

Rader, Laura. *Mother Hubbard's Cupboard. A Mother Goose Surprise Book.* New York: Tambourine Books, 1993.

Rand, Ann and Paul. *Sparkle and Spin.* New York: Abrams, 1991.

Rayevsky, Robert (Ill.). *Aesop's Fables* retold by Tom Paxton. New York: Morrow Junior Books, 1988.

Reid, Barbara. *Zoe's Rainy Day.* New York: Cartwheel Books, 1991.

Rockwell, Anne. *In Our House.* New York: Thomas Y. Crowell, 1985.

Rounds, Glen. *Three Little Pigs and the Big Bad Wolf.* New York: Holiday House, 1992.

Savage, Stephen. *Making Tracks.* New York: Dutton Children's Books, 1992.

Scary, Huck. *Looking Into the Middle Ages.* New York: Harper and Row, 1984.

Scruton, Clive. *Mary's Pets.* New York: Lothrop, Lee & Shepard, 1989.

Sendak, Maurice. *The Nutshell Library.* New York: Harper and Row, 1962.

Shachtman, Tom. *Parade.* New York: Macmillan, 1985.

Shapiro, Arnold. *Triangles.* New York: Dial, 1992.

Spier, Peter. *Father, May I Come?* New York: Doubleday, 1993

———. *Noah's Ark.* Garden City, New York: Doubleday, 1977.

Steig, William. *Roland the Minstrel Pig.* New York: Windmill Books, 1968.

Stow, Jenny (Ill.). *The House That Jack Built.* New York: Dial Books for Young Readers, 1992.

Ungerer, Tomi. *Zeralda's Ogre.* New York: Harper and Row, 1967.

Van Allsburg, Chris. *The Wreck of the Zephyr.* Boston: Houghton Mifflin, 1983.

Watts, Bernadette (Ill.). *George's Garden.* New York: North-South Books, 1985.

Weller, Linda. *Turn and Learn: Colors* by Peter Seymour. New York: Macmillan Pub. Co., 1984.

Wildsmith, Brian. *Daisy.* New York: Pantheon Books, 1984.

Wilsdorf, Anne. *Princess*. New York: Greenwillow Books, 1993.

Zemach, Margot (Ill.). *Henry's Fourth of July* by Holly Keller. New York: Greenwillow, 1985.

————(Ill.). *The Princess and the Froggie* by Harve and Kaethe Zemach. New York: Farrar, Straus, and Giroux, 1974.

Zwerger, Lisbeth. *Aesop's Fables*. Saltzburg, Aus: Neugebauer Press, 1989.

————. *Hans Christian Andersen Fairy Tales*. Saxonville, MA: Picture Book Studio, 1991.

Professional references

Annual '89, Illustrators of Children's Books. Natick, MA: Picture Book Studio.

Burke, E. M. (1990). *Literature for the Young Child* (2nd ed.). Boston: Allyn & Bacon.

Carpenter, H., & Pritcard, M. (1984). *The Oxford Companion to Children's Literature*. New York: Oxford University Press.

Cleaver, B. P. (1990, July 11-13). "Silhouette Illustration as Visual Information in Children's Books." Paper presented at The International Visual Literacy Association Symposium, London.

Cobb, N. (1992, May). "The Show-and-Tell Tale(s) of the Great Explainer." *The Smithsonian Magazine*, pp. 71-80.

Cooper, I. (1991). "Pop Goes the Book." *Booklist*, 88(2), 154.

Crago, M., & Crago, H. (1983). *Prelude to Literacy*. Carbondale, IL: Southern Illinois University press.

Donahue, R. (1992). "Books Big and Small." *Publishers Weekly*, 239(9), 13-15.

Dooley, P. (1980, October). "The Window in the Book: Conventions in the Illustration of Children's Books." *Wilson Library Bulletin,* pp. 108-112.

Eggum, Arne. (1984). *Edvard Munch*. London: Thames and Hudson.

Feaver, W. (1977). *When We Were Young. Two Centuries of Children's Book Illustration*. New York: Holt, Rinehart and Winston.

Glaister, Geoffrey. *An Encyclopedia of the Book*. Cleveland: World Publishing, 1960.

Goddard, C. (1992). "Alive with Color." *Publishers Weekly*, 239(9), 18-19.

Goldenberg, C. (1993). "The Design and Typography of Children's Books." *The Horn Book*, 69(5), 559-567.

Greenlaw, M. J. (1988, October/November). "Using Picture Books in the Middle School." *Reading Today*, p. 20.

Groban, B. and R.G. Lowe. (1982. October). "Book Binding Considerations." *School Library Journal*, 101-104.

Halsey, M. (1992). "Putting Humor in the Pages." *The Artist's Magazine*, 9(2), 70-76.

Harms, J. M., & Lettow, L. J. (1989). "Book Design: Extending Verbal and Visual Literacy." *Journal of Youth Services in Libraries*, 2(2), 136-142.

Haviland, V. (1980). "Questions to an Artist Who Is Also an Author." In V. Haviland (Ed.), *The Openhearted Audience* (pp. 25-45). Washington, DC: Library of Congress.

Irvine, J. (1992). *How to Make Super Pop-Ups*. New York: Beechtree Books.

Lacy, L. (1986). *Art and Design in Children's Picture Books*. Chicago: American Library Association.

Macaulay, D. (1991). "1991 Caldecott Acceptance Speech." *Journal of Youth Services in Libraries*, 4(4), 340-347.

MacCann, D., & Richard, O. (1992). "Picture Books for Children." *Wilson Library Bulletin*, 66(9), 101-103.

Marantz, S., & Maranz, K. (1987, May/June). "Interview with Ann Jonas." *The Horn Book Magazine*, pp. 308-312.

Moss, E. (1986). *Part of the Pattern*. New York: Greenwillow Books.

Nodelman, P. (1984, December). "How Children Respond to Art." *School Library Journal*, pp. 40-41.

Nodelman, P. (1988). *Words About Pictures, The Narrative Art of Children's Picture Books*. Athens, GA: The University of Georgia Press.

Paley, N. (1992). "Postmodernist Impulses and the Contemporary Picture Book: Are There Any Stories to These Meanings?" *Journal of Youth Services in Libraries*, 5(2), 151-162.

Pitz, Henry C. (1963) *Illustrating Children's Books*. New York: Watson-Guptill.

Schwarcz, J. H., & Schwarcz, C. (1991). *The Picture Book Comes of Age. Looking at Childhood Through the Art of Illustration*. Chicago: The American Library Association.

Steig, W. (1993). "The Artist at Work." *The Horn Book Magazine*, VLXIX(2), 170-174.

Stewig, J.W. (1994, January/February) "New Lives for Old Favorites." *The Five Owls*, 8 (3), 49-51.

Taylor, J., Whalley, J. I., Hobbs, A. S., & Battrich, E. M. (1987). *Beatrix Potter 1866-1943. The Artist and Her World*. London: F. Warne & Co., The National Trust.

Weber, N. F. (1989). *The Art of Babar*. New York: Harry N. Abrams.

Zemach, Margot. *Self-Portrait: Margot Zemach*. Reading, MA: Addison-Wesley, 1978.

The Influence of Art Movements

6

Understanding the effect of artistic antecedents on book illustration can enhance children's appreciation of illustrations. Many ideas, techniques, and themes of painting have been incorporated into book illustration.

All art forms a continuous flow, a largely unbroken stream of influences and followers. Techniques and concepts artists use today will lead to new techniques and concepts for future artists. A group of German painters working near the end of the nineteenth century can be lumped together and called expressionists, and we can study the phenomenon of expressionism. But the work of the expressionists didn't exist in a vacuum; it grew out of the movements that went before and it led into the movements that followed. Teachers can help children sense this flow by pointing out the links that exist between art movements and the art in children's books.

Realistic or representational art

The style of art most adults know best is the type which adheres closely to the way things really look to us in the world that surrounds us. This art is, as Cianciolo says, "… exact and precise, as if one is viewing the scene closely." She goes on to comment on "literalism and realism," in which only a "limited amount of distortion is permitted to emphasize the artist's message."[1] Many adults are most comfortable when pictures look as much like the real thing as it is possible to make them look (MacCann & Richard, 1980).

The best of representational art often grows from extensive, detailed study. If a realistic artist is depicting the world today, s/he will examine the objects to be shown with care, looking at how the surface textures, for example, vary, and how the underlying shapes of the objects can be most accurately depicted. If a representational artist is showing an historic time period, the preparation will often also include extensive study of that time period, perhaps by using reference books, or perhaps by going to a particular place to be shown.

Among the most skilled of representational artists whose work often springs from a particular time period is Nancy Ekholm Burkert. Her *Snow-White and the Seven Dwarfs*, for instance, remains a touchstone work against which other artists working in this visual style must be measured, some 20 years after its publication. Using double-page spreads on every other opening, alternating with full spreads of text, Burkert achieves a sufficiently spacious context for the many small details she shows to convince viewers of the authenticity of these pictures. Details of costume, architecture, household goods, all are combined to give us a view of a time and place unfamiliar to us, but understandable because of the clarity and precision with which they are rendered. On the fifth opening, for instance, we see so clearly the subtle neck treatment on Snow-White's dress, the black piping found there (and reflected in her belt color) but not found on the hem of the garment's arm. Many children won't notice such small details, which are in themselves unimportant. What is important is the way this accumulation of historically accurate detail enables Burkert to transport us to a time and place we've not experienced directly. She guides us through that environment, because of her care in depicting realistically what she wants us to see.

Burkert used the same realistic style in *Valentine and Orson*, a much honored book which received a Special Citation for Creative Excellence from the Boston Globe-Horn Book Awards Committee. This book, set in sixteenth-century Flanders, allows Burkert a similarly spacious venue for her penchant for details, presented this time in a horizontal format, not a vertical one as in *Snow White*. On the 11th opening we see, for example, the contrasting textures of the cook's pot, the hood over the fire, the hair garment the Wild Man is wearing, the wood of the floor, and the fur of the cat. Each is evoked with photographic clarity, and yet as Dooley points out, Burkert's precision and delicacy never results in "her intricacy look[ing] forced or dry ... [rather] they retain a pristine freshness." Dooley is saying here what could be

Activity

With children, you might compare and contrast Burkert's art in Snow-White and the Seven Dwarfs *with the illustrations done by Angela Barrett (1991), which take on a romantic look in which details are less important than the overall effect.*

said of the very best of representational artists, whether they are depicting life today or in some previous time period: they are able to transcend the details to give us a compelling overall picture that draws us into the work. In a contrasting point of view, May has described *Valentine and Orson* as a "highly decorative 'coffee table' book, a production which is an art object more than it is a story."[2]

Trina Schart Hyman is another skilled practitioner of what might be called "romantic realism"; that is, her art renders realistically the details of texture, shape, and color of objects and people she depicts, but it is a world of verdant landscapes and beautiful people, far more ideal than we would really encounter. In fact, Zipes (1988) speaks of the "rugged-looking prince" and the "young, beautiful, smiling princess" Hyman gives us in *The Sleeping Beauty*. We see that kind of idealized depiction in her *The Kitchen Knight* as well. The broad-shouldered men and nubile young women who inhabit Hyman's paintings make us wish them well because of her skill in this style.

Impressionism

Impressionism, an art movement centered in France between 1860 and 1920, probably had more effect on more artists than any other single art movement (Bailey, Rishel, & Rosenthal, 1989). Exemplified by such widely known painters as Claude Monet (1840-1926) and Auguste Renoir (1841-1919), impressionism influences painting and book illustration even today. Impressionism was revolutionary, growing up largely as a reaction against the conventional, representational art of that time. Impressionists were rebelling against the naturalistic style of such artists as Camille Corot (1796-1875), who painted landscapes in realistic colors. The work of the impressionists bursts with unmixed color and with unusual subjects. These artists were concerned with the changing effect of light on surfaces at different times of day and under different atmospheric conditions. They used anything for subject matter, and their asymmetrical compositions presented an unusual view of temporary events.

Nonny Hogrogian, although known for her woodcuts, has also worked in an impressionistic manner. In her book *Apples*, she uses light, bright crayon colors in a pleasantly hazy rendition of objects and the environment. The strokes of several different shades of color define the forms, rather than line. This Caldecott

About the book
Burkert (1991) has written about the process of creating this book.

For more information
This is one of several versions of The Sleeping Beauty *analyzed by Betsy Hearne (1988), in an article examining the recent proliferation of illustrated versions of old tales. In the article, Hearne claims that market forces may be responsible for the many new editions of these tales; she warns about the lack of authenticity in some of these presentations.*

For more information
A fine, though brief, explanation of impressionism intended for children is given by Marshall B. Davidson in A History of Art.

Another description of this movement which teachers may find helpful in broadening their own knowledge is the writing by Reyero (1990).

Figure 6.1: Mr. Rabbit and the Lovely Present

This is one of 14 full-page paintings Sendak did, presented bled to the page edge, in a pleasantly cozy small (8" x 6³/4") format, facing each text page. The text is set in a compact block, leaving a generous amount of white space to further enhance the colors Sendak used.

Medal-winning artist returned to this style more recently, in doing illustrations for her husband, David Kherdian's gentle story of a small girl's walk home from school. In *By Myself*, the poet describes the things the girl sees: birds, flowers, stones, and clouds among them, giving a lyrical look at the commonplace. Hogrogian's light and bright palette features the kind of blending of small dabs of related colors which characterizes impressionist painting. She's particularly effective in evoking the sunshiny effect of light on grass and leaves.

Maurice Sendak prepared as beautiful an example of impressionism as any in children's literature, in his illustrations for the story of *Mr. Rabbit and the Lovely Present*, by Charlotte Zolotow. Using soft, wonderfully varied shades of watercolor, Sendak creates a pastoral environment. The muted blues, greens, and purples of the scene where Mr. Rabbit meets the little girl are evidence of a gentle approach to watercolor that is characteristic of impressionism. The work may be overshadowed by some of Sendak's later, better-known books, but it is among the very best of his work in this style.

More recently, Brian Wildsmith has continued to mingle impressionistic elements in his work, often interspersed with hard-edged geometric forms which are not characteristic of impressionism. In *A Christmas Story,* he retells a familiar set of events through the eyes of a young girl and a young donkey. Some of the pages, like the fifth opening, include a very geometrically-based rendering of the city of Jerusalem that isn't impressionistic. But on other pages, like the second, third, and sixth openings, we see the loosely defined shapes, daubs of color to represent shapes of objects, and subtle color mixings indicating the effect of light on surfaces, that is very typical of impressionism. The book illustrates that artists can and do incorporate a variety of influences in one book.

Impressionistic strokes of color, which at times become so small that they approach pointillism, the next category to be discussed, are apparent in Neil Waldman's illustrations for *America the Beautiful* by Katharine Lee Bates. After a tour through the scenic wonders of this country, Waldman was moved to depict scenes for Bates's poem, widely known because of its musical setting. The broken color strokes in the opening "for spacious skies" is reminiscent of the most typical of impressionist painters. In contrast, on the opening for "From sea …" the tiny dots of color on the hills are more typically pointillistic. No matter how they are described, the unblended strokes of color, juxtaposed one over the other, lead to a vibrancy that enlivens each page.

Steve Johnson's paintings for *Up North at the Cabin* by Marsha Wilson Chall, provide another example of the principles of impressionism presented in book format. The young female narrator remembers the sensory delights of swimming, boating, and other outdoor activities in the woods, which she can recreate in her mind's eye, because of the vividness of the images. Johnson's full-page, unbordered pictures, continually play with the contrasts between light and dark, delighting in the differences. An opening double-page spread precedes the first text page, and sets the tone for the rest of the book. The brightness of the blue sky and the white clouds, with the sunlight shining on the cabin roof and the grass, contrasts with the heavy darkness of the pine woods, deep greens and blues but shading almost to black in several places. On the third opening, the sunlight of early morning casts shadows across the breakfast table, and once again the differences between the light and the dark is readily apparent. The sunlight sparkling on the water in the fourth opening is a spread which recalls the way impressionists often played with the effect

Activity

A similar, bucolic setting is depicted impressionistically by Gary Blythe in art for Under the Moon *by Dyan Sheldon. You might have children study these two books, and do a comparison chart of ways they show a rural setting.*

About the artist

Details about the artist's life are included in the biography by Ernest Raboff.

Another Expressionist, Vincent Van Gogh, was the subject recently of a book for intermediate grade or middle school students, in Richard Muhlberger's What Makes a Van Gogh a Van Gogh? *from a series of six books which focuses on the visual elements of each of the painters included.*

of light on water. On the 12th opening, in the softness of the focus, and the momentary quality of the illustration as the little girl leaves the house with her suitcase, we see again impressionist precepts.

Expressionism

In this style of art, the artist moves away from concern with how light affects the external surfaces of objects, and into a deeper concern with how the objects make the artist feel. The essential nature of objects, interpreted through the feelings these evoke, is the main focus. The expressionist artist isn't concerned with accurate representations of real objects, but instead paints to show his/her subjective emotional reaction to these.

Marc Chagall (1887-1985), the Russian emigre who lived most of his adult life in France, is a leading expressionist painter (Compton, 1985). This book for adults includes many large reproductions you could use with children. Look at Chagall's work in the context of the art in *When Cats Dream* by Dav Pilkey which begins and ends with large black and white illustrations showing real life. The middle section, a dream fantasy, explodes into vibrant full color, replete with the kind of floating objects, people, and animals so typical of Chagall's paintings. On the fourth opening, for instance, the relationship is quite evident. The woman sitting in her chair is floating, with a green face, through the air (just under the moon) while behind her, a huge cat, nearly twice her size also floats, arms akimbo, through the air. Sizes, shapes and colors of objects are changed to suit the artist's desires, with no particular emphasis on realistic representation. On the sixth opening, the village shown is also reminiscent of Chagall's villages. The tenth opening is related visually to the jungles of Henri Rousseau (1844-1910), whose work is discussed later in the Folk Art section.

When we turn to children's books, we find several examples of artists whose work exemplifies Expressionist principles. Cianciolo identifies Ludwig Bemelmans, the artist/author of the long-beloved *Madeline* series of books, as a particularly noteworthy expressionist artist. Commenting on the "rather childlike" nature of this art, she commends this artist for having made this style his own.[3]

More recently, Katya Arnold did illustrations for *Baba Yaga*, and in the process exemplified expressionistic characteristics.

The shapes make the objects, like Baba Yaga's body, trees, fire-places, birds, and tables recognizable. But Arnold isn't concerned with literal representation of any of these: on the dust jacket we quickly see, in Baba Yaga's blue face, that this artist wants us to know what she is feeling about this tale. Notice on the second opening, how the size of the fish is exaggerated, and how its shape is curved above young Tishka. Both of these emphasize the emotional tone of the picture, rather than a realistic, or an impressionistic style. This gives us the feeling of emotion, of how huge the fish seems to the child. On the fifth opening, the way Tishka's body is depicted shows clearly in the visuals how the artist feels about the words she is illustrating. We feel the stretch and contortion of Tishka's body because of this art. Throughout the illustrations for this book, we understand the structure of the objects shown. For example, the trees are clearly trees. Yet they are not representationally done, nor does Arnold concern herself with how light affects these objects. Rather we see, for instance on the eighth opening, how the artist wants us to feel about these trees, hemming in Baba Yaga in her frustration and rage, as she tries to vent her anger on Tishka.

Ed Young, in his double-page illustrations done in pastel for *Goodbye Geese*, exemplifies an expressionist concern with feelings evoked, not with literal representation of objects. Nancy White Carlstrom's mood piece about the passing of autumn, the leaving of the geese, and the coming of winter, similarly uses language to evoke feelings of loneliness, of hopefulness, through the use of memorable images. Many children may not understand this nonliteral language, i.e., winter hearing "even the beat of our hearts" is more evocative than language children usually encounter. On the fourth opening, an illustration of the geese feet is interestingly done with no outline at all. Rather, Young simply fills in the background and lets viewers sense the webbed feet by seeing where the background stops. Expressionist art like this sees detail as relatively unimportant. In some pictures, like the one on the sixth opening of the village, we view the scene from a great distance, and detail is unimportant. In contrast, on the ninth opening, where we see winter's arms, "strong as the wind's spirit," we feel we're almost in the art, because we're given such a close-up view; here again, the detail is unimportant. Young achieves any expressionist's main aim: to give the viewer a dynamic and dramatic view of what the artist was feeling about the subject.

Figure 6.2: Follow the Drinking Gourd
Though the individual pieces of art are placed separately on two facing pages (rather than a double spread, per se), the size of this horizontal rectangle is luxuriously ample when opened. The art is 9" x 5³/4" on a page that is 11" x 10". Winter used a similar heavily painted style in illustrations for *Diego*, a biography of the famed Mexican revolutionary mural painter, Diego Rivera. Look at the art in that much smaller book, which is printed in both English and Spanish, to see how it is alike and different than this art.

Activity

To help children see that artists' styles evolve over time, compare this art with some done four years earlier, for Hush Little Baby, *in which Winter uses a more realistic palette and soft, recognizable shapes.*

Jeanette Winter's pictures for *Follow the Drinking Gourd* are dramatically strong expressionistic paintings in which realistic representation isn't a major preoccupation. She's telling the story of Peg Leg Joe and a group of runaway slaves who used the Underground Railroad to escape from the South to freedom in the North. These brooding, highly patterned paintings convey the sense of danger we should feel in this ominous story of danger and near escape. In the illustration reproduced here, we can sense the enfolding, sheltering nature of the cornstalks. In other places, as on the 12th opening, we feel the desperation of the slaves, trying to elude the soaking rain. Winter exaggerates size and body shape to convey the feeling of fear. On the second opening, for example, we see only the legs and hands of the slave master, close to us, and larger than life size, to emphasize the fear of the slave, cowering in the cotton.

It is an interesting coincidence that the African American painter, Jacob Lawrence, much earlier, used an Expressionist style for his retelling of a story set at the same time, in *Harriet and the Promised Land*. Named New York Times Best Illustrated Book when it was originally published, this has been reissued, making available again art which is noteworthy for its ability to draw us into empathy for the characters. There isn't a more exemplary expressionistic illustration than the one of Harriet scrubbing the floor, on the "Harriet, grow bigger" page (sixth opening) in this book.

Jacob Lawrence used the same visual style to tell a more personal story in *The Great Migration*, derived from a series of paintings he did in 1940-1941, chronicling the journey of hope many black Americans began in traveling from the rural South to seek job opportunities in the urban North. In dramatically dark paintings, full of simplified shapes arranged for their aesthetic, rather than representational qualities, Lawrence conveys the feeling of danger that this journey entailed. For the most part, the people shown are not distinguished one from another visually; they become part of a pattern in much the way they must have felt themselves part of the sweep of humanity moving anonymously from one area to another. There's much use of symbolism. For example, in painting number 19, "Segregation divided the South," we see bold, blocky figures representing the white and black population, detached from each other and kept apart by the river flowing between them. This particular painting is interestingly reminiscent of those done by the American painter, Milton Avery (1893-1965), of quite different subject matter.

Milton Avery's work wasn't available in a book for children, until Karla Kuskin put words to a set of paintings he did over 40 years ago. Now *Paul*, who wanted to sing his made up song to someone, is available. His father and mother are too busy, so Paul sets out on a journey to his "magic grandmother." Along the way he encounters a pig who is flying out west, a blue-eyed caterpillar whose tail was a cloud of smoke, and a plump policeperson who had "a short, snappy way of speaking," among many unexpected people and animals. Avery's double-spread paintings, bled to the page edge, eschew small detail in favor of abstracted sweeps of color. Some of the paintings are all angles, like the one of wolves surrounding Paul (pp. 40-41). Others, like the painting of the winged pig and the caterpillar (pp. 17-18) are more curvilinear.

About the artist

Hughes (1993) describes at greater length the context in which Lawrence's paintings were done.

About the artist

Kramer (1962) presents an in-depth focus on one part of this artist's life, calling him a "modernist" whose paintings are "divested of identifying detail and simplified to flat, cut-out forms...then reinvested with the strength of (his) color." The 16 color plates included are large enough for serious study of the work.

Throughout, the text pages are decorated with smaller figures lifted from the complete paintings. This provides a look at the whimsical paintings of a major American expressionist.

Pointillism

The pointillists, also called neoimpressionists, carried the idea of placing strokes of pure color side by side as far as it could go without the subject's disappearing entirely. They broke up large surfaces into countless small, separate dots (or points) of complementary color—a tedious, time-consuming process. The viewer's eye mixes these colors visually. Pointillism attracted few followers. The best known were Georges Seurat (1859-1891) and his student Paul Signac (1863-1935). Interest in pointillism waned after Signac died. Book illustrators do occasionally use the technique, however.

Children will enjoy the opportunity to learn about the paintings of Seurat, many of which are splendidly reproduced in books for adults (Thompson, 1985 and Madeline-Perdrillat, 1990). Seurat's best-known painting, *La Grande Jatte*, is a precisely organized, solidly planned composition depicting the afternoon recreational excursion of a great number of people. These solid citizens, so weightily arrayed, seem like figures carved of wood. The close-ups in the book of this and other paintings show the thousands of tiny color daubs Seurat used to create the images. Signac's work is available in a book for adults by Ratliff (1992). Though these books are for adults, children will enjoy their large, full-color reproductions.

Although few illustrators today use pointillist techniques to any great extent, some do use small dots of color to build up form. On the "r is for rain" page of Gyo Fujikawa's *A to Z Picture Book*, the author/illustrator uses many round dots of different shades of green and brown to suggest, rather than literally depict, the tree leaves.

Though she doesn't use it throughout the book, artist Colleen Browning does provide some interesting examples of pointillism in *Can't Sit Still* by Karen E. Lotz. This is the story of a young girl whose exuberant energy makes her hop, skip, and dance through the year. On the fifth opening, we seen "winter in the city" through the accumulation of many hundreds of dots of color. Again on the eighth opening, in the snow, the artist creates

For more information

For a tongue-in-cheek takeoff on the composition of Seurat's painting, see the dust jacket of I Want a Dog *by Dayal Kaur Khalsa. The organization, where things are located, and the stiffness of the figures are humorously derived from this painting, though Khalsa has painted in solid, unmodulated colors. Her paintings often are derived from other artists: in* My Family Vacation, *for example, in the flatness of bright color, and in the patterning evident, there is a similarity to some of the work of Matisse. Frank (1990) has talked about why Khalsa'a experimenting is important.*

the clothing the young girl wears by putting together the tiny dots of color pointillists use.

Ellen Raskin modified the pointillist technique by using black dots in *Spectacles*, a humorous account of the problems Iris Fogel has because she resists wearing glasses. The author/illustrator alternates full-color pages with others featuring only black-ink pointillist designs made up of thousands of tiny dots. For example, the giant pigmy nuthatch on Iris's front lawn, depicted in black dots on a solid green background, turns out—in full color on the next page—to be Iris's good friend Chester.

Author/illustrator Rachel Isadora, in *City Seen from A to Z*, incorporates pointillist techniques in black-and-white drawings depicting the many environments and inhabitants of an urban area. Some of the drawings are richly complex, and others are interestingly spare. For example, the "p" (for pigeon) page provides many people, buildings, and objects to study, all done in myriad tiny black and white dots, but the "h" (for hat) page is dramatically understated, with no background at all. Throughout the book, Isadora presents fully rounded, three-dimensional forms, created as the dots converge to create shadows.

More recently, Craig Brown has been experimenting with overlaying many tiny black dots on top of watercolor washes, to create light and shadow in his illustrations. When the dots are clumped together, they also create lines for Brown, who doesn't use continuous pen lines. In *My Barn* he plays with the environmental sounds and shows both panoramic views of the outside scenes, and closeup views of the stalls in the barn. A companion book, *City Sounds*, features the same technique enhanced by the use of different type faces of varying sizes to emphasize the sounds being represented.

Examples of this style, by painters, not book illustrators, are included in *Looking at Paintings. Landscapes* by Peggy Roalf. This is from a fine new series of books about art, all under the general title *Looking at Paintings*... (and then a second category word is included). A distinguishing characteristic of this set of art books is that the reproductions, all in full color, are also all full-page size. In this particular volume, Roalf includes a painting by Paul Signac, and another by the French artist Camille Pissaro, which could be used to help children understand this way of dealing with paint. Roalf's books on *Dancers* and on *Circus* also include paintings by Seurat.

For more information

In a book for middle schoolers, which librarians and teachers would find helpful in expanding their own understanding of post-impressionism, Wiggins (1993) uses many reproductions of paintings from the Art Institute of Chicago to examine the work of these painters.

Plate 10: Stevie

Notice how all of the characters face toward Stevie himself, a way to focus the composition on the main character. In this early work, Steptoe developed an impressive richness of color by layering one over another. That isn't always apparent in subsequent reprintings of the book, especially when in paperback. A reproduction, photographed from the original art, is available in *Reading Pictures. John Steptoe* by John Warren Stewig.

Plate 11: Mufaro's Beautiful Daughter

Notice the tight composition the artist uses here. Follow with your eyes the invisible line inscribed from the left bird's wing up to the topmost birds in the right corner and in a circle around Nyasha's head. The line travels a path like this:

Be sure to look at this art in comparison with the art Steptoe did for *Stevie*, some 18 years earlier.

Les Fauves

Following in the footsteps of Vincent Van Gogh and Paul Gauguin, some painters achieved eminence as part of a French group called les fauves (Gassier, 1983). This name translates as "wild beasts," and art critics used it scornfully to reject paintings these artists submitted to an important exhibit in 1905. Today, the label is neutral and simply describes a group whose works share certain visual similarities, as well as a stylistic verve that incorporates lively linear effects and boldly clashing colors.

Georges Roualt (1871-1958) was one of the best known of les fauves but used a more somber palette than the others. The most distinctive characteristic of his paintings is the heavy black lines that enclose each color area. These lines and the austere forms create an effect much like stained glass, a craft Roualt pursued as a young man.

John Steptoe, some of whose early work was similar to Roualt's, was an artist of many styles. As a young black man, Steptoe wrote realistic stories about black children and illustrated them in vibrant shades of color separated into areas by heavy black line. *Stevie (color plate 10)* is the universally appealing story of a young child who feels displaced when a younger child comes to stay in his home. The book has been praised by Tremper (1979/1980) for the authenticity of its black English. The illustrations are done in brilliant chalk, with one color skillfully layered over the one below to increase the intensity of both. *Stevie* has, according to Lewis, "remained the most popular of these early books," perhaps because its "situation is universal."[4] In *Uptown*, two boys contemplate what they will be when they grow up. *Train Ride* tells of four adventuresome boys who find that sneaking onto a train is not an unalloyed joy. The illustrations in *Uptown* and *Train Ride* are done in opaque watercolor. In addition to black line, Steptoe skillfully uses applied white. For example, in *Train Ride*, the decorative use of white smudges to depict the lights of movie marquees in one illustration contrasts starkly and yet pleasingly with the darker color range of the background.

Beautifully crafted drawings, done in colored inks, illustrate *Mufaro's Beautiful Daughters (color plate 11)*, also by John Steptoe. Done is a realistic style, not les fauves, the illustration here allows a comparison in the range that Steptoe demonstrated in his work. This large-scale visualization of an African tale shows Steptoe's skill in creating fine detail, realistic people and backgrounds, and roundness of form and deep space. The book is thus a striking contrast with his earlier works, such as *Stevie*. Many fine lines, hatched and crosshatched invite viewers to examine the authentic depiction of birds and flowers from this continent.

In Fiona French's *City of Gold*, the stiff figures with stylized faces, done in brilliant color and outlined heavily in black, recall the stained-glass windows that influenced Roualt's work. Author/illustrator French uses brighter colors than Steptoe does and mixes them less frequently. You might look at this in the context of the more recent *The Savior is Born* by Brian Gleeson, with illustrations by Robert Van Nutt, in which the artist purposely did illustrations in the style of stained glass windows. Children could be helped to notice how different these two books are. The French and the Van Nutt illustrations are tighter in execution than the far looser interpretation in the Steptoe books.

The illustrations for *Christmas at Anna's* by Kate Spohn accompany a simple, contemporary story of young children going to visit an adult friend. The paintings make much use of the kind of vivid colors immediately juxtaposed, a delight in patterns for their own sake, and the intensification of the surfaces because of the contours of shapes in contrasting colors. The double-page spreads on the fifth and sixth openings, for example, are the direct artistic descendants of the paintings of Henri Matisse (1869-1954), a French painter with whose work these could be compared.

Folk art

Unlike formal art movements, whose originators were localized in a particular time or place, folk art is the naive, unselfconscious creation of untrained artists of any time or place. These people, often engaged in other work to earn a living, paint because they feel impelled to express themselves in this way. Folk art is often characterized by imaginative use of color, repeated stylized patterns, lack of perspective, and simple, childlike forms.

Henri Rousseau (1844-1910) is a striking example of a self-taught artist who painted because he felt compelled to (Descargnes, 1972). Unschooled in formal approaches to painting, Rousseau used strong lines to fill his canvases of jungle scenes with wildly imaginative plant forms and animals. His flat patterns evoke an unworldly but appealing landscape in which all natural detail is subordinated to his sense of repeated design. To introduce this artist to children, you could use the book about him from the "Art for Children" series by Ernest Raboff. The text, throughout this set of books, asks children to think about what they are seeing. Raboff says, for example: "By reading a painting slowly, like a poem or a book, we can receive much pleasure as details of the picture recall happy scenes from our own store of memories."[5] Even young children can be encouraged to think about what they see, and how it relates to what they have experienced.

Rousseau-like patterning is evident in the illustration for the "l is for lullaby" page in Gyo Fujikawa's *A to Z Picture Book*. The artist used basic plant forms and, by accenting the curves and repeated aspects of their lines, made a pattern that is more a symbol for the plants than a realistic representation.

Another book reminiscent of the art of Henri Rousseau is the art by Ann and Reg Cartwright for *In Search of the Last Dodo*.

Figure 6.3: In Search of the Last Dodo

Reg Cartwright won the Mother Goose Award, given in England for the "most exciting newcomer to children's book illustration." He introduces this book with endpapers that share the common design motifs apparent throughout the illustrations: a repetition of highly controlled plant shapes, of the ocean waves, and indeed of the people themselves. His endpapers for *The Winter Hedgehog* by Ann Cartwright introduce this book in the same way. It is interesting to compare how the curvilinear aspects of his style can be applied to a more realistic nature tale.

The rhythmic, repeated forms of the jungle plants are clearly related to Rousseau's jungle forms, and even the repetition of the waves in the several pictures set on the ocean are similar to the way Rosseau repeated curves in his work. The text, as is often the case with ecological books, is somewhat didactic but the art is worth sharing for the calm, ordered world it creates.

Durga Bernhard's highly saturated colors, flat (two dimensional), repeated patterns revel in the delight of juxtaposing one shape against another. In *What's Maggie Up To?* she tells the slight story of a cat beloved by many people in the neighborhood, until she disappears, causing them to worry. In the end, the answer to the question is provided. The pictures resolutely eliminate everything that isn't necessary and have in places a quality, though not the coloring of the Swedish craft of rosemaling.

Though she is not technically a folk artist, since she had extensive art training, nonetheless Margot Zemach often worked in a folk-like manner. For example, her illustrations for a variation of an old Swedish tale, *Nail Soup*, by Harve Zemach, capture the quality of folk art. Zemach's humorous ink and wash drawings show a squatty tramp and a rotund old lady, whose tiny house is stuffed with hidden food. Using only watercolor shades of brown, gold, and pink and applying them loosely, the artist creates charming peasant patterns on the clothes of the lady and the tramp. The black outline of the trees and the lack of perspective in the house add to the folk-art quality.

In her *Duffy and the Devil*, a Caldecott Award winner, the artist presents a popular nineteenth-century story from Cornwall in England as retold by her husband Harve Zemach, in soft pastel shades showing Squire Lovel and his servant girl, Duffy. The scratchy black pen line gives definition to the loosely painted watercolors, largely done without background details so viewers can focus on the antics of these people. The story, a variation on the Rumplestiltskin motif, ends with the Squire, in all his pink corpulence, coming home to Duffy, who resolves she'll never again knit another thing.

The colors in *Mommy, Buy Me a China Doll* are more solidly painted, in somber shades of earth tones, but warmed by the addition of a robust red, which echoes the strength of the family Margo Zemach depicts in a folk-like style.

Lester Abrams created decorative patterns in his illustrations for *The Four Donkeys* by Lloyd Alexander. These patterned pas-

Activity

Have children look at the art in What's Maggie Up To?, *with that which Bernhard did for one in which she consciously used folk motifs from another culture as the basis for her own work. In a Yuit tale,* How Snowshoe Hare Rescued the Sun *she used flat colors and repeated patterns to depict objects.*

tel illustrations successfully evoke a different time and place. Abrams also added many unusual, unsymmetrical borders made up of repeated decorative patterns in related colors.

Brightly colored, highly simplified decorative shapes abound in *My Little Island*, by Frane Lessac, done without any attention to realistic perspective. This book tells of the visit of the narrator and his best friend to the little Caribbean island on which the narrator was born. The figures are all two-dimensional; the patterns in the clothes they wear are delightful. The waves in the water, leaves on the trees, scales on the fish—all show a similarity to the works of the American primitive painter Grandma Moses. More recently, the artist has continued to use her brilliantly colored palette, and repeated shapes, to illustrate a collection of poems by several different poets, in *Caribbean Canvas*. In a large (9¼" x 12¼") vertical format, she showcases both vertical and horizontal paintings, set around with generous amounts of white space to enhance the intensity of the colors.

Lessac also used this style to illustrate a series of unrhymed poems by Monica Gunning in *Not a Copper Penny in Me House*. The poems evoke the elements of Caribbean culture, like the "Roadside peddlers, [with] their tangerines strung on strings …" (p. 8), the whitewashing of houses in celebration of Christmas, and includes much imaginative language, i.e., "We swim like the whales, racing giant waves to beat them ashore" (p. 29). On each page, Lessac's paintings vibrate with both repeated patterning and highly saturated color.

The paintings of Mattie Lou O'Kelley in *From the Hills of Georgia* and *Circus* also present flat, decorative patterns, which are delightful for their own sake, rather than for any attempt to represent the world realistically. In *From the Hills of Georgia*, subtitled "An Autobiography in Paintings," the artist presents the richly detailed panoramic views of fields, hills, and forests where all the elements are patterned together to make an overall design. The block of text which runs vertically on either side of the gutter leaves room for ample white space which sets off the intensely colored paintings. In both books, the text simply serves to string the pictures together, but O'Kelley's folk art—especially the richly luminous night scenes—will quickly engage children's attention.

From a very different location, but showing some visual similarities to other of the folk art discussed here, is the set of pictures which Timothy Rhodes did for *The Singing Snake* by Stefan

Figure 6.4: From the Hills of Georgia
A characteristic of folk art is that often there's less distinction between focal point and background than is found in the work of artists who have been more formally trained. We can go—visually—from place to place in this painting, finding each stopping point equally interesting. The panoramic view says to us that finding a single center of interest isn't important. This in fact reflects the nature of the text, which is a set of related, but non-sequential anecdotes/reminiscences, rather than a coherent plot with a single climax and conclusion.

Czernecki. Using a pervasive orange/brick red tone contrasted with blues and greens, Rhodes drew on the design motifs common in aboriginal Australian art, to produce completely flat paintings which—within their patterned borders—almost give the impression of being fabric or wallpaper designs. Tiny dots of various colors break up the large spaces, and we get interior views of, for example, Lark inside Snake's throat, and the bones of an animal inside Crocodile's stomach!

Abstraction

Stuart Davis (1884-1964) was an American painter who painted so abstractly that the shapes of objects become more important than their details. Davis's colorful landscapes juxtapose flat but lively patterns against other patterns (Lane, 1978).

An artist who works in a style reminiscent of Davis's is American illustrator Leonard Weisgard. For both *The Noisy Book* and *The Winter Noisy Book*, by Margaret Wise Brown, Weisgard painted bold blocks of solid, unshaded colors. He uses these blocks of color to create illustrations that stand for but do not realistically depict his subject matter. In the two cityscapes in *The Noisy Book*, solid orange, light blue, yellow, and black geometric shapes represent buildings. These bold abstractions capture the essence of the buildings without showing details. Individual details are eliminated or made into patterns that are subordinated

Figure 6.5: Red Light, Green Light
The solidness of the barn and silo evoke a bucolic rural setting now rapidly disappearing in the U.S. Nevertheless, the story and this new art, will still appeal to young viewers. Many of Brown's texts, written decades ago, are being reissued now. Her *Four Fur Feet* is a rhymed story that children will delight in learning by rote and repeating with you. Illustrations by Woodleigh Marx Hubbard done in brightly colored gouache, make use of repeated visual forms which mirror the text repetition.

to the overall design of the page. In the same way, the artist abstractly portrays fathers coming home in *The Winter Noisy Book*. These two books, with their fine abstract illustrations, were first published during the 1940s, when most books were firmly anchored in the realistic representational style. The publisher made a new edition of *The Noisy Book* available in 1993, printed on a pleasant coated paper which intensifies Weisgard's highly saturated colors.

More recently, Weisgard has used casein, watercolor, crayon, and ink to reillustrate Margaret Wise Brown's text, *Red Light, Green Light* (1992). This book follows in the same general stylistic path of the earlier books, but there is a wider range of colors used, and there is more subtle blending of colors than was evident in previous illustrations.

Similar to Weisgard's work are some of the illustrations by Marcia Brown, an artist whose work has been characterized by continuous experimentation in various styles and mediums. In her *Henry—Fisherman*, Brown creates pleasant, abstract forms that tell a tale of a young boy growing up in the Caribbean. In another early book, *The Little Carousel,* Brown used bright, flat shades of coral red, yellow, pale green and grey, accented with black, to show an urban environment in which the patterning is also reminiscent of her teacher, Stuart Davis. The boldly simple shapes, and the repeated patterns in illustrations that are often mostly without backgrounds are a delight to examine, if you can find a copy in a library. There is interesting balance in these illustrations between forms defined by *line* (i.e., an applied line of a contrasting color) and by those defined simply by *edge* (the form stops, without any containing line). Though Stuart Davis portrayed a different geographic area, the visual similarities between his work and Brown's are impressive.

A kinetic energy similar to that found in Stuart Davis's paintings is evident in *Little Chicks' Mothers and All the Others*, by Mildred Luton. The handsome endpapers feature strong geometric patterns in highly saturated colors that vibrate against one another. The animals in the book are equally intense: the curved line of the goat, the straight line of the horse's blanket, and the teardrop-shaped feathers on the chicken are juxtaposed to produce a greater intensity than any of the patterns would have by itself. The effect is further intensified by the latticelike patterns that border the pages. The rhyming text facing the full-page illustrations has less impact than the visual qualities of the pictures.

A rather sophisticated book, both visually and textually, is *Sun Moon Star*, written by Kurt Vonnegut and illustrated by Ivan Chermayeff. This handsomely produced oversized volume has a black linen cover stamped in gold, silver, and black, that opens to reveal black endpapers with an impressive heft. Inside, the glossy, coated paper sets off the highly saturated colors used by Chermayeff, who made the pictures before Vonnegut wrote the words. It is often asserted that abstract art is inappropriate for children, but Dressel (1984) believes that they can indeed deal with abstraction, but "in a concrete way."

Surrealism

Surrealists juxtapose contrasting realistic elements to create a vague, dreamlike world of surprises; their paintings are usually puzzling and sometimes shocking. Cianciolo spoke of the "gleeful freedom of the imagination" which characterizes such artists.[6] The imaginative qualities of such paintings do not appeal to viewers who want to feel firmly grounded in reality.

A Spanish painter, Salvador Dali (1904-1989) is undoubtedly the best-known surrealist. Although his paintings are seminal to the surrealist movement, the work of another Spaniard, Joan Miró (1893-1983), and that of the Swiss painter Paul Klee (1879-

Activity
A teacher might share Brown's book with students and then present reproductions of Davis's work, encouraging the children to notice how they are alike.

For more information
Sun Moon Star *is one of a small number of books described by Dressel (1984), who examines the appropriateness of abstract art for young children.*

For more information
Clark (1986) wrote about Klee for children in one of a series of articles on art that appear regularly in the magazine Highlights for Children, *and Ernest Raboff has written more extensively about this artist in a book for children.*

Chiaroscuro

Is the intensification of light and dark in a painting to provide greater contrast. From the Italian words meaning bright and dark, this came into use during the seventeenth century when artists like Caravaggio and Rembrandt began to exaggerate the effect of light on objects (Chilvers & Osborne, 1988).

For more information

Another interesting example of chiaroscuro is available in Heron Street *with art by Lisa Desimini; in this her lights are brighter, and her shadowy areas darker than they would be under ordinary circumstances.*

About the artist

Schwarcz (1982) has commented on the illustrator's Story Number 2, *pointing out that there are allusions (for example, to Noah and the Great Flood) which children of picture book age will probably not understand.*

About the artist

Drescher has talked about his work in an interview he did with Ferguson (1991).

1940) hold more appeal for children. A book written for adults about Miró by Bernier (1991) and one about Klee by Grohmann (1985) could be used to introduce boys and girls to surrealism.

Surrealism has not had an extensive impact on children's book illustration, though sometimes surrealistic elements appear in books of fantasy. One of the most significant examples is *The Moon Jumpers,* by Janice Udry. Pictures by Maurice Sendak set a surreal mood, as on the title page, which features a cat that is as big as the house. Framed by sunflowers, his tail tightly encircling a moon, the cat stares with unequal almond-shaped eyes at the reader. In full-color, double-page spreads, Sendak creates an eerie, other-worldly environment, using the sharp contrast between rich deep purples and blues and the light cast by the moon. Such intense *chiaroscuro* is not common in children's books but is a usual feature in surrealistic paintings. The recurring figure of the cat, in one case peering from the crotch of a tree, is reminiscent of the Cheshire cat in *Alice in Wonderland*. This book represents Sendak's finest work in surrealistic interpretation, but, like his work in *Mr. Rabbit and the Lovely Present*, it has been overshadowed by his more popular books.

Story Number 4, by the absurdist French playwright Eugene Ionesco, tells of an inquisitive little girl, who searches for her father under the kitchen table and other peculiar places. Illustrations by Jean-Michel Nicollett are as strange and otherworldly as the almost plotless tale about a father who wants to elude his daughter while he gets ready to go to work. The illustrations are modestly in the tradition of Salvador Dali—not as complex but equally surreal. What is real and what is a dream is not resolved either in the illustrations or in the story. Another story by Ionesco that also moves from dreamlike states to apparent reality and back again is *Story Number 1*, which has illustrations by Etienne Delessert designed for children under three (according to the author). Though these books have been out of print for some time, they are well worth searching for in a library collection.

Recently, Henrik Drescher incorporated a feeling of surrealism in his *Look-Alikes*, which chronicles one unexplainable happening after another, beginning when a boy and his obstreperous monkey flee the dinner table for the treehouse. In the treehouse, they play with toy look-alikes that suddenly run across the lawn and up to the treehouse, just as Rudy and Buster did. The boy and his monkey are drawn into the toys' adventure—or are the toys drawn into theirs? Reality and fantasy merge in the full-color

Figure 6.6: Pictures of Home
Full-page paintings on each right page face a left text page—featuring word descriptions of the qualities of homes—set above a smaller related picture. Throughout, one gets a feeling of a visual relationship to the art of Anthony Browne. Many of the details will be unfamiliar (for example, the 1930s art deco house on page 19), and will thus need careful examination.

illustrations, and the book is decorated throughout with tiny black ink drawings reminiscent of the work of Paul Klee.

Colin Thompson's *Pictures of Home* isn't a story, per se, but rather a collection of full-page and smaller pictures showing what children have in words said about qualities of a home. The single sentences are accompanied by elaborately detailed pictures, which show surprising details that catch our eye. For example, in one a charming half-timbered house is perched on two huge tree trunks, growing out of a bathtub. In another example, there is a canvas deck chair, past which we can see a view of the ocean. The perplexing thing is the tiny complete house, sitting on its landscaped lawn, which is in turn ensconced on the deck chair. The sense of scale here, as in other of the illustrations, is what makes the pictures perplexing in an interesting way.

Full-page illustrations and small vignettes placed above and below text, each done in a subtle array of ombre shades, use a surrealistic style to illustrate *The Voice of the Wood*. Paintings by Frederic Clement accompany a story by Claude Clement in a tall, vertical-rectangle format which effectively showcases these acrylic paintings. The story is a slight one, of a gifted musical instrument maker who, after the death of a beloved tree, crafts the wood into a cello which can only be played by a musician whose heart is in tune with the music in the wood. The paintings are done in a highly realistic manner, showing clearly the juxtaposition of unexpected elements. On the second opening, for example, oarsmen steer gondolas toward and into the heavy foliage of a large tree, the leaves of which are in fact comprised of many small, meticulously rendered trees. On the eighth opening, the impetuous young musician finds the craftsman is right: the cello makes only "brutal, grating noises." The text compares the noises to crocodiles chewing and clawing their way across the floor. The illustration shows parts of the floor becoming crocodile bodies! Their front legs and heads emerge from the cobblestones of the floor. Unexpected changes occur: on the 11th opening, the cello's neck begins to spout leafy branches, and a flock of songbirds lands and begins to add their music to the voice of the wood, in an illustration reminiscent of the best of Salvador Dali.

Figure 6.7: Changes

There's often something slightly unexpected lurking just beneath the surface in art by Browne, and this set of illustrations exemplifies that. We see a middle-class British family, and don't know just what changes to expect: everything seems a little askew in the pictures. If your class enjoys these illustrations, share with them *Piggybook* in which a fairly didactic message about gender equity is sugar-coated with some delightful changes.

Anthony Browne plays with surrealism in *Changes*, which he makes readily apparent in the cover illustration, where the teapot is alarmingly cat-like. In the story, young Joseph notices "On Thursday morning at a quarter past ten," that strange things are beginning to happen. Yet, as in surrealist paintings, this occurs surrounded by the ordinary and commonplace. We're told that in the kitchen, everything was in its place, and the room even smelled as it ought to. Since that's the case, what is happening? We follow Joseph and see other strange transformations: a slipper into a bird, a bathroom wash basin into a head with nose, eyes, and mouth, and a chair into a gorilla, among other things. All of this is depicted with painstaking reality: Browne shows texture, color, and shape so realistically that there's no doubt what he's depicting, except that what seems real slips into something else without warning. There's a pleasant twist to the ending: we discover what his father meant when he said earlier in the day that everything would be changing. It's a book that deals with a common fear of older siblings, in a surrealist way.

In Browne's *The Tunnel*, working in a much smaller format, he tells a journey story (i.e., Jack and Rose, brother and sister, crawl through the tunnel into a different place). The trees they discover "in a quiet wood" are strikingly reminiscent of the trees Arthur Rackham did much earlier in this century. They're human, in eerie ways. Once again, details are rendered so minutely and realistically that we wonder what is real and what is imagined. In that way, Browne's work in this book, too, is surrealistic.

Both the narrative poem and the illustrations in *The Hungry One* are surreal, resulting in a book we must return to several times to determine our reactions. Kurt Baumann's poem tells about voracious Rum Tum Tum, who devours conventional food like carrots, unconventional things like tree trunks, and improbable/impossible things like the chains which bind him in jail. In the end, the miller and his daughter, who have spurned the creature's attentions, are themselves eaten. The pictures combine photographs of human hands and what seems to be a body in human clothing, but these juxtapose in unpredictable ways with eerie drawings that depict the less human aspects of Rum Tum Tum. The resulting montages by Stasys Eidrigevicius are as darkly brooding as is the story itself.

For more information

Information about illustrators and authors is often available from the promotion department of publishing houses. In addition, CBC Features *is available from the Children's Book Council, 568 Broadway, NY 10012. It often features notices of materials about illustrators available from the individual publisher members of the CBC.*

Involving children in studying the influence of art movements

An effective way to expand children's awareness of illustrators and their work is to plan and present an illustrator-of-the-month program. This approach is effective at all grade levels and is simple enough even for kindergartners (Pippel, 1984). The teacher or librarian selects an artist whose work will interest students. A bulletin board features a large, full-color reproduction of one of the artist's paintings or illustrations which are often easily available as promotional posters from the publishing house. Around this central focus the librarian can arrange smaller reproductions of some of the artist's other works. On a table nearby, books featuring the work of the artist can be displayed. To initiate discussion of the artist and his or her work, you may want to make a few introductory statements about the person, being careful not to give a formal lecture inappropriate for children. Ask children to share their observations about what they see in the art and encourage them to speculate as to why the artist painted something in a particular manner, emphasizing that more than one speculation is always possible. After several months of studying one artist a month, adults can ask children to comment on how what they are viewing is like or unlike something they saw earlier.

The illustrator as a person

One goal of studying illustrators is to help children understand each illustrator as a person and thereby become sensitive to the full range of his or her work. Too frequently children may feel that artists work in only one given style. Help children understand that an illustrator's visual expression often varies depending on the book; a particular story may evoke a kind of illustration very different from what the illustrator has previously produced. In addition, a painting created at the height of an illustrator's powers may be quite different from one produced in younger years. By locating and sharing as much as possible of one illustrator's work, the teacher or librarian shows children a wide range of visual expression.

The development of an illustrator

If teachers at every grade level in a particular school utilize illustrator-of-the-month experiences, the work of particular artists can be returned to at different times during elementary school, and children will, as a result, develop a deeper understanding and appreciation of artists' work. Marcia Brown, for example, is an artist whose illustrations could be studied at several different grade levels for the differences in media and style they represent. Brown herself has said: "Each book should look different from the others, whether or not the medium used is the same. … A technique learned as a formula to apply willy-nilly to any subject often knocks the life out of the subject." A master of several techniques, Brown believes that: "… books are as individual as people, and each book must elicit from the artist a unique set of feelings if it is to be a unique experience for the child looking at it."[7]

Brown's many books illustrated in paint, ink line, and chalk are probably the most familiar. Her *Cinderella* in this combination medium won the artist her first Caldecott Medal. Other of her books show an equally competent use of this mix. For *Skipper John's Cook*, the artist did bold ink-line and dry-brush paintings of the skipper and the dog. In *The Little Carousel*, she paints the adventures of Anthony and Mr. Corelli with flat shades of red, green, blue, and yellow. Though the environments of these two stories are different, children can see similarities in the use of flat, solid color shapes and of dry brush and chalk. Other books in which Brown uses a similar technique are *Felice, The Neighbors*, and *Tamarindo*.

Very different from this style is Brown's work in woodcut. She uses just one color—a soft sage green—in a book for intermediate-grade students, *Backbone of the King*. Appearing on every other page or so, the half- and full-page woodcuts make extensive use of the wood's grain and are predictably angular. The artist uses silhouette shapes and different textures to evoke an island world. Another example of this style is *Dick Whittington and His Cat*.

In two books about animals, Brown uses a wider color spectrum in her woodcuts. She also uses the print of the uncut board to create backgrounds. The pattern is strong and angular, but not overwhelming. Light and dark olive green and burnt orange evoke the jungle setting in a retelling of an old Indian fable, *Once a Mouse*, for which Brown won her second Caldecott Medal. The wood grain and the gouges made by the woodcut tools themselves are incorporated in the design. A white silhouette of a dog barking in the woods is a fine use of negative shape; the feline

Activity

Look with your children at two other artist's work in woodcut. ABC Book *by C.B. Falls is probably still available in libraries: it is truly remarkable for the intensity of its large, simplified images which seem hewn out of the page. Kent (1962) describes why Falls is important in the history of illustration. More recently, in an elegantly bound showcase, Christopher Wormell presented* An Alphabet of Animals, *the visual descendent of Falls' earlier book. The strength of these images remains with viewers long after looking at the book.*

grace of the tiger stretching to fill the page makes a convincing two-dimensional rendition. In a nonstory format, in *All Butterflies*, which won a Boston Globe-Hornbook Honor designation, the artist used woodcuts of animals, domestic and wild, to present the alphabet via linked pairs of words (cat dance, mice nibbling).

With the publication of *Listen to a Shape, Touch Will Tell, and Walk with Your Eyes*, Brown's fans became aware of her interest in photography. Her beautiful photos are taken from an amazing variety of perspectives. Closeup and wide-angle shots are displayed in full-, half-, and quarter-page sizes on clay-coated paper. The subjects are nearly all from the natural world, though the pictures include a wide variety of shapes, colors, forms, and textures. This visually stimulating series of books is somewhat marred by inept and clumsy text. Poetic language is interspersed with pedestrian language, and inappropriate words jar the reader's ear. Readers may become confused trying to determine what is text and what is caption. Nonetheless, these books should be shared with children to expand their sense of Brown's development as an artist.

With *Shadow*, a story originally written in French by Blaise Cendrars, Brown returns to the medium of woodcut. There is the same interesting use of transparency and subtle color that marked her earlier efforts. In addition, in several places she utilizes an unusual effect produced by putting a blank piece of paper on top of a piece of wood covered with wet paint and then removing it. The sharp outline and intense blackness contrast well with the highly saturated and pastel colors. With this book, Brown became the first artist to win the Caldecott Medal three times.

The book provoked widely varying responses. *The Bulletin of the Center for Children's Books* (1982) was one of several reviewing sources that commented positively on the book, noting especially its "strong use of pure color … eerie wisps of superimposed images … strong silhouettes, all in handsome double-page spreads that are remarkable in their composition." In contrast, the *Interracial Books for Children Bulletin* (1983) was highly critical of the text, saying it ("presents no authentic cultural clues" and "reinforc[es] the idea of Africa as 'The Dark Continent'") and of the illustrations (the figures do not "reflect the actual grace of an African dance" and there is "casual use of African spiritual/religious symbols"). Which represents the more accurate assessment? Teachers may want to examine the book themselves in

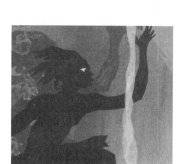

Plate 12: Shadow
The large scale of these double-spread illustrations, bled to the page edge, allows ample space for the artist to combine: cutpaper shapes, woodblock prints, and lift techniques related to monoprinting, into a densely varied whole. The use of transparent shapes, particularly as they contrast with the much more definite silhouette shapes, is effective. More recently, Brown contributed art to a section of *Sing a Song of Popcorn*, a selection of poems selected by Beatrice Schenk de Regniers. In this volume, Brown joins eight other Caldecott Medal artists, in a book named an ALA Notable book. Brown's section of weather poems sweeps along exuberantly, with definition provided only by her brush strokes.

light of these varying points of view, which illustrate that even award-winning books are by no means universally accepted.

Loranger commented on Brown's winning the Laura Ingalls Wilder Award for the entire body of her work. In closing, she concluded that Brown "has served both with real dedication and rare distinction."[8]

No school library is likely to have copies of all books by a single illustrator, but a teacher interested in doing illustrator-of-the-month programs for children will have no trouble securing a selection of books using the interlibrary loan services available either through the school library or the local public library. By encountering an array of books at appropriate times during elementary school, students will gain a firmly established sense of the range of possibilities within one artist's work. A coordinated study similar to that outlined for the work of Marcia Brown is possible for other illustrators, such as Trina Schart Hyman, Roger Duvoisin, and Maurice Sendak. The variety in the works of such artists as Paul Cezanne, Pablo Picasso, and Georges Braque makes them also particularly fitting for such study.

In addition to such study of a body of an illustrator's work, we can also encourage children to examine the work of illustrators to see relationships with artists' paintings. For example, even young children can see the similarities in the use of line and splashy color in the work of the French artist, Raoul Dufy (1877-1953) and the illustrator Ludwig Bemelmans. Using the adult art books widely available in libraries, choose some of Dufy's paintings and then compare them with the full-color pages in *Madeline*, for instance. Children can be helped to see that both use large blocks of color applied generally in the area of a particular form, and then overlaid with an energetic line which gives definition to these more general shapes. The differences in subject matter apparent in comparing Dufy's paintings with Bemelmans' illustrations doesn't obscure the stylistic similarity.

With older children, one might also look at the work of Anthony Browne for the many influences apparent on his work. Schwarcz and Schwarcz (1991) point out, in doing an extended analysis of this illustrator's work, that he has in various places been influenced by such diverse sources as the contemporary American realist David Hockney, the Belgian surrealist Rene Magritte, the French painter Edouard Manet, and the American popular illustrator, Norman Rockwell.

Activity

Stewig (1987) developed a kit of materials, including a resource guide, to help librarians and teachers plan a unit of study on Marcia Brown.

Activity

Indeed, a classroom teacher has described in detail her work highlighting Sendak for children (McKay, 1982).

In addition to the idea of how an artist's work changes over time, we can also help children learn to look for relationships between the art in books and the art in museums. A useful comparison would be to look at the work of Virginia Lee Burton and the painting of the American Regionalist painter, Grant Wood, who lived 1881-1942.

Comparing an illustrator and an artist

During her lifetime, Burton was an immensely popular children's book illustrator. We see in *Choo. Choo.* indications of Burton's fascination with the circle as an enclosing compositional element. This developed later to its artistic peak in her perenially-popular *The Little House.* But in this earlier book, illustrated throughout in black and white, we see the beginnings of her style. On the four-color endpapers, Burton uses the railroad tracks to lead our eye from bottom left, where we see the soon-to-be runaway train, to the far top right, leading off into the title page. The tracks loop in swirling circles, counterbalanced by the less-noticeable road which also is an arc. The rhythm of the rounded hilltops further accentuates the circular nature of the shapes. In all, this is a composition to which Grant Wood could relate.

On the title page, the black and white tracks and the clouds swoop in a circle across the double spread. On the third opening, the engine is encircled in the smoke it generates, as is engineer Jim. On the right page of the fifth opening, in two vignettes separated by text, we see the kind of tightly constrained, circular composition which is Burton's trademark. All that happens goes on within the enclosing circle.

Throughout the book, on nearly every page, we see the kind of rounded, natural shapes Burton favored. At times these are manufactured objects (like the streamlined passenger train on the 16th opening, or the rounded bridge arches on the next opening). In other places (like the 14th and 20th openings), she uses the circularity in such natural forms as tree branches and trunks.

In *Katy and the Big Snow*, Burton uses a clear palette composed mostly of solid, vivid red, turquoise, and yellow, to tell the story of the personified "beautiful red crawler tractor."

Even in the borders of this book we see Burton's fascination with curves. On the opening pages, pictures are small, contained within a rectangle, sized to allow for a border comprised of small, circular designs showing various aspects of Katy's life. On the third opening, for example, the tiny labeled diagrams in the border show such things as a seven-ton truck, a stone crusher, a compressor, and a steamroller with scarifier, among others.

The circular patterning continues: even the highway department building is, somewhat improbably, bent into a semi-circle, echoed in the tracks in the snow, the same shape.

When it begins to snow, and continues, and continues…, Burton switches type of border, and provides a solid blue swirled design which borders each of the pages until the last one, when "…only then did Katy rest."

Burton even plays with type placement, as on the 17th opening. When the design of the traffic in its plowed corridor of snow circles from left to right and back, the text shifts to accentuate and accommodate this.

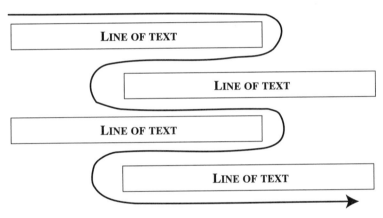

But it is in her Caldecott Award winning *The Little House*, that we see most clearly Burton's design kinship with her male counterpart, Grant Wood. This heart-warming, if slightly sentimental tale of a pretty Little House who was "strong and well built," tells of how it was encroached upon by civilization and ultimately relocated to a peaceful country setting.

On the first opening, we see the stylized trees, each a design variation of the others, a generic symbol of tree, rather than portrayals of individual trees. The next opening shows multiple images of the sun sequence in a golden arch across both pages, a protective canopy for the house and its attendant field of daisies. On the fourth opening, we have an illustration which could be easily mistaken for a painting study by Grant Wood. The panoramic view of fields stretches back to the horizon, but is still securely encompassed in the encircling border of the roads. The next four pages we see the seasonal sequence: the trees vary from the bare twigs of spring to the full foliage of summer, and back to the bare branches of winter. No matter, we easily recognize the similarity of the scene because of the strong pattern.

Finally, on the eighth opening, we see the advent of civilization, i.e., in the form of the road builders. And it is interesting to note that this—the threat personified, is a straight slash through the otherwise rounded countryside. The turmoil develops, with more and more uncompromising straight lines, i.e., the tenement houses on the 18th opening, and this compresses the still slightly convex Little House.

In this book, as in *Katy*, Burton sets the type in interesting ways. On the 36th opening, for example, the shape of the swirling road on which the Little House is moved back to the country is paralleled by the way the type on the right page swirls from side to side.

In the end, of course, the controlled tranquility so common in Burton's work prevails. On the last two openings we see the house in its newly regained country location. In the daylight scene, the protecting half circle of the sun's rays enfolds the house. In the final night scene, it is the half circles of stars which enfold the house, so we see visually what the text tells us: "all was quiet and peaceful in the country."

So this visual message of protection, tranquility, and the enfolding quality of nature is a pervasive visual element in Burton's work. She uses the circle, both in form, and in composition, to create that tranquil environment.

Children can be helped to see that the same use of form, and of composition, pervades the work of the American Regionalist painter, Grant Wood.

About the artist

Tully (1983) has written more extensively about Wood, who formalized on canvas the fecundity of the American Midwestern landscape.

Though Grant Wood, a Midwesterner, never turned his talents to illustrating children's books, many full color reproductions of his paintings are available in art books for adults, in sizes large enough to make them useful in sharing with a class of children. You could look at books by Corn (1983), Czestochowski (1981), or Dennis (1986) for samples of his paintings. In these you will find the same sort of patterned treatment of nature that systematizes and regularizes trees, plants, clouds, and other elements into a repeated design.

After studying Burton's work, we could, for example compare the trees in his painting, "The Birthplace of Herbert Hoover" (Plate 19, Dennis, 1986), or in "Near Sundown," (Plate 26, same source). We could look at the art in Burton's books in the context of such paintings as "Young Corn" (Plate 22, Dennis) or "Stone City" (Plate 12, Dennis); these two paintings show clearly the visual relationship between the rounded, balloonlike hills and the curvilinear composition in Burton and Wood.

Some of the art which Tom Leonard did for a book of poetry by Margaret Wise Brown, also resembles the work of Grant Wood. In *Under the Sun and the Moon and Other Poems*, this artist shows the kind of rural landscape which was common in Wood's paintings. Beyond the subject matter, however, the style is similar. Notice the way the hills are regularized into repeated patterns, and the way the trees are not individual trees but rather part of a larger pattern of trees. The individual differences between objects shown is minimized, and regularized, so that an overall pattern is set up. Margaret Wise Brown was one of the most popular children's authors until her death in 1952; these 19 poems were previously unpublished.

After studying Burton and Wood, it would be interesting to look at *The Story of May* by Mordicai Gerstein to see if children could recognize the similar use of curvilinear lines and composition that pervaded the work of the other two artists. This allegorical story of the months follows young May around the year visiting each of her month-relatives, until she ends up with her mother, April, once again. On the second opening, for example, we see the rounded sweep of stylized trees so typical of Burton and Wood, and a similar circular composition shown in the rows of plantings (third and fifth openings).

Another linking could be established between Grant Wood, Virginia Burton, and the kind of trees so prevalent in *The Stranger* by Chris Van Allsburg. Set in the late fall, this mysterious tale features the autumnal coloration found in many of Wood's paintings. But it is in the regularization and patterning of the trees, where individual differences are subsumed into the overall design of a page, that the illustrations in Van Allsburg's book bear the closest resemblance to Burton and Wood. Notice how these are done, on the first, second, seventh, and 13th openings. On the 11th opening, a panoramic view of the farm, we can see an immediate kinship with the rolling hills in many of Wood's paintings. Throughout the book, the static or posed quality of the pictures, purposely devoid of any appreciable action, also reflects Wood. Even the scene of dancing is curiously frozen

About the artist

For a commentary about Brown by one of her contemporaries, see Bechtel (1955).

in time, perhaps due to the monumental quality of the people Van Allsburg depicts throughout the book.

Looking at books within a style

One thing we might do with children is select a visual element, such as those described in chapter two, and look at several books representing a particular art movement, to see how different artists use that element. For example, each of the artists in the folk art section of this chapter use line. But the kind of line the artist Henri Rousseau used in his paintings is different than the kind which Margot Zemach used in her books. Frane Lessac's line is more pervasive and connected than is the line in Mattie Lou O'Kelley's art. Any of these could be compared with the elegantly thin, uninterrupted line which Sharon McGinley-Nally used in her illustrations for a story by John Cech, *My Grandmother's Journey*. The flat shapes of the people, objects, and environments shown are made even flatter by the unvarying line McGinley-Nally uses. These create decorative patterns (as for example on Gramma's vest shown on the second opening), and march resolutely up—but not farther back—on the page (as in the tablecloth design shown on the fifth opening). These bright pages, full of folk-like motifs, i.e., the flowers and birds surrounding the text and picture on the 14th opening, are ones to which children will return time and time again.

Another link librarians and teachers might make is between the art in *This Home We Have Made*, and the mural art of the Mexican artist, Diego Rivera. The book, subtitled in Spanish, *Esta Casa Que Hemos Hecho* is by Anna Hammond and Joe Matunis and recounts the efforts of a community group which included artists, and formerly homeless children, painting on the side of the building with the children, ages four through 15, were then living. The muralists were working in the South Bronx, a poor area of New York City, but the images are vivid and hopeful. Smaller, closeup parts of the mural throughout the book lead into the double foldout sheets at the end which show the entire art work. Throughout, the text is printed in both English and Spanish, the language of most of the artists and children involved.

In the monumentally sized, simplified shapes, and the flat, decorative quality of the art, the project is similar in visual quality to the work of Rivera (1886 to 1957), a painter known primarily for his mural work. His large scale works, which conformed to the architectural shapes of which they became an integral part, are boldly painted in flat colors. The shapes are stylized into patterns, rather than trying to represent realistically the people they represent.

Books about art and artists

A number of high-quality books about art and artists are available today. These books are typically written by experts who are well acquainted with the art forms they describe. They bring art to life, through clarifying descriptions, helpful photographs, and/or imaginative illustrations. Teachers should seek out and use appropriate books about art and artists; an annotated list of such titles begins on page 229.

Summary

The purpose of this chapter is to emphasize the possibility of studying illustration as an independent visual artifact. The outcome of such conscious study is the development of children's visual sensitivity so that they can be knowledgeable consumers of art in books.

Book illustrators are often influenced by different art movements, such as impressionism, pointillism, abstractionism, and others. Teachers can help children develop their visual awareness by leading them in studying the relationship between art movements and their parallels in book illustration (Purves & Monson, 1984).

Classroom teachers need to share art experiences with children. Since many students attend schools that offer no separate art program staffed by trained teachers, they will only be exposed to an array of art experiences if their classroom teachers and/or librarians provide such experiences. Many fine books describe how to offer an art-making program. Fewer discuss how to share art books with children or suggest books to use. The bibliography will help librarians and teachers give boys and girls experiences in looking at works of art. That is a helpful addition to looking at the art in picture books.

Recommended children's books

Abrams, Lester (Ill.). *The Four Donkeys* by Lloyd Alexander. New York: Holt, Rinehart and Winston, 1972.

Arnold, Katya. *Baba Yaga*. New York: North-South Books, 1993.

Activity
The adult art book by Rochfort (1987) includes reproductions of Diego Rivera's art in sizes large enough to use with groups of children.

Avery, Milton (Ill.). *Paul* by Karla Kuskin. New York: HarperCollins, 1994.

Barrett, Angela (Ill.) *Snow White.* New York: Alfred A. Knopf, 1991.

Bemelmans, Ludwig. *Madeline.* New York: The Viking Press, 1939.

Bernhard, Durga. (Ill.) *How Snowshoe Hare Rescued the Sun. A Tale from the Arctic* by Emery Bernhard. New York: Holiday House, 1993.

———. *What's Maggie Up To?* New York: Holiday House, 1992.

Blythe, Gary (Ill.). *Under the Moon* by Dyan Sheldon. New York: Dial Books for Young Readers, 1993.

Brown, Craig. *City Sounds.* New York: Greenwillow Books, 1992.

Brown, Craig. *My Barn.* New York: Greenwillow Books, 1991.

Brown, Marcia. *All Butterflies.* New York: Scribner's, 1974.

———. *Backbone of the King.* New York: Scribner's, 1966.

———. *Cinderella.* New York: Scribner's, 1954.

———. *Dick Whittington and His Cat.* New York: Scribner's, 1950.

———. *Felice.* New York: Scribner's, 1958.

———. *Henry—Fisherman.* New York: Scribner's, 1949.

———. *Listen to a Shape.* New York: Franklin Watts, 1979.

———. *The Little Carousel.* New York: Charles Scribner's Sons, 1946, o.p.

———. *The Neighbors.* New York: Scribner's, 1967.

———. *Once a Mouse.* New York: Scribner's, 1961.

———. *Shadow.* New York: Scribner's, 1982.

———. *Sing a Song of Popcorn* by Beatrice Schenk de Regniers. New York: Scholastic Inc., 1988.

———. *Skipper John's Cook.* New York: Scribner's, 1951.

———. *Tamarindo.* New York: Scribner's, 1960.

———. *Touch Will Tell.* New York: Franklin Watts, 1979.

———. *Walk With Your Eyes.* New York: Franklin Watts, 1979.

Browne, Anthony. *Changes.* New York: Alfred A. Knopf, 1990.

———. *Piggybook.* New York: Alfred A. Knopf, 1986.

———. *The Tunnel.* New York: Alfred A. Knopf, 1989.

Browning, Colleen (Ill.). *Can't Sit Still* by Karen Lotz. New York: Dutton Children's Books, 1993.

Burkert, Nancy Ekholm. *Snow-White and the Seven Dwarfs.* New York: Farrar, Straus and Giroux, 1972.

———. *Valentine and Orson.* New York: Farrar, Straus and Giroux, 1989.

Burton, Virginia Lee. *Choo. Choo. The Story of the Little Engine Who Ran Away.* Boston: Houghton Mifflin Co., 1937.

———. *Katy and the Big Snow.* Boston: Houghton Mifflin, 1943.

———. *The Little House.* Boston: Houghton Mifflin, 1942.

Cartwright, Ann and Reg. *In Search of the Last Dodo.* Boston: Joy Street, Little Brown and Co., 1989.

———. *The Winter Hedgehog.* New York: Macmillan, 1989.

Chermayeff, Ivan (Ill.). *Sun Moon Star* by Kurt Vonnegut. New York: Harper & Row, 1980.

Clement, Frederic (Ill.). *The Voice of the Wood* by Claude Clement. New York: Dial Books for Young Readers, 1989.

Davidson, Marshall B. *A History of Art*. New York: Random House, 1984.

Davis, Stuart (Ill.). *Little Chicks' Mothers and All the Others* by Mildred Luton. New York: Viking, 1983, now o.p.

Delessert, Etienne (Ill.). *Story Number 1* by Eugene Ionesco. New York: Harlan Quist, 1967.

Desimini, Lisa (Ill.). *Heron Street* by Ann Turner. New York: Harper & Row, 1989.

Drescher, Henrik. *Look-Alikes*. New York: Lothrop, Lee and Shepard, 1985.

Eidrigevicius, Stasys (Ill). *The Hungry One* by Kurt Baumann. New York: North-South Books, 1993.

Falls, C.B. *ABC Book*. Garden City: Doubleday and Co., 1923.

French, Fiona. *City of Gold*. New York: Henry Z. Walck, 1974, now o.p.

Fujikawa, Gyo. *Gyo Fujikawa's A to Z Picture Book*. New York: Grosset and Dunlap, 1974.

Gerstein, Mordicai. *The Story of May*. New York: HarperCollins Publishers, 1993.

Golembe, Carla. *How Night Came from the Sea*, retold by Mary-Joan Gerson. Boston: Little, Brown and Co., 1994.

Hammond, Anna and Joe Matunis. *This Home We Have Made. Esta Casa Que Hemos Hecho*. New York: Crown Publishers, Inc., 1993.

Hogrogian, Nonny. *Apples*. New York: Macmillan, 1972.

———(Ill.). *By Myself* by David Kherdian. New York: Henry Holt, 1993.

Hubbard, Woodleight Marx (Ill.). *Four Fur Feet* by Margaret Wise Brown. New York: Hyperion Books for Children, 1994.

Hyman, Trina Schart (Ill.). *The Kitchen Knight. A Tale of King Arthur*, retold by Margaret Hodges. New York: Holiday House, 1990.

———. *The Sleeping Beauty*. Boston: Little, Brown and Co., 1977.

Isadora, Rachel. *City Seen from A to Z*. New York: Greenwillow, 1983.

Johnson, Steve (Ill). *Up North at the Cabin* by Marsha Wilson Chall. New York: Lothrop, Lee & Shepard Books, 1992.

Khalsa, Dayal Kaur. *I Want a Dog*. New York: Clarkson N. Potter, Inc., 1987.

———. *My Family Vacation*. New York: Clarkson N. Potter, 1988.

Lawrence, Jacob. *The Great Migration. An American Story*. New York: The Museum of Modern Art, the Phillips collection, and HarperCollins Publishers, 1993.

———. *Harriet and the Promised Land*. New York: Simon and Schuster, 1968, 1993.

Leonard, Tom (Ill.) *Under the Sun and the Moon and Other Poems* by Margaret Wise Brown. New York: Hyperion Books for Children, 1993.

Lessac, Frane. *Caribbean Canvas*. New York: J. B. Lippincott, 1987.

———. *My Little Island*. New York: Lippincott, 1985.

———(Ill.). *Not a Copper Penny in Me House* by Monica Gunning. Honesdale, PA: Wordsong/Boyds Mills Press, 1993.

——— (Ill.). *The Wonderful Towers of Watts* by Patricia Zelver. New York: Tambourine Books, 1994.

McGinley-Nally, Sharon (Ill.). *My Grandmother's Journey* by John Cech. New York: Bradbury Press, 1991.

Muhlberger, Richard. *What Makes a Van Gogh a Van Gogh?* New York: The Metropolitan Museum of Art/Viking, 1993.

Nicolett, Jean-Michel (Ill.). *Story Number 4* by Eugene Ionesco. New York: Harlan Quist, 1973.

O'Kelley, Mattie Lou. *Circus*. Boston: Atlantic Monthly Press, 1986.

———. *From the Hills of Georgia*. Boston: Atlantic Monthly Press, 1983.

Pilkey, Dav. *When Cats Dream*. New York: Orchard Books, 1992.

Raboff, Ernest. *Henri Rousseau*. New York: J. B. Lippincott, 1988.

———. *Marc Chagall*. New York: J. B. Lippincott, 1988.

———. *Paul Klee*. New York: J. B. Lippincott, 1988.

Raskin, Ellen. *Spectacles*. New York: Atheneum, 1972.

Rhodes, Timothy (Ill.). *The Singing Snake* by Stefan Czernecki. New York: Hyperion Books for Children, 1993.

Roalf, Peggy. *Looking at Paintings. Circus*. New York: Hyperion Books for Children, 1992.

———. *Looking at Paintings. Dancers*. New York: Hyperion Books for Children, 1992.

———. *Looking at Paintings. Landscapes*. New York: Hyperion Books for Children, 1992.

Sendak, Maurice (Ill.). *Mr. Rabbit and the Lovely Present* by Charlotte Zolotow. New York: Harper and Row, 1962.

———(Ill.). *The Moon Jumpers* by Janice Udry. New York: Harper & Row, 1959.

Spohn, Kate. *Christmas at Anna's*. New York: Viking, 1993.

Steptoe, John. *Stevie*. New York: Harper and Row, 1969.

———. *Train Ride*. New York: Harper and Row, 1971.

———. *Uptown*. New York: Harper and Row, 1969.

Stewig, John Warren. *Reading Pictures. John Steptoe*. Hilton Head Island, SC: Child Graphics Press, 1988.

Thompson, Colin. *Pictures of Home*. New York: Green Tiger Press, 1992.

Van Allsburg, Chris. *The Stranger*. Boston: Houghton Mifflin, 1986.

Van Nutt, Robert. *The Savior is Born* by Brian Gleeson. Saxonville, MA: Picture Book Studio, 1992.

Waldman, Neil (Ill.). *America the Beautiful* by Katharine Lee Bates. New York: Atheneum, 1993.

Weisgard, Leonard (Ill.). *The Noisy Book* by Margaret Wise Brown. New York: Harper and Row, 1939, 1993.

———(Ill.). *Red Light, Green Light* by Margaret Wise Brown. New York: Scholastic Hardcover, 1992.

———(Ill.). *The Winter Noisy Book* by Margaret Wise Brown. New York: Harper & Row, 1947, 1975.

Wildsmith, Brian. *A Christmas Story*. New York: Alfred A. Knopf, 1989.

Winter, Jeanette. *Diego*. New York: Alfred A. Knopf, 1991.

———. *Follow the Drinking Gourd*. New York: Alfred A. Knopf, 1988.

———. *Hush Little Baby*. New York: Pantheon Books, 1984.

Wormel, Christopher. *An Alphabet of Animals*. New York: Dial Books, 1990.

Young, Ed (Ill.). *Goodbye Geese* by Nancy White Carlstrom. New York: Philomel Books, 1991.

Zemach, Harve & Margot. *Duffy and the Devil*. New York: Farrar, Straus, & Giroux, 1973.

————. *Mommy, Buy Me a China Doll*. New York: Farrar, Straus, & Giroux, 1966.

Zemach, Margot (Ill). *Nail Soup* by Harve Zemach. New York: Farrar, Straus, & Giroux, 1964.

Professional references

Alderson, B. (1993, May/June). "Maurice Before Max: The Yonder Side of the See-Saw." *The Horn Book Magazine*, pp. 291-295.

Bailey, C. B., Rishel, J. J., & Rosenthal, M. (1989). *Masterpieces of Impressionism and Post-Impressionism*. New York: Harry N. Abrams, Inc.

Bechtel, L. S. (1955). *Books in Search of Children*. New York: The Macmillan Co.

Bernier, R. (1991). *Matisse, Picasso, Miró As I Knew Them*. New York: Alfred A. Knopf.

The Bulletin of the Center for Children's Books, 35 (July-August 1982), 203.

Burkert, N. E. (1991, January/February). "Valentine and Orson." *The Horn Book Magazine*, pp. 45-47.

Chilvers, I., & Osborne, H. (1988). *The Oxford Dictionary of Art*. Oxford: The University Press.

Cianciolo, P. (1976). *Illustrations in Children's Books*. Dubuque: Wm. C. Brown Company Publishers.

Clark, H. (1986, January). "Paul Klee." *Highlights for Children*, pp. 20-21.

Compton, S. (1995). *Chagall*. London: Royal Academy of Arts.

Comte, P. (1991). *Paul Klee*. New York: The Overlook Press.

Corn, W. M. (1983). *Grant Wood: The Regionalist Vision*. New Haven: Yale University Press.

Czestochowski, J. S. (1981). *John Steuart Curry and Grant Wood: A Portrait of Rural America*. Columbia: University of Missouri Press.

Dennis, J. M. (1986). *Grant Wood: A Study in American Art and Culture*. Columbia: University of Missouri Press.

Descargues, P. (1972). *Le Douanier Rousseau*. Geneve (Suisse): Editions d'Art Albert Skira.

Dooley, P. (1989). "Contemporary Illustrators: Tomorrow's Classics?" In P. Nodelman (ed.), *Touchstones* (Vol. 3) (pp. 153-163). West Lafayette, IN: Children's Literature Association.

Dressel, J. H. (1984). "Abstraction in Illustration: Is It Appropriate for Children?" *Children's Literature in Education*, 15, 103-112.

Ferguson, J. (1991, September/October). "Interview with Henrik Drescher." *The Horn Book Magazine*, pp. 556-561.

Frank, J. P. (1990, January 19). "New Levels of Subtlety Mark Children's Book Jacket Art." *Publishers Weekly*, pp. 76-77.

Gassier, P. (1983). *Manguin Parmi les Fauves*. Paris: Fondation Pierre Gianadda.

Grohmann, W. (1985). *Paul Klee*. New York: Harry N. Abrams, Inc., Pubs.

Hearne, B. (1988). "Booking the Brothers Grimm: Art, Adaptations, and Economics." In J. M. McGlather (ed.), *The Brothers Grimm and Folktale* (pp. 220-233). Urbana: University of Illinois Press.

Hughes, R. (1993, November 22). "Stanzas from a Black Epic." *Time*, pp. 70-71.

Interracial Books for Children Bulletin, 14 (1983), 34.

Jardi, E. (1991). *Paul Klee*. New York: Rizzoli International Publications, Inc.

Kent, N. (1962, February). "C.B. Falls, 1874-1960. A Career in Retrospect." *American Artist*, pp 34-41+.

Kingman, L., Hogarth, G. A., & Quimby, H. (1978). *Illustrators of Children's Books 1967-1976*. Boston: The Horn Book, Inc.

Kramer, H. (1962) *Milton Avery: Paintings, 1930-1960*. New York: Thomas Yoseloff.

Lane, J. R. (1978). *Stuart Davis. Art and Art Theory*. New York: The Brooklyn Museum.

Lewis, C. (1989). "John Steptoe." In T. Chevalier (ed.), *Twentieth-Century Children's Writers* (pp. 918-919). Chicago: St. James Press.

Loranger, J. A. (1992). "Marcia Brown." *The Horn Book Magazine,* 68(4), 440-443.

Madeleine-Perdrillat, A. (1990). *Seurat*. New York: Rizzoli International Publications, Inc.

MacCann, D., & Richard, O. (1980, October). "Picture Books for Children." *Wilson Library Bulletin*, pp. 132-135.

McKay, J. A. (1982, October). "Making the Most of Maurice." *The Reading Teacher,* pp. 90-91.

May, J. P. (1991). "Exploring Book Illustration as a Work of Art." *The CLA Bulletin*, 17(2), 2-4.

Pippel, M. (1984, April). "Guess Who Visited Our Class? Artist Appreciation With Flair." *Early Years*, p. 25.

Purves, A. C., & Monson, D. L. (1984). *Experiencing Children's Literature*. Glenview, IL: Scott, Foresman.

Ratliff, F. (1992). *Paul Signac and Color in Neo-Impressionism*. New York: Rockefeller University Press.

Reyero, C. (1990). *The Key to Art from Romanticism to Impressionism*. Minneapolis: Lerner Publications Company.

Rochfort, D. (1987). *The Murals of Diego Rivera*. London: Journeyman Press Limited.

Schwarcz, J.H. (1982). *Ways of the Illustrator: Visual Communication in Children's Literature*. Chicago: American Library Association.

Stewig, J. W. (1987). *Reading Pictures: Marcia Brown*. Hilton Head Island, SC: Child Graphics Press.

Thomson, R. (1985). *Seurat*. Oxford: Phaidon Press Limited.

Tully, J. (1983, May). *Portrait of Americana*. Horizon, pp. 37-43.

Whalen-Levitt, P. (1986, March). "Breaking the Frame: Bordering on Illusion," *School Library Journal*, 32: 100-103.

Wiggins, C. (1993). *Eyewitness Art. Post-impressionism*. New York: Dorling Kindersley.

Zipes, J. (1988). *The Brothers Grimm. From Enchanted Forests to the Modern World*. New York: Routledge, Chapman, and Hall.

Books About Art and Artists

Bjork, Christina and Lena Anderson. *Linnea in Monet's Garden.* Stockholm: R & S Books, 1985.

In brief compass (53 pages) and small size (9^1/4" x 6^1/2"), the authors tell a pleasantly fictionalized account of a small girl who goes to Paris and visits the garden made famous by the French Impressionist master. This book includes four-color photographs of flowers actually taken in the garden, black and white photos of the Monet family and small decorative paintings in the margins, but the major emphasis is on Monet's work. Endpaper prints of water lilies give way to close-ups of over a dozen other works. This is altogether an unintimidating, appealingly personal introduction to an artist children should know.

Brown, Laurene Krasny and Marc Brown. *Visiting the Art Museum.* New York: E. P. Dutton, 1986.

Rather than dealing with the work of a single artist as many books do, this book presents works by many artists. The Browns unobtrusively use the device of a fictional family's visit to a museum to tie together the presentation of a wide variety of artworks ranging from an ancient Egyptian mummy case to works by John Singleton Copley, Pierre Auguste Renoir, and Roy Lichtenstein. Most works are presented in photographs which are quite true to the color in the original. In some cases where permissions couldn't be obtained, the work is rendered by the Browns themselves.

Cirlot, Lourdes. *The Key to Modern Art of the Early 20th Century.* Minneapolis: Lerner Publications Co., 1990.

A comprehensive, scholarly resource for teachers, which may also be used directly with middle school students, this includes small full-color reproductions on virtually every page (some are, in fact,

Dada was an art movement begun in Zurich during World War I by Hans Arp and others. It valued unusual methods and materials in antipathy to traditional style and materials, exalting the commonplace by taking it out of context. Pop art, a recent American art movement, is sometimes called neo-dada. T. A. R. Neff explains this at greater length in In the Mind's Eye. Dada and Surrealism *(Chicago: Museum of Contemporary Art, 1986). Fauvism and surrealism are defined elsewhere in this book.*

full-page—$5^1/2$" x 8" in size). Before examining such movements as fauvism, dadaism, and surrealism in depth, the author opens with sections on general appreciation, geography and chronology, and on the artist and contemporary society. Throughout the text, terms defined in the glossary are presented in boldface type. Even for those readers not interested in mastering all the historic details presented, the illustrations provide a pleasantly wide overview of artists and paintings in a convenient format. There are five other titles by various authors in this series, including *The Key to Painting* and *The Key to Gothic Art.*

Cumming, Robert. *Just Imagine. Ideas in Painting.* New York: Charles Scribner's Sons, 1982.

This book asks children to look at—and speculate about—art from a wide variety of schools and times. Continuous text, which is not divided into subsections, accompanies the full-color reproductions. Sometimes there is just one (as large as 8" x 6") reproduction on a page; at other times three (as small as $2^3/4$" x $5^1/4$") reproductions are juxtaposed to highlight contrasts. Placing an ultra-realistic Peter Paul Rubens painting done in 1632 next to a completely nonobjective Jackson Pollock painting done in 1950 is sure to stimulate a variety of responses. The text, which assumes an intermediate-age reader, considers content and technique and frequently asks the reader questions about the paintings without providing answers.

Davidson, Marshall B. *A History of Art.* New York: Random House, 1984.

This pleasantly large ($9^2/3$" x 11") book covers the years from 25,000 B.C. to the present. The vast majority of reproductions are in full color, and many are as large as $5^3/4$" x $9^3/4$"; even the small ones ($2^1/2$" x $2^3/4$") are reproduced very clearly. The text is brief, allowing more room for the art itself. Generous margins set off the reproductions and keep pages from appearing crowded.

Epstein, Vivian Sheldon, *History of Women Artists for Children.* Denver: VSE Publishers, 1987.

Opening with a brief consideration of the unnamed female artists who wove baskets, made clay pots and dyed thread for cloth, the author moves into the decorative arts of the Middle Ages which were often produced by women who were either royalty, members of wealthy families or were living in convents. Following this, on a single page for each of 39 artists, she presents a brief paragraph or two and a large (4" x 6") reproduction—15 of them in color. The artists range from Sonfonisba Anguissola (born in Italy in 1532) through Judy Chicago (born in 1939). The color reproductions are clear and accurate; the text is concise and devoted to fact rather than to speculation.

Florian, Douglas. *A Painter.* New York: Greenwillow Books, 1993.

Rather than focusing on a particular artist, the author here, as in other books in his "How We Work" series, deals generically with how one can be involved in this category of work. Here, he describes the mediums artists use ("With pastels he can draw strokes of shimmering light."). Florian talks about scale in art, subjects artists paint and feelings they express, and concludes with a page of technical information about such things as easels, palettes, and the qualities of materials. All of this is accompanied by Florian's own pleasant watercolor and pencil illustrations. His book, *A Potter,* is similar and available from this publisher.

Gardner, Jane Mylum. *Henry Moore. From Bones and Stones to Sketches and Sculptures.* New York: Four Winds Press, 1993.

The brief text, ranging from one sentence to two paragraphs on a page, is a device to string together a series of black and white photographs by David Finn, a close personal friend of Moore for over 30 years, and internationally known for his skill in photographing sculpture. The book includes photos of Moore drawing, sculpting, studying his own work, and riding his bicycle. The text is full of homely details: Henry's favorite lunch was cold meat and pickles. The words focus with admirable clarity on the work itself: extraneous details like names, places, and dates are minimal. Throughout, the author emphasizes how important seeing was to Moore, and how carefully he looked, and relooked at his work, trying to visualize it in new ways, to uncover new possibilities. We do learn something about his process, i.e., moving from sketches, into a maquette, into a full-sized piece, though we don't learn any of the details involved in the casting of his large bronze works, for example. At the end there is a more complete biographical note for adults.

Gherman, Beverly. *Georgia O'Keeffe.* New York: Atheneum, 1986.

For children interested in biography, this recounts the exciting life of the major American woman painter of our century. When she began in 1916, women simply did not compete in the all-male world of "real" artists. Yet before she died in 1986, she had carved for herself a unique position in the annals of art history. Her oversized, exuberantly abstract paintings had captured the imaginations of Americans more thoroughly than any other woman. Another biogra-

Maquette

A maquette is a small model in wax or clay made as a preliminary study, presented to a client for approval, for submission to a competition, or because craftsmen will actually make the full-size sculpture designed by the sculptor.

For more information

Felt, M. E. (1993, Winter/Spring). "The Lives of Artists: A Bibliography of Biographies." *CBC Features, unp.*

phy of O'Keeffe is included by Felt (1993) in her annotated list of biographies of artists.

A very different sort of talent, life, and training is described in *Grandma Moses. Painter of Rural America* by Zibby Oneal (Viking Kestrel, 1986). For slightly younger readers, and told in just 58 pages, this shares the drawback which limits Gherman's book—the few small black and white reproductions in no way capture the glories of these two amazingly different art forms. The books must be read in conjunction with some adult art books featuring large, full-color reproductions of the art itself.

Goffstein, M. B. *Lives of the Artists.* New York: Farrar, Straus & Giroux, 1981.

The writer/artist here turns her usual minimalist style of understating everything in tiny books to a somewhat larger format (6" x 8¹/2") and to five artists—Rembrandt, Guardi, Van Gogh, Bonnard, and Nevelson. This collection is not as easily and immediately appealing to young readers/viewers as the colorful Impressionist painters. Nonetheless, with just six brief pages for each artist, Goffstein catches and holds our attention. Each section features one full-color and one black and white reproduction. In brief text (that for Bonnard is only nine sentences long), Goffstein selects a particularly memorable aspect of the work. Some of this is biographic (of Guardi, "Your father, your two brothers, and your sons were painters, too"). Some of it is evaluative (of the same artist, "His highways of green water and their reflective twin, the skies, were brushed dramatically").

Following this first book, Goffstein published *An Artists Album* (same publisher, 1985), which takes readers from Johannes Vermeer's birth (1632) to Claude Monet's death (1926). Using just two reproductions for each of six artists (only for Vermeer are both in color), the artist captures vividly her own personal reaction to the works. As an example, she writes about the paintings by Vermeer, "The more worn they are, the clearer they become." This assumes an audience mature enough to respond to such non-literal statements, for Goffstein is never bogged down in the factual minutia which engrosses many art historians.

Heslewood, Juliet. *Introducing Picasso.* Boston: Little, Brown and Co., 1993.

Compressing the enormously fertile creative life of this artist who lived to be 91 years old, creating until he died, is a challenging task. This will indeed introduce a child reader, and the effort is helped by the large number of full-color reproductions from all periods in the artist's life. It is further helped by the contexts the author sets up:

Picasso's work is juxtaposed with reproductions of work by Tou-louse-Lautrec, Gauguin, Monet, Gris, Matisse, and even much earlier works by El Greco and Velazquez, from whom Picasso derived painting ideas. The time line, and the several photographs of the artist and his associates helps make details of his life interesting.

Holme, Brian. *Enchanted World: Pictures to Grow Up With*. New York: Oxford University Press, 1979.

This elegant, expensively produced volume includes 96 illustrations, nearly half of which are reproduced in accurate full color. Margins are narrow and print is small to allow more room for reproductions. Subject matter includes artists (like Jean Honore Fragonard) and children's book illustrators (like Beatrix Potter). Art from the eleventh to the twentieth centuries is included, and paintings on the same subject are often placed opposite each other to facilitate comparisons. The book assumes no previous art background.

In *Creatures of Paradise* (Thames and Hudson, 1980), Holme focuses on common and extraordinary animals depicted by such diverse artists as Edward Hicks and Joan Miro. Both the lavish use of color and the large size of the pictures make the book easy to study.

Isaacson, Philip M. *Round Buildings, Square Buildings, and Buildings That Wiggle Like a Fish*. New York: Alfred A. Knopf, 1988.

The most comprehensive examination of architecture for children published recently, this is illustrated with remarkably clear full-color photographs by the author. When it received an honor award from the *Boston Globe-Hornbook* committee, that group commented on the poetic nature of the language with which Isaacson describes the array of buildings ranging from Stonehenge, built some 3,500 years ago, to a 1985 art gallery. There are examples of vernacular architecture, done by anonymous builders whose work is still revered for its honesty of craftsmanship, as in the example of houses in Nepal. In contrast, there are the highly polished architectural creations of internationally known architects like the airline terminal Eero Saarinen designed in 1956, located at Kennedy Airport. Isaacson deals with such things as building structure in a chapter called "Old Bones and New Bones," and his language is never just informative. Of a five hundred year old stone barn in England, he said "Its grizzled parts are like the bones of an old sea animal." His juxtapositions are always enlightening: this building is contrasted with the 1978 addition to the National Gallery of Art, all thin sleek steel support. Each of these is compared with the cathedral at Durham, which "... stands high above a river like a sturdy soldier."

Isaacson continued sharing his wide-ranging knowledge with middle school readers in *A Short Walk Around the Pyramids and Through the World of Art* (Knopf, 1993), giving his insights about such disparate forms as a pyramid in Saqqara built 4600 years ago, a Marsden Hartley painting from 1938, and a Frank Stella painting. This was named a "Best Book of the Year" by *School Library Journal*.

MacClintock, Dorcas. *Animals Observed. A Look at Animals in Art*. New York: Charles Scribner's Sons, 1993.

This topical art book ranges from large animals like elephants, to small animals like bats, including painting, sculpture, engravings, and pen drawings. The art ranges in age from a four thousand year old Egyptian sculpture to one done in 1989. It includes art from such well-known artists as Sir Edwin Landseer and lesser known ones like the Scottish artist Joseph Crawhall. The focus in most of the commentary is on the animals themselves: how they live, habitat, feeding habits, and other matters, rather than on the art work itself. There are minimal comments about the artists' lives, the circumstances in which the work was produced, and where it is now displayed. One piece of particular interest is a squirrel done by Dorothy Lathrop, an artist who won the first Caldecott Medal, awarded for her book, *Animals of the Bible* (J. B. Lippincott, 1937).

Marks, Claude. *Go In and Out the Window*. New York: The Metropolitan Museum of Art and Henry Holt and Company, 1987.

This is not a book about art, but rather a songbook illustrated on nearly every page with full-color reproductions of artworks. This book combines high quality reproductions of original work with concise and informative commentaries. The art ranges in age from a 136 B.C. Egyptian dynasty painting to a 1979 painting by Yvonne Jacquette. The reproductions vary in size from a 1" x 2" jeweled automation frog to a 9" square oil by François Boucher.

Similarly, in *Talking to the Sun* selected by Kenneth Koch and Kate Farrell (The Metropolitan Museum of Art and Henry Holt and Co., 1985), viewers find paintings, sculptures, photographs, porcelains, fabrics, prints, and drawings. Unlike Marks' book, the layout in *Talking to the Sun* is small with tighter margins. The sources and dates of the art are acknowledged, but commentary is not provided.

Mayhew, James. *Katie's Picture Show*. New York: A Bantam Little Rooster Book, 1989.

A fictionalized treatment about little Katie's first trip to a museum with her Grandma, this is a fantasy in which Katie steps into a series of paintings by John Constable, Jean-Auguste-Dominique Ingres, Pierre-Auguste Renoir, Henri Rousseau, and Kasimir Malevich. Grandma needs to rest a bit, and so sends Katie off to look at the pictures. In each case Katie looks at the photographic reproduction of the painting and then steps through it into the place it is set, and has a short adventure there with the people in the painting. In the end she returns to Grandma, now rested up enough to take Katie out to tea. There's a brief "More about Katie's Pictures" informational page at the end of the book.

Micklethwait, Lucy. *A Child's Book of Art. Great Pictures, First Words.* New York: Dorling Kindersley, 1993.

The oversized format ($10^3/4$" x $14^1/4$") is ideal for presenting these full-color reproductions of art, ranging in time from an Egyptian coffin painting (ca. 1050 BC) through an oil painting by David Hockney done in 1978. The art is primarily western; some of it, like a vibrant Hans Hoffman is presented full-page size, while others, like an oil painting of a girl herself painting, by Louise Vigee-Lebrun, are small (4" x $4^3/4$"). There's an introductory note to parents and teachers, plus a complete bibliographic list at the end. Other than these two sections for adults, the pictures are left to speak for themselves. They're grouped generally into categories: some of these—like "Wild Animals" and "Colors" are expectable; others— like "Six Ways to Travel" and "A Time to Sleep" are more unusual.

Micklethwait, Lucy. *I Spy Two Eyes. Numbers in Art.* New York: Greenwillow Books, 1993.

Use this with children for the superb reproductions of art, varying in time from a circa 1405 reproduction of "The Emblem of the Hare" by an unknown artist, used for the page, "I spy eleven hares," to a 1961 Robert Indiana painting, "The American Dream I," used for the "I spy nineteen stars" page. It's a clever idea, asking children to look for a certain number of the named objects included in the paintings. Some are quite easy, i.e.: finding the three puppies in a Paul Gauguin still life; others take more effort, like finding all 15 hands and feet in a Ferdinand Leger painting. Throughout, however, the reproductions are large enough and clear enough so children will be entranced with the details. *I Spy. An Alphabet in Art* (same publisher, 1992) moves from Rene Magritte for the letter A, to Wybrand de Geest for the letter Z, looking for objects in this array of paintings.

Charles Sullivan took the same idea, of walking young viewers through the alphabet using paintings, in *Alphabet Animals*, (Rizzoli, 1991). In the process, he acquaints viewers with art ranging from an

Iranian sculpture done in the 6–5th century BC, through a metal sculpture done in 1987 by the American Jim Gary. Paintings range from the realistic (like one by John James Audubon) to the abstract expressionist, as in one by Richard Pousette-Dart.

Munthe, Nellie. *Meet Matisse.* Boston: Little, Brown, 1983.

In this book the large ($8^{1}/4$" x $9^{3}/8$"), nearly square shape and intensely white, coated paper set off the reproductions to their best advantage. For the most part, there is just a single reproduction on each page. The instructional pages, which involve children in experimenting with color and manipulating collage forms, have smaller diagrams and illustrations. The text is sometimes descriptive ("Matisse had a catalogue of images in his head") and sometimes directive ("when your brush is filled with paint, start stroking the color on the paper"). The intent is to help children learn to see with more insight and to encourage them to try their hand at several techniques this artist used.

Newlands, Anne. *Meet Edgar Degas.* Toronto: Kids Can Press, 1988 (distributed by Harper and Row).

A brief introduction and conclusion (each only a few paragraphs) frame the main text which is written in first person narrative. Pages of text face full-color reproductions of thirteen major paintings, a piece of sculpture and two small sketches, all large enough so details can be studied. The text offers explanations of the artist's motives and responses to his paintings and provides technical information (size, media, etc.).

Pekarik, Andrew. *Sculpture. Behind the Scenes.* New York: Hyperion Books for Children, 1992.

The author begins by pointing out that when most people hear the word *art*, they think of painting; he then goes on to make the case that sculpture is an important kind of art—different in some ways and similar in other ways to flat painting. The first section, dealing with processes of making sculpture, includes attention to such things as "Removing" and "Constructing," among others. Each section is accompanied by a full-color photograph of a piece exemplifying the process, including information about title, artist, date, materials, and size of original. The latter is particularly helpful in some cases, for instance, when we learn that a Claes Oldenburg cloth hamburger, shown 4" x $5^{1}/2$" in the book is actually 52" x 84". A following section is on form, as the author explains such things as contour (the outside shape), enclosure (the inside shape), weight, and movement. The latter topic deals with design movement in a stable piece of sculpture, as well as the other kind of movement shown in a mobile by Alexander Calder. Another section deals with the topic of scale and discusses pieces ranging in height from 151 feet high to $5^1/2"$. A final, and in some ways the most problematic, aspect of sculpture is surface texture; the tactile qualities of many sculptures beg to be touched, which is usually impossible. Throughout, the author asks readers questions to help them perceive art in new ways. "Could the diagonal plates be arms and legs?" asked about a David Smith sculpture, can indeed cause us to see possibilities that might have before eluded us.

Raboff, Ernest. *Pablo Picasso.* New York: Lippincott, 1987.

Pablo Picasso is part of the "Artstart" series. The books in this series are distinguished by a large-sized format, high-quality reproductions and hand-lettered text. The fact that a single full-color illustration appears on a page makes the book especially useful for sharing with a whole class at once. This book features fifteen full (or nearly full) page illustrations in full-color, with many smaller black and white drawings and designs. The series includes *Paul Klee, Marc Chagall, Rembrandt van Rijn* and others.

Reef, Pat Davidson. *Dahlov Ipcar, Artist.* Falmouth, ME: The Kennebeck River Press, Inc., 1987.

This, the second title in "The Maine Art Series for Young Readers," is a 48-page paperback, 11" x 8" in size, which allows plenty of room for color as well as black and white reproductions of the artist's work on nearly every page. We get personal data (she is the daughter of the famous sculptor, William Zorach) as well as technical information (lithography is a medium in which many prints can be made from an original drawing done on stone). This is all set within a generally chronological account of her life as an artist, with specially identified subsections on such topics as cloth sculpture and children's books. Some of the reproductions are full page in size while others are smaller. This follows an earlier (1985) title, *Bernard Langlais, Sculptor*, by the same author and same publisher, which was printed in the same general format, but with just black and white reproductions.

Samton, Sheila White. *Beside the Bay.* New York: Philomel Books, 1987.

The unnamed young first-person narrator steps along through an almost deserted environment (blue water and grey sky are introduced first) and gradually acquires an entourage of creatures. The sharp-edged, flat-colored shapes in the illustrations—a new color is introduced on each page—match the swatch of the same color underlining the color word on the facing text page. The cumulative text introduces each color in this book for very young readers/viewers.

Books about colors continue to be the most numerous of those dealing with art elements. Also recommended are *Growing Colors* by Bruce McMillan (Lothrop, 1988) with full-page, full-color photographs remarkable for their textures; *Colors* by Shirley Hughes (same publisher, 1986) in which appealing small children experience many different shades of the colors in natural settings; *Color Zoo* by Lois Ehlert (Lippincott, 1989) in which children may match the highly saturated colors throughout the book with color chips at the end; and *Color Dance* by Ann Jonas (Greenwillow, 1989) in which three young leotard-clad girls create many new shades by moving with transparent sheets of color they manipulate.

Schick, Eleanor. *Art Lessons.* New York: Greenwillow, 1987.

Small scale pencil drawings printed on a pale orange ground appear on single pages. These show the adult woman artist, Adrianne, and a young friend who becomes her student. They draw in various environments (featured in short chapters like "At the Museum") where she helps him learn not only how to see, but how to capture on paper what he sees.

Turner, Robyn Montana. *Mary Cassatt.* Boston: Little, Brown & Co., 1992.

From a series, "Portraits of Women Artists for Children," this exemplifies the strengths of the other books in the set. There are large, full-color reproductions on nearly every opening: four are full page in size and only two are so small that they presuppose a single viewer. These books are biographies, written in a casual style to draw the young reader in. The author does, incidentally, include dates, places, exhibitions, names of other artists, but these don't overwhelm the forward movement of the interesting story Turner is telling. At places we get clear explanations of processes; on page 24, for instance, the description of Cassatt learning to make etchings is thoroughly enough described so readers unfamiliar with the process will understand it. Unfamiliar words are given a phonetic pronunciation in parentheses. Other titles to date in the series include *Georgia O'Keeffe*, *Rosa Bohneur*, *Faith Ringgold* and *Frida Kahlo*.

Venezia, Mike. *Rembrandt.* Chicago: Children's Press, 1988.

From the "Getting to Know the World's Greatest Artists" series (which also includes Picasso and Van Gogh), this book includes 19 full-color reproductions of Rembrandt's paintings within 32 pages. Though visual elements are discussed, the focus is on Rembrandt's life. The style is informal and nontechnical. For example, the author comments that sometimes Rembrandt painted smoothly while at others he would "pile on the paint." Commentary is followed by a reproduction of the entire painting it describes, as well as a close-up of one aspect of the painting which documents the explanation.

Ventura, Piero. *Michelangelo's World.* New York: G. P. Putnam's Sons, 1989.

The text, which opens with a chronology, compresses into just 39 pages the 89 turbulent years of the artist's life. Condensing that amount of church and civil intrigue—much of which directly affected Michelangelo's artistic output—into such a brief space leaves little room for more than a sketch of the motivations and feelings of this complex artist. The detail-oriented child will enjoy the minute drawings, while the text may open interests to more extended biographies.

Even larger than the Michelangelo sculptures is the lion image of Pharaoh Khafre done centuries ago and still gazing across the desert sand. The process of creating this sculpture monument is described by Mary Stoltz in a fictionalized account, *Zekmet. The Stone Carver* (Harcourt Brace Jovanovich, 1988). The book is enlivened by Deborah Nourse Lattimore's art that relies on Egyptian hieroglyphics for its motifs.

Walsh, Ellen Stall. *Mouse Paint.* San Diego: Harcourt Brace Jovanovich, 1989.

This is a brief introduction for the youngest listener to color mixing, done in cut paper collage. The torn-edged mice will remind young viewers of the art of Leo Lionni, with which it could be compared. The artist shows viewers just three color mixes (to obtain orange, green, purple) which are repeated twice, and the last page ties back to the opening. The book is effective because of its understated simplicity.

Waterfield, Giles. *Faces.* New York: McElderry Books, 1982.

From the "Looking at Art" series, which also includes *People at Home* and *People at Work*, this book is distinguished by the size and quality of its color reproductions. From the face of "Hermes" by Praxiteles created in 350 B.C. through Picasso's "Woman Weeping,"

Activity

Lattimore always draws heavily on her wide-ranging knowledge of art history in preparing her art. In The Flame of Peace. A Tale of the Aztecs *(Harper and Row, 1987) she incorporates Aztec motifs, and in* The Winged Cat, A Tale of Ancient Egypt *(HarperCollins, 1992) she uses Egyptian motifs. Use these with children, who will enjoy identifying ideas presented in the catalogue endpapers when they occur later in the book illustrations themselves.*

this book presents no more than one piece of art on each large (8^1/2" x 10^1/2") page. The placement of reproductions on facing pages is sometimes conventional (a self portrait by Durer faces one by Rembrandt), and sometimes imaginative and unexpected (peasants by Hogarth contrasted with royalty by Winterhalter).

Welton, Jude. *Drawing. A Young Artist's Guide.* New York: Dorling Kindersley, 1994.

An oversized (10" x 13") format provides ample space for an exploration varying from foundational topics like "Keeping Your Drawings," and "Drawing tools," to more conceptually complex topics like "Speed and Energy," in a book featuring drawing done by adults (from Albrech Durer in 1502 to Sarah Cawkwell in 1993) and by children. This is a helpful combination of analysis of famous artists like Fernand Leger's use of line, and practical activities designed to help children understand more about this visual element. The section on imagination and storytelling even touches briefly on the art in children's books, using an example from Edward Ardizzone. The book is designed to expand children's concepts about the topic, for example, in devoting a double spread to drawing with a brush, a tool most children wouldn't usually associate with drawing. The children shown in full-color photographs appear to be intermediate grade level, though the material is sophisticated enough to be helpful in expanding what teachers themselves know.

Winter, Jonah. *Diego.* New York: Alfred A. Knopf, 1991.

Activity

In a much larger format, Winter has illustrated a very different kind of story, in Klara's New World *(Knopf, 1992), but used essentially the same sort of visual style. After studying both books, you might talk with children about which text is most effectively supported by this style.*

A simple biography of this renowned Mexican artist for young readers, with but one to four sentences on each page, springs to vivid life because of Jeanette Winter's paintings, in full color, on every page. The text, set in both English and Spanish, is utilitarian and doesn't in the brief compass chosen, allow for much explanation of complications and motivations. But the paintings, highly patterned, primitive in style, and intensely colored in dark shades, capture the essence of this muralist's approach, without being derivative. There's lots of rhythmic repetition, intensified because of the small scale of the illustrations. The book ends with a factual note about the artist's life.

A more extensive, fictionalized treatment of the tumultuous life of this artist with social reformer tendencies is presented by Anne E. Neimark, in *Diego Rivera. Artist of the People* (HarperCollins, 1992). The biography begins with Diego's birth, describes in humorous detail the various family members, and progresses at a thorough pace to his death in 1957. The book includes black and white reproductions but only four color ones; a problem in both books is that the scale of Rivera's mural work prevents it from being captured adequately in a small format.

Woolf, Felicity. *Picture This: A First Introduction to Painting*. Garden City: Doubleday, 1989.

This book is for readers who "don't know anything about art but know what they like." Woolf uses 24 examples of paintings made between 1400 and 1952, as she guides viewers through the development of Western art. She demonstrates that looking at paintings can be as instructive as history and as exciting as a treasure hunt. The text is enlightening and the range of paintings wide enough to catch the interest of even the most reluctant viewer. An introduction explains why some of the paintings were chosen, the reason the book stops in the 1950s, and why so few women are represented. The book provides background information for teachers and librarians and is also accessible to middle school and older readers.

Woolf, Felicity. *Picture This Century. An Introduction to Twentieth-Century Art.* New York: A Doubleday Book for Young Readers, 1992.

This covers the development of art in both Europe and North America, progressing historically; it begins with a Henri Matisse painting of his wife done in 1905 and ends with a 1982 sculpture by Niki de Saint Phalle. There are full-color reproductions on every opening, though many of them are of a size accessible only to individual viewers. The artists include such familiar names as Andy Warhol and his pop art images of Coke bottles, and less familiar ones like Boris Kustodiev's representational painting of the revolution in Russia. The author carefully includes a variety of sculpture among the paintings: an Alexander Calder mobile is a more familiar image than is the ice sculpture by Andy Goldsworthy. Woolf makes a valiant effort to help viewers understand such perplexing works as Joseph Beuy's "Felt Suit," though her detailing of the particular experience which prompted this art doesn't really convince that it communicates to others.

Pop Art
A form of art which depicts common objects from everyday life and uses visual techniques from commercial art, like comic strips.

Yenawine, Philip. *Colors*. New York: The Museum of Modern Art; Delacorte Press, 1990.

In brief format (just 22 pages of text) that includes large, full-color reproductions of paintings from 1890 (by Paul Signac) to 1981 (by Jaspar Johns), the author directs children's observations about the visual element of color. With a single sentence or two, the author points out the variety of ways artists have used colors. Language is simple—a Josef Albers painting, for example, is described as using "just one color"; it actually includes several different shades of the color, but no attempt is made at introducing the term or concept of "shade." Other books in the series include *Shapes, Lines, and Stories* (same publisher and date).

Another useful book is *A Color Sampler* by Kathleen Westray (Ticknor & Fields, 1993), using just abstract blocks of color, rather than reproductions of paintings. As Yenawine does, this artist shows how to mix colors, how black and white changes basic hues, how backgrounds seem to affect the color of shapes placed on them, how the intensity of hues seems to make them advance or recede and how the size of the color shapes make them seem distinct or blurry. The bold graphics make this appealing to middle grade readers for whom the difficulty of the text is appropriate.

Zemach, Margot. *Self-Portrait: Margot Zemach.* Reading, MA: Addison-Wesley, 1978.

A chatty, informal account of the artist's life, enriched with her own illustrations in color and in black and white. Many of the real-life characters Zemach draws turn out to look very similar to the fictional characters in the artist's book illustrations. This is one of the few books for children that focus exclusively on a book illustrator. It is part of a series which includes *Erik Blegvad* (1979) and *Trina Schart Hyman* (1981). Each book is a personalized, "behind the scenes" look at the artist's life and work rather than a serious, critical analysis of the significance of his/her art. (Although only the book on Trina Schart Hyman is still in print, the other books in the series may be available in your local library.)

Zhensun, Zheng and Alice Low. *A Young Painter.* New York: Scholastic Hardcover, 1991.

An elegant production job provides a showcase for this biography of a prolific young prodigy who has created over 10,000 paintings in a centuries-old tradition. Photographs of the 15-year-old painter at work are interspersed with large reproductions of her paintings which are characterized by spontaneous brushwork and playfulness. The appendix describes the tools, the styles of painting, the brush techniques, including explanations of cun (texture), ca (rubbing) dotting, and jimo. The interaction between her father/mentor and the youngster is described: a section on how he questions her about what and why she has painted is an interesting commentary on the desire to encourage creativity and thoughtfulness. The quick, energetic brushstrokes and the limited array of color used show a different sensibility than is present in much Western art.

Ethnic Bibliography

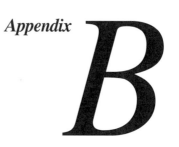

Books by and/or about Blacks

Africa Dream by Eloise Greenfield (p. 101)
All the Magic in the World by Niki Daly (p. 68)
All Night, All Day by Ashley Bryan (p. 70)
The Ballad of Belle Dorcas by Brian Pinkney (p. 116)
Beat the Story Drum, Pum Pum by Ashley Bryan (p. 70)
Bitter Bananas by Ed Young (p. 28, 46)
Brown Angels by Walter Dean Myers (p. 128)
Can't Sit Still by Karen E. Lotz (p. 200)
The Cat's Purr by Ashley Bryan (p. 70, 103)
Celebrating Kwanzaa by Laurence Migdale (p. 117)
Chicken Sunday by Patricia Polacco (p. 155)
Climbing Jacob's Ladder by Ashley Bryan (p. 106)
Crafty Chameleon by Adrienne Kennaway and Mwenye Hadithi (p. 9, c.p. 1)
Dinner at Aunt Connie's House by Faith Ringgold (p. 67)
Do Like Kyla by Angela Johnson (p. 23)
Everett Anderson's Friend by Ann Grifalconi (p. 36)
Everett Anderson's Year by Ann Grifalconi (p. 110)
Follow the Drinking Gourd by Jeanette Winter (p. 23, 198)
Freight Train by Donald Crews (p. 143)
Grandmother's Pictures by Sam Cornish (p. 162)
The Great Migration by Jacob Laurence (p. 199)
Harriett and the Promised Land by Jacob Laurence (p. 199)
The Honey Hunters by Francesca Martin (p. 170)
Hot Hippo by Adrienne Kennaway and Mwenye Hadithi (p. 9)
Jake and Honeybunch Go to Heaven by Margot Zemach (p. 19)
King of Another Country by Fionna French (p. 43)
Mother Crocodile by John Steptoe (p. 40)
My Mama Needs Me by Pat Cummings (p. 68)
Parade by Donald Crews (p. 43)

Seven Candles for Kwanzaa by Brian Pinkney (p. 117)

Shadow by Marcia Brown (p. 216, color plate 12)

The Snowy Day by Ezra Jack Keats (p. 118–119)

Stevie by John Steptoe (p. 202)

Sweet Clara and the Freedom Quilt by Deborah Hopkinson (p. 23)

Tar Beach by Faith Ringgold (p. 67)

Tell Me a Story, Mama by Angela Johnson (p. 23)

Train Ride by John Steptoe (p. 202)

Tricky Tortoise by Adrienne Kennaway and Mwenye Hadithi (p. 10)

Uptown by John Steptoe (p. 202)

Books by and/or about Hispanics

Abuela by Elisa Kleven (p. 85-87, color plate 5)

The Gold Coin by Neil Waldman (p. 63, 88)

I Lost My Arrow in a Kankan Tree by Noni Lichtveld (p. 20)

The Mexican Story by Lynd Ward (p. 126)

My Little Island by Frane Lessac (p. 206)

Not a Copper Penny in Me House by Frane Lessac (p. 206)

Pedro & the Padre by Verna Aardema (p. 24)

This Home We Have Made Esta Casa Que Hemos Hecho by Anna Hammond and Joe Matinis (p. 222)

Books by and/or about Native Americans

(including Indian tribes of Central and South America)

Crow Chief by Paul Goble (p. 70)

Desert Voices by Peter Parnall (p. 74)

The Girl Who Loved Wild Horses by Paul Goble (p. 70)

The Great Race of the Birds and Animals by Paul Goble (p. 71)

How Rabbit Tricked Otter and Other Cherokee Trickster Tales by Murv Jacob (p. 26)

If You Are a Hunter of Fossils by Peter Parnall (p. 74)

Ladder to the Sky by Helen K. Davie (p. 24)

Little Eagle Lots of Owls by Jane Ross (p. 124)

Ma'ii and Cousin Horned Toad by Shanto Begay (p. 25)

Pyramid of the Sun, Pyramid of the Moon by L.E. Fisher (p. 10)

Rain Player by David Wisniewski (p. 122)

Spotted Eagle and Black Crow by Durga Bernhard (p. 25)

The Tree That Rains by Durga Bernhard (p. 28)

Where the Great Bear Watches by Lisa Flather (p. 112)

Why There Is No Arguing in Heaven by Deborah Nourse Lattimer (p. 160)

Books by and/or about Asians

A to Z Picture Book by Gyo Fujikawa (p. 200, 204)

A to Zen by Yoshi (p. 124)

Brown Honey in Broom Wheat Tea by Floyd Cooper (p. 62)

Chin Yu Min and the Ginger Cat by Mary Grandpre (p. 25)

The Funny Little Woman by Blair Lent (p. 175)

The Girl Who Loved the Wind by Ed Young (p. 46)

The Great Wall of China by Leonard Everett Fisher (p. 10)

Little Silk by Jacqueline Ayer (p. 13)

The Moles and the Mireuk by Holly Hyeshik Kwan (p. 24)

The Nightingale by Nancy Burkert (p. 53-54, color plate 3)

The Paper Crane by Molly Bang (p. 88)

Sam Panda and the Thunder Dragon by Chris Conover (p. 160)

The Sea and I by Harutaka Nakavatari (p. 143)

Seven Blind Mice by Ed Young (p. 46, color plate 2)

SH-KO and His Eight Wicked Brothers by Ashley Bryan (p. 70)

The Tale of the Mandarin Ducks by Leo and Diane Dillon (p. 39, 172)

Tree of Cranes by Allen Say (p. 60-61)

The Wave by Blair Lent (p. 111)

When Sheep Cannot Sleep by Satoshi Kitamura (p. 3, 90)

Books by and/or about Native People in Other Places

The Backbone of the King by Marcia Brown (Hawaiian, p. 215)

Enora and the Black Crane by Raymond Meeks (Aboriginal Australian, p. 24)

Henry-Fisherman by Marcia Brown (Caribbean, p. 208)

The King's Chessboard by Devis Grebu (India, p. 78)

The Mountains of Tibet by Mordicai Gerstein (p. 83)

Paper Boats by Grace Bochak (India, p. 121)

The Singing Snake by Timothy Rhodes (Aboriginal Australian, p. 206)

Picture Book Genres

Chapter one defined a picture book, to distinguish it from other kinds of books. Here, we'll explore another distinction, between two terms. Literature experts often discuss *genre*, defined as "a kind or type of literature in which the members share a common set of characteristics."[1] We might think that, therefore, a picture book is a genre of literature. That's not the case, however. A picture book is a *format*—most usually 32 pages, though at times 48 or 64 pages. Within the format of some text and more picture (or pictures) on the page, authors can present any genre. We can, for instance, have historic or modern fiction in a picture book format. We can also find examples of poetry, information, biography, fantasy and folk literature genres presented in picture book format Though most of these are told in a combination of words and pictures, sometimes book creators tell a wordless story only through illustrations. This section describes a variety of exemplary picture book presentations in various genres.

Alphabet

An Edible Alphabet. Bonnie Christensen. New York: Dial Books for Young Readers, 1994.

From A for apple to Z for zucchini, the artist leads us to reflect on such familiar foods at grapes, unfamiliar ones like ipomea, and even some most people consider in another category, i.e.: nasturtium! In the tightly constrained style which wood engraving usually invokes, the artist shows us young children harvesting (figs), enjoying (watermelon), and just contemplating (dill), alone (pumpkin), with other children (blueberry) or with adults (quince). The black, patterned borders encompass the picture, capital and lower case letters, and a single word, contrasting effectively with the intense white glossy finish of the paper. Bright colors enliven the black of the engravings.

Counting books

On Halloween Night by Ferida Wolff and Dolores Kozielski. Illustrated by Dolores Avendano. New York: Tambourine Books, 1994.

This progresses from one witch, seen in owl's eye view, to conclude with 13 ghosts, seen straight on, by the two children who are careful, but not frightened away by this array of creatures. We see the bears tramping through the haunted woods from an ant's eye view; this shifting of viewpoint throughout makes Avendano's art more interesting. The gauzy wisps of fog which swirl through all of these double spreads, subtly bordered in brown, add a rhythm to the pictures. But the shapes of the creatures themselves, from the cat's twitching tails to the owl's flapping feathers (and even including the feelers of the bugs) create other, equally interesting visual rhythms.

Biography

In writing about biographies, experts often divide them into two categories, those that deal in depth with a single figure, and those which group together different individuals who share some common thread. We'll here look at two recent examples. A single figure biography:

Tutankhamen's Gift. Robert Sabuda. New York: Atheneum, 1994.

This is what is also called a partial biography, which deals with one period of the person's life, rather than trying to encompass the life from birth to death. In this case, we learn about the Egyptian pharaoh, only from birth until he ascended the throne at age ten. Sabuda incorporates much historic information, i.e.: about burial and mourning practices, and yet throughout tries to keep the focus on the young child and his skills, thoughts, and insecurities. Here, as in other of his books, Sabuda has used a heavy black outline to surround all of his shapes; the firmness and regularity of the line makes it as important in the overall composition as are his flat, highly saturated colors. It's interesting to learn, from an artist's note, that this isn't ink line. Rather, each illustration was made from a "single cut piece of black paper adhered to painted handmade Egyptian papyrus."

Another kind of biography is the *group biography*, in which several people whose lives are in some way related are written about in the same book. An example is:

Eve and Her Sisters. Women of the Old Testament by Yona Zeldis McDonough. Illustrated by Malcah Zeldis. New York: Greenwillow Books, 1994.

Zeldis uses gouache paints in highly saturated colors to create this flat, folk-like art. The illustrations swirl with repeated shapes that can barely be contained within the borders. She does one, full-page painting for each of the single page biographies of the 14 women included here. The text pages themselves are encircled with brush line drawings, done in a single color that emphasizes the movement of the line. Each text page is topped with part of a verse from the King James version of the Bible, and in just a paragraph or two, the author elaborates a bit, giving readers the briefest insight into the life of these unusual women.

Fantasy

Hotel Animal. Keith Duquette. New York: Viking, 1994.

A staple of fantasy: talking animals who wear clothes and live in human architecture, reappears here in a story of Camille and Leon Lizardo, overworked owners of the local insect market. The author-illustrator develops his premise that being lizard-sized can be a real disadvantage, when surrounded by naturally sized, but much larger animals, like a hippo. The scale and the problems it creates, are maintained convincingly throughout the smooth-edged art, done in a variety of pastel colors.

Unlike fantasy, which can be set in the past, the present, or the future, *science fiction* is typically set in the future. Another characteristic of the genre is that it depends on scientific apparatus to create events and objects which may seem imp9ossible to us now, but may well become possible in the future. Here is an example of science fiction in picture book format:

Willy Whyner, Cloud Designer. Michael and Esther Lustig. New York: Four Winds Press, 1994.

In a wide horizontal format, the artists use a limited array of colors: black pencil drawings are enhanced with flat color washes applied in a few places on each page. Young Willy's interest in science wasn't supported by his too-serious parents (who adults will recognize as lifted from a famous Grant Wood painting).

They didn't like Willy "building totally useless things." The illustration showing the cloud machine Willy cobbled together is delightfully full of the kind of erratic bits and pieces often used to depict wild-eyed inventor's creations. Will it in fact someday be possible to create advertising clouds for business? This might have sounded impossible until the recent television newscasts of the company developing billboards in space. Science fiction ideas are seldom as strange as they might originally seem! You might compare this science fiction with *Richie's Rocket* by Joan Anderson (Morrow Junior Books, 1993) which is the same genre. What makes it unusual is that, through George Ancona's full-color photography, we see that fiction can be illustrated with this medium.

Folk Literature

We most usually think of the short folk (sometimes called fairy) tales when we think of this genre, and many of these—from a widening variety of cultures worldwide, have been appearing in retold versions in picture book format.

Beware the Brindlebeast. Anita Riggio. Honesdale, PA: Boyds Mills Press, 1994.

Drawn from an English source collected originally by Joseph Jacobs, this features Birdie, "a cheerful old woman," who lived with her marmalade cat. In the small bucolic village setting, the Dread Brindlebeast raises his havoc. Riggio's opaquely painted, full-page pictures facing each text page bleed to the edge, though the text is bordered with a think brown rule, which also encloses the small silhouettes of the same color, at the bottom corner. Because Birdie is brave, despite the fearsome double wordless spread when she confronts her nemesis, all ends with a cozy chat over supper. In addition to the impressive pictures, there's elegantly crafted language here: "The dusk crept behind her across the meadow, slipping into snug places, tucking itself into burrows and hollows."

Myth and legend is another sub-category of folk literature. An example is:

The Robber Baby. Stories from the Greek Myths. Anne Rockwell. New York: Greenwillow Books for Children, 1994.

In this book, Rockwell presents 15 myths about god and goddesses worshipped in ancient Greece and Rome. Some of these, like "Pandora's Box," are better known than others, like "The Goat-Footed God." All of her retellings are accompanied by Rockwell's usual two-dimensional, decorative drawings; this time the flat colors she uses are encompassed within a brick red, rather than black, line. The mostly half-page or smaller illustrations with one or more per story, really serve as page decorations, rather than providing additional information, or drawing us into the character's feelings and actions, as Rockwell has in other of her books.

Historic Fiction

Josepha. A Prairie Boy's Story by Jim McGugan. Illustrated by Murray Kimber. San Francisco: Chronicle Books, 1994.

Set around 1900, this is narrated in first person, by another child bidding good-bye to Josepha, who has decided to leave school. This common-enough occurrence—in the Midwest at that time—is shown and told poignantly. The narrator is aware that, "our words must have sounded like sheep talk," to the 14-year-old immigrant boy, at a time when teachers routinely eradicated any original language by insisting on English. The oversized boy was driven from the classroom by the taunts of others. But when he leaves, the younger narrator thinks of the gift he can give to Josepha, who would be "my friend for aye." This gift, the key to the story, is shown in pictures, not mentioned in words. The monumental, often detail-less, and softly unfocused full-page paintings, are as unadorned as the landscape they depict. And they are more powerful because of their simplicity. The angular planes of people and landscape are reminiscent of the work of French painter, Paul Cezanne.

Information Books

Here is the Tropical Rainforest by Madeleine Dunphy. Illustrated by Michael Rothman. New York: Hyperion Books for Children, 1994.

Using the accumulated form we're familiar with from "This is the House That Jack Built," Dunphy begins with her single sentence (the book title) and expands it to a 17-line conclusion in which each of these chaining phrases is cleverly linked together. The fully painted illustrations in a variety of lush jungle colors are bordered with a solid, dark green band which stretches across the opening to also border the text, set on paler green. The paintings spread across three quarters of each opening, leaving a predictable space on the left where the words are set, allowing the reader to focus on the expanding text. The book concludes with a page of ink line drawings showing in more precise detail that the paintings do, the animals, as well as giving their names.

Modern Realistic Fiction

Smoky Night by Eve Bunting. Illustrated by David Diaz. San Diego: Harcourt Brace and Co., 1994.

Taking a very current event, the Los Angeles riots, Bunting turns it into memorable fiction, by focusing on the psychological and sociological effects on the humans involved. This is narrated by young Daniel, who with his mother lived through the devastation. The way tragedy brings together people who earlier hadn't been able to get along seems quite convincing. The story succeeds because it is seen, and told, through the immediacy of Daniel's thoughts and feelings, particularly his worry about his missing cat. What could have been an event to engender didactic, distanced statements about right and wrong, turns out rather to elicit a compassionate, subtle assertion about the possibilities of getting along with those different than ourselves. Diaz's art is nothing short of spectacular: a vivifying combination of heavy paint and imaginative collages. The bold, simplified and patterned paintings which face the text pages are heavily outlined in black, reminiscent of both stained glass, and the early work of John Steptoe. Under and around the text are Diaz's collages of many different types of paper and cloth, objects (even shoe soles) printed labels, and broken glass. Despite the diverse array of materials used, the tonalities unify each page so that the book has a coherent overall look.

Poetry

At times the picture book format is used for a collection of poems by many different authors:

A Caribbean Dozen edited by John Agard and Grace Nichols. Illustrated by Cathie Felstead. Cambridge, MA: Candlewick Press, 1994.

The baker's dozen of poets, including the editors themselves, features a one page statement by each poet (with a picture) and brief biographies at the book's end. The poems vary from Valerie Bloom's two line "Ode to Twelve Chocolate Bars," to Telcine Turner's "Charley and Miss Morley's Goat," which extends to ten stanzas. They vary in style from Faustin Charles's rhymed

"Steel Band Jump Up," to John Lyons's unrhymed "Chicki-chong." Accompanying all this variety are Felstead's illustrations, done in several different types of paints, and collage. Sometimes she uses paint with soft-edged grace, as in the picture for Marc Matthews's "A Shower A Shave A Shampoo A Chin." At other times, she relies on the sharp-edged, simplified shapes of collage, as for Opal Palmer Adisa's "Fruits." Sometimes the line is dominant and omnipresent, as in the illustration for David Campbell's "Corn and Potato," while at other times it is nonexistent, as in the art for Lyons's "The Pun Na-na Frog."

At other times, picture book may contain a single, connected poem by one poet, focussing on a smaller range of topics and events. For example:

Knoxville, Tennessee by Nikki Giovanni. Illustrated by Larry Johnson. New York: Scholastic Hardcover, 1994.

This unrhymed poetry recounts the delights of a remembered summer, listing the tastes and sounds and tactile sensations (i.e.: going barefoot) of childhood. Giovanni evokes a simpler, family oriented time, in which the extended family of the church played an important role. The warmth of the relationships shines through. Johnson's heavily painted double-page spreads bleed to the edges. They eschew detail to concentrate instead on an impressionistic rendering of light and shadow, expressed through casual stroking of a variety of tones.

At still other times, several poems by the same poet are grouped together into a picture book. For example:

Crocodile Smile by Sarah Weeks. Illustrated by Lois Ehlert. New York: HarperCollins, 1994.

Ten songs of the earth, "as the animals see it" by Weeks's animal narrators, are full of humor. As, for example, when the dragon protests that he'd never eat a princess, for "what with the frou-frou and ticklish hairdo," she'd probably stick in his throat! Ehlert shows us a komodo dragon, spread cumbersomely across her 22" wide, horizontal double-page spread, accompanied by an elegant, sans-serif typeface set in white. The egret spreads its feathers across a similarly generous dimension (though most child readers won't remember and thus won't understand, the hats decorated with feathers, clearly an adult reference.) Ehlert gives flat, intensely colored backgrounds, combined with her usual collage, featuring papers with interesting applied colors and textures. The soft bleeding of paint applied to wet paper contrasts effectively with her sharp, cut-edged forms. A cassette tape of the poet performing the songs accompanies the book.

An example of art not originally done specifically for a poem, but selected for use with it, is available in *O Beautiful for Spacious Skies*, written by Katharine Lee Bates in 1894 and here illustrated with paintings of Wayne Theibaud (Chronicle Books, 1994). The 17 paintings by this important contemporary American artist are different than the ones analyzed by Greenberg and Jordan in their book, *The Painter's Eye*, described in chapter 2.

Wordless Books

Time Flies. Eric Rohmann. New York: Crown Publishers, Inc., 1994.

From the solid, oatmeal-colored endpapers, through the plain white borders which surround each large, (20" x 10") double-page spread, the design decisions in this book are all calculated to enhance the serious presentation of the art. This is in interesting contrast to the more light-hearted nature of many wordless books. There is a panoramic sweep to the art apparent from the title page onward, whether set in the museum hall where the dinosaur skeletons are housed, or in the less-constraining outside world to which they magically return. These oil paintings contain a lot of detail presented close up to be studied (for example, the detail of the bird on the 12th opening), and yet Rohmann's design sense always manages to subordinate detail to the total effect he's creating in any given painting. The detail doesn't overwhelm as it sometimes does in the hands of a less-skilled artist. He's particularly good at evoking textures (for example, the skin of the dinosaur on the fifth opening). The unifying tonality which pervades the book from beginning to end is also skillfully done.

Notes

Chapter 1

1. S. A. Egoff. (1981). *Thursday's Child. Trends and Patterns in Contemporary Children's Literature*. Chicago: American Library Association, p. 248.

2. Z. Sutherland. (1977). *Children and Books*. Glenview, IL: Scott, Foresman, p. 54.

3. G. Oakley. (1992). "Graham Oakley." In S. Marantz and K. Marantz (eds.), *Artists of the Page. Interviews with Children's Book Illustrators*. Jefferson, NC: McFarland & Co., Inc., Publishers, p. 163, 166.

4. D. Evans. (1991, November/December). "An Extraordinary Vision." *The Horn Book Magazine*, p. 714.

5. J. W. Stewig. (1992). "Ten from the Decade: Visually Significant Picture Books and Why." *The Dragon Lode*, 10(1), 1-9. p. 3.

6. S. Lurie (1991). "First the Word: An Editor's View of Picture Book Texts." *School Library Journal*, 37(10), 50-51. (p. 50)

7. S. Schmidt. (1977, March). "Language Development and Children's Books in Intermediate Classrooms." *Insights Into Open Education*, p. 5.

8. In *Illustrations in Children's Books* (Dubuque, Iowa: William C. Brown, 1976), Patricia Cianciolo describes different styles in art and comments on the importance of sharing the best book designs with children. The book is a comprehensive examination of styles and media. Suggestions for using illustrations found in books are included in chapter 4.

9. O. Richard and D. MacCann. (1984, September). "Picture Books for Children." *Wilson Library Bulletin*, p. 50.

10. B. Cullin. (1991). "Ezra Jack Keats Bookwriting Award." *USBBY Newsletter*, 16(2), p. 14

11. D. MacCann and O. Richard. (1993). "Picture Books and Native Americans: An Interview with Naomi Caldwell-Wood." *Wilson Library Bulletin*, 67(6), p. 30

Chapter 2

1. L. Dillon and D. Dillon. (1992). "The Tale of the Mandarin Ducks." *The Horn Book Magazine*, 68(1), p. 35.

2. J. Doonan. (1993). *Looking At Pictures in Picture Books.* Stroud, Glos., U.K.: Thimble Press, p. 23.

3. Jan Greenberg and Sandra Jordan. (1993). *The Painter's Eye. Learning to Look at Comtemporary American Art.* New York, Delacorte Press, pp. 47, 34.

4. P. Dooley. (1989). "Contemporary Illustrators: Tomorrow's Classics?" *Touchstones*, ed. by P. Nodelman, *3*, p. 158.

5. R. S. Gainer. (1982). "Beyond Illustration: Information about Art in Children's Picture Books." *Art Education*, *35*, p.19.

Chapter 3

1. L. Smith. (1993). "The Artist at Work." *The Horn Book Magazine*, p. 68.

2. L. Cirlot. (1990). *The Key to Modern Art of the Early 20th Century.* Minneapolis: Lerner Publications Company, p.60.

3. M. Bang. (1991) *Picture This. Perception and Composition.* Boston: Little, Brown and Co., p. 80.

4. B. Bader. (1976). *American Picturebooks from Noah's Ark to the Beast Within.* New York: Macmillan Publishing Co., Inc., p. 269.

5. C.J. Hewett and J.C. Rush. (1987). "Finding Buried Treasures: Aesthetic Scanning with Children." *Art Education*, *40*(1), p. 42.

Chapter 4

1. M. Brown. (1986). *Lotus Seeds. Children, Pictures and Books.* New York: Charles Scribner's Sons, p. 7.

2. S. Fressolini. (1992). "Glossary of Terms in Art and Design of Children's Books." *CBC Features*, *45*(2), n.p.

3. D. Evans. (1992, November/December). "An Extraordinary Vision: Picture Books of the Nineties." *The Horn Book Magazine*, p. 762.

4. M.L. Becker (1939, Arpil 30). Review. *Books*, p. 10; E. L. Buell, (1939, June 18). Review. *The New York Times*, p. 10; K.T. Horning (1988). "Are You Sure that Book Won the Caldecott Medal?

Variant Printings and Editions of Three Caldecott Medal Books."
Journal of Youth Services in Libraries, 1(2), p. 173.

5. B. Lent (1971). "How the sun and the moon got into a film."
The Horn Book Magazine, 47, p. 591.

6. K. Stone. (1988). "Three Transformations of Snow White." In
J.M. McGlathery (ed.), *The Brothers Grimm and Folktale.* Urbana:
University of Illinois Press, p. 61.

Chapter 5

1. C. Goldenberg. (1993). "The Design and Typography of Children's Books." *The Horn Book Magazine, 69*(5), p. 559.

2. M. Fisher. (1975). *Who's Who is Children's Books.* New York:
Holt, Rinehart and Winston, p. 336.

3. W. Steig. (1993). "The Artist at Work." *The Horn Book Magazine, VLXIX*(2), p. 174.

4. J.M. Harms and L.J. Lettow. (1989). "Book Design: Extending
Verbal and Visual Literacy." *Journal of Youth Services in Libraries,
2*(2), p. 137.

5. L. Lacy. (1986). *Art and Design in Children's Picture Books.*
Chicago: American Library Association, p. 35.

6. D. Macaulay. (1991). "1991 Caldecott Acceptance Speech."
Journal of Youth Services in Libraries, 4(4), p. 346.

Chapter 6

1. P.Cianciolo. (1976). *Illustrations for Children's Books.* Dubuque: Wm. C. Brown Company Publishers, p. 32.

2. P.Dooley. (1989). "Contemporary Illustrators: Tomorrow's
Classics?" In P. Nodelman (ed.), *Touchstones* vol.3 West Lafayette,
IN: Children's Literature Association, p. 159; J.P. May. (1991).
"Exploring Book Illustration As a Work of Art." *The CLA Bulltein,*
17(2), p. 3.

3. Cianciolo, p. 35.

4. C. Lewis. (1989). "John Steptoe." In T. Chevalier (ed.), *Twentieth-Century Children's Writers.* Chicago: St. James Press, p. 919.

5. E. Raboff. (1988). *Henri Rousseau.* New York: J. B. Lippincott,
p. 11.

6. Cianciolo, p. 40.

7. L. Kingman, G.A. Hogarth, and H. Quimby, (1978) *Illustrator's of Children's Books 1967-1976.* Boston: The Horn Book, Inc. ,
p. 104.

8. J.A. Loranger. (1992). "Marcia Brown." *The Horn Book Magazine*, *68*(4), p. 443.

Appendix C

1. R. J. Lukens, (1990. 4th ed.). *A Critical Handbook of Children's Literature*. New York: HarperCollins.

Index